John Wesley:
Contemporary P

John Wesley:
Contemporary Perspectives

edited by John Stacey
with an introduction by Frank Baker

EPWORTH PRESS

British Library Cataloguing in Publication Data

John Wesley: contemporary perspectives.
1. Methodist churches. Wesley, John, 1703–
1791. Biographies
I. Stacey, John, *1919–*
287'.092'4

ISBN 0–7162–0449–5

First published 1988
by Epworth Press,
Room 195, 1 Central Buildings,
Westminster, London SW1H 9NR

Typeset by the Spartan Press Ltd
Lymington, Hants
and printed in Great Britain by
Richard Clay Ltd, Bungay, Suffolk

Contents

Preface

John Wesley: Contemporary Perspectives originated through the enterprise of Brian Thornton, General Manager of the Methodist Publishing House, Peterborough, England but has been taken over by the Epworth Press under the provisions of the Methodist Conference for the publication of books. It is published as a contribution to the commemoration of the 250th anniversary, in 1988, of the conversions of John and Charles Wesley.

The symposium has a list of distinguished contributors and a wide variety of subjects relating to John Wesley. It contains much informative and imaginative writing and makes good reading for the inquirer into the life and work of this honoured churchman and evangelist. The Epworth Press is pleased to offer the volume as an appropriate tribute to the one who was, substantially, its own founder.

John Stacey
Epworth Press

Contributors

Frank Baker   *Professor Emeritus of English Church History in Duke University, North Carolina*

Ole E. Borgen   *Bishop in the United Methodist Church, Northern Europe Area*

Aelred Burrows, OSB   *Priest and Monk of Ampleforth Abbey*

Wesley A. Chambers   *Minister and President of the Wesley Historical Society, New Zealand*

W. R. Davies   *President of the Methodist Conference 1987–8*

Melvin E. Dieter   *Director, Wesleyan Holiness Project, Asbury Theological Seminary, Kentucky*

A. Raymond George   *Warden of the New Room, Bristol*

David Guy   *Literary Secretary of the Salvation Army*

Joe Hale   *General Secretary of the World Methodist Council*

Richard P. Heitzenrater   *Editor of the Bicentennial Edition of the Works of John Wesley, Perkins School of Theology, Texas*

Bruce Kent   *Vice-Chair, Campaign for Nuclear Disarmament*

Morris Maddocks   *Bishop and Adviser for the Ministry of Health and Healing to the Archbishops of Canterbury and York*

John Newton   *Chairman of the Liverpool District*

Donald Soper   *Former Superintendent of the West London Mission*

Christopher Stell   *Investigator for the Royal Commission on the Historical Monuments of England*

W. P. Stephens   *Professor of Church History in the University of Aberdeen*

C. Norman R. Wallwork   *Superintendent of the Keswick and Cockermouth Circuit*

Pauline M. Webb   *Former Director of Religious Broadcasting, BBC Overseas Service*

A. Skevington Wood   *Former Principal of Cliff College*

Frances Young   *Professor of Theology in the University of Birmingham*

Introduction

Frank Baker

Whether we realize it or not, welcome it or not, most of us have multiple personalities. It is rarely, if ever, that a woman or a man is seen as exhibiting exactly the same traits of character at home, at work, and in social activities, in delivering a speech, or driving a car, or dealing with a youthful problem. We may be able to discourse with authority in some fields, but only hesitantly in other related fields; we may become excited about some forms of art or music, but remain cold or even antagonistic towards others. Every man – and every woman – is an island, nurturing some forms of his or her natural landscape, but letting other features run to waste, or attempting to replace them. To capture in a formula, even an extremely complex formula, the unique combination of characteristics comprising any human being, let alone assess their actions and achievements over a long lifetime in the public eye, is clearly impossible.

This becomes even less possible – if indeed there is anything less possible than impossible – when one is removed by a quarter of a millennium from the subject of one's assessment. Yet with a public and universal figure such as John Wesley it becomes tantalizingly desirable to discover what he was *really* like. Even in his own long lifetime he had become much of a legend, and because he was the founder of their family in the Church Universal, loyal Methodists experienced a strong urge to set him on a pedestal, not allowing any foibles to be seen in official biographies, and even refusing to admit that he might indeed have been sullied by any weaknesses. That time is long past, of course, and we are now trying to sort out what has happened to the various images people had of him; we are still asking what he was really like as a person, and what were his lasting contributions to church and society and to the world in general. And all the time we are coming to realize more and more that whatever we discover must be fragmentary at best.

Anyone who sets out to be different from his fellows, of course, is bound to attract criticism, and mild criticism was certainly present in a half-humorous title bestowed on Wesley by one of the literary ladies in a Cotswold coterie with whom he eagerly corresponded, a title which perceptively diagnosed how he was striving to be different – 'Primitive Christianity'.[1]

Plenty of much more unpleasant mud was thrown at John Wesley from his Oxford days onward, though little of it stuck. The brands of mud that were thrown, and the measure in which they stuck, may indeed be used as one method of attempting to assess his true character – a kind of negative biography which is at least worth trying once, on a very small scale. The very title 'Methodist' was used as a jeering nickname, and the first printed attack upon Wesley and his colleagues, which appeared in a London newspaper, *Fog's Weekly Journal* for 9 December 1732, accused the Oxford Methodists of being hypocrites who 'use religion only as a veil to vice'. As the early Christians at Antioch had accepted their nickname as an honourable description, so did the Methodists, and Wesley similarly welcomed 'The Holy Club' as a 'glorious title'.[2] Although at times Wesley seemed to court persecution as if it were a sign of the favour of God, his more considered principles were explained in his 1732 apologia for Methodist self-discipline: 'We do indeed use all the lawful means we know to prevent "the good which is in us" from being "evil spoken of"; but if the neglect of known duties be the one condition of securing our reputation, why, fare it well.'[3]

Actually it was out of similar defamation that Wesley's *Journal* came – or at least its publication. It is indeed a sad and tortuous story which we read in Vol. 18 of the Bicentennial Edition, where we follow his tactless and fumbling love affair with Sophy Hopkey in Savannah – in which it is difficult to find any valid charge of impropriety or of even minimal ecclesiastical error, but merely a lack of worldly wisdom. Captain Robert Williams of Savannah, however, a Bristolian, was one of Wesley's enemies, and when he also returned to Bristol, he hawked about the streets a scurrilous broadsheet implying that Wesley had seduced Sophy. This scandal might well have undermined the nascent revival in the city, so that Wesley felt it incumbent upon him in 1740 to present a genuine account of the affair by publishing (again in Bristol) the first *Extract of the Rev. Mr John Wesley's Journal*. This led eventually to twenty further extracts, the last only a few months after his death.[4]

Thirty-six years later his own estranged wife began a further round of vilification, having allowed an almost pathological jealousy to fester over the years because of her husband's warm pastoral familiarity with the many gifted women in his society. (It was indeed true, to use Alexander Knox's stilted phrase, that he 'had a predilection for the female character.'[5]) Mrs Mary Wesley handed over to a newspaper some of her husband's private pastoral letters to female followers, garbled in such a way as to imply his immorality. His brother Charles urged John to stay in London to defend his good name instead of taking his proposed trip to Canterbury with his niece. To which John replied: 'Brother, when I devoted to God my ease, my time, my life, did I except my reputation? No. Tell Sally I will take her to Canterbury tomorrow.'[6]

Another focal point of criticism was Wesley's supposed greed. He was reputed to have accumulated immense wealth from the contributions of his societies and from his multitudinous publications. Wesley grew weary of rebutting such charges by pointing to his simple life and his constant charities, though these were never flaunted. Among other concerns, he cared for widows and orphans, for the education of the young, and began the first free public dispensary in London. Hundreds of his tiny awakening pamphlets were distributed freely, and almost all of his larger works were published in the inexpensive duodecimo form at twopence or threepence instead of in the more fashionable octavo, at sixpence or a shilling. The spiritual and intellectual profit of his followers was what he sought, and their small but regular monetary contributions were intended simply to secure the payment of their expenses – and to help the poor. The true wealth accruing from his publications was in their devotional and intellectual stimulus to his preachers and to his societies.

Neither his early followers nor the more critical students of later generations have been able to discover any real vices in him, only the undue exaggeration of some of his virtues, which may indeed have occasionally caused unintended distress. Increasingly over the years the law of love was his major motive, although he nevertheless sought also lesser virtues such as punctuality and courtesy, as well as strict honesty and truthfulness in all things. Occasionally his gentle trusting affection led him to neglect other things more important in worldly eyes, as in the instance of Sally's outing. He himself continued to hope that others would forgivingly follow his own precept: 'It is a rule with me to take nothing ill that is well meant.'[7]

This, however, did not prevent his occasional impatience with those well-meaning bumblers who frustrated his careful administration of the Methodist societies, and therefore – as he certainly saw it – the clear purposes of God. 'I hate delay:' he once wrote to his brother, 'The King's business requires haste!'[8] We have sometimes described as autocracy that firm control over people and preachers which he claimed was rooted in their own request that he should be their spiritual director.[9] His expectations of them were quite clear: 'All our preachers should be as punctual as the sun, never standing still, or moving out of their course.'[10] He constantly reminded them that his brand of Methodism made no pretence of being a democratic institution, and that their remedy was quite simple: if they felt dissatisfied with his authoritarian leadership, they were always at liberty to leave.[11]

He was sometimes accused of boasting, yet pride was an enemy with which he was constantly and consciously at war. One of his favourite expressions about the Methodist success story was Numbers 23.23, 'What hath God wrought!' His general demeanour made it clear, however, that this was by no means personal boasting, but a genuine desire to give glory to God for the providential rise of Methodism. He was truly humble, in accordance with his own definition: 'The knowledge of ourselves is true humility; and without this we cannot be freed from vanity, a desire of praise being inseparably connected with every degree of pride. Continual watchfulness is absolutely necessary to hinder this from stealing in upon us.'[12] When the anonymous clergyman 'John Smith' accused him of 'over-done humility' he replied: 'I am to this day ashamed before God that I do so little, [compared] to what I ought to do . . . I do not spend *all* my time so profitably as I might, nor all my strength, at least not all I might have if it were not for my own *lukewarmness* and remissness, if I wrestled with God in constant and fervent prayer.'[13] In fact, of course, he set himself what seem to us impossibly high standards, and was genuinely distressed when he fell short of them.

Even then, in his forties, he was (as he later came to realize) too breathlessly energetic about his religious exercises. He diagnosed this possible flaw in himself in a letter to his brother Charles in 1766: 'I find rather an increase than a decrease of zeal for the whole work of God, and every part of it. I am φερόμενος [*pheromenos*, 'driven'], I know not how, [so] that I can't stand still.'[14] In a measure he had achieved calmness of spirit through most of his life because of his firm belief in a special providence, and his acceptance of people and events as they came and as they were.[15] However, just as 'John Smith' criticized Wesley's 'overdone humility', others might well regard as 'over-done equanimity' his claim: 'By the grace of God I never fret; I repine at nothing; I am discontented at nothing. And to have persons at my ear fretting and murmuring at everything is like tearing the flesh off my bones . . . This I want – to see God acting in everything, and disposing all for his own glory and his creatures' good.'[16] Perhaps it was the mood of the moment: but there were a million such moments in his over-busy life.

He continued to be guilty of many errors in dates and in facts, as he had been even during his middle years. He foreshortened in his 1782 memory the account of how he had dedicated himself in a few days to the practice of early rising – instead of over several months in 1729–30, as his diary proves to have been the case.[17] This was not because he intended to mislead his hearers, but because he was living in a golden glow of what God had managed to do with his life, in which the glorious end completely overshadowed the actual drudgery of the means.

John Wesley felt no shame in utilizing the actual words – usually condensed – of many authors whom he did not name, a literary crime which we now pejoratively term 'plagiarism'. To him, however, and to many of his contemporaries, this was a normal literary device, and the apt phrase or the cogent argument was to him far more important in itself than the remembering or repeating of its author's name. Sometimes, indeed, he may deliberately have withheld the identity of his source, for fear that it might set up a reaction that would diminish the impact of the quotation, as was possibly the case when he recited a devastating argument against the folly of war as by 'a late eminent hand' –

instead of referring to Jonathan Swift's *Gullivers's Travels!*[18]. All of his hundreds of editings or re-writings of the works of others, however, were deliberately carried out to the glory of God, and he felt that he would serve God less effectively by spending precious time in composing an original essay expounding the works of God's grace if it were much simpler to reshape the writings of someone else. Always, however, his aim was clear: 'Goldsmith's *History* and Hooke's are far the best. I think I shall make them better. My view in writing history (as in writing philosophy) is to bring God into it.'[19]

Only very gradually did Wesley's furious pace slow down somewhat. In his *Journal* for 28 October 1765 he contrasted himself favourably with his former pupil, George Whitefield, who 'seemed to be an old, old man, being fairly worn out in his Master's service, though he has hardly seen fifty years'. 'And yet,' he continued, 'it pleases God that I . . . in my sixty-third year, find no disorder, no weakness, no decay, no difference from what I was at five-and-twenty, only that I have fewer teeth and more gray hairs.' On 28 June 1770, his sixty-seventh birthday, he wrote: 'I . . . am now healthier than I was forty years ago. This hath God wrought!' And a year later: 'I am still a wonder to myself. My voice and strength are the same as at nine-and-twenty. This also hath God wrought.'

The almost annual birthday reflections in his *Journal* from 1770 to 1790 remain equally buoyant into his seventies, but in his eighties reveal a slight relaxing of the interminable pressure, though (as shown by his daily diary from 1782 onwards) there was little change in his activities or timetable. His friends noticed, however, that his calmness amidst the busy turmoil was developing into a deep serenity. He was widely regarded among Methodists and non-Methodists alike as having something of the halo of saintliness about him. After the death of his younger brother in 1788 no one felt able to use his first name: he was 'Mr Wesley' to his followers, from the lowest to the highest. Most remarkable and revealing are his later birthday reflections. The longest was penned on 28 June 1788, written at his birthplace, Epworth, where he preached twice that day, and prepared the agenda for his forthcoming Conference. Apparently he considered the memorandum so significant that he had an amanuensis transcribe it, and he himself addressed the copy to Samuel

Bradburn, the most junior member of his preaching staff at the New Chapel, City Road, London – and the only non-cleric among them. It is lengthy, but it offers a suitable climax to our efforts to portray Wesley as he saw himself among his detractors:

> I this day enter my eighty-fifth year. And what cause have I to praise God, as for a thousand spiritual blessings, so for bodily blessings also! How little have I suffered yet by 'the rush of numerous years'! It is true I am not so *agile* as I was in times past: I do not run or walk so fast as I did. My *sight* is a little decayed. My left eye is grown dim, and hardly serves me to read. I have daily some pain in the ball of my right eye, as also in my right temple (occasioned by a blow received some months since), and in my right shoulder and arm, which I impute partly to a sprain, and partly to the rheumatism. I find likewise some decay in my memory, with regard to names, and things lately passed; but not at all with regard to what I have read or heard twenty, forty, or sixty years ago. Neither do I find any decay in my hearing, smell, taste, or appetite (though I want but a third part of the food I did once); nor do I feel any such thing as weariness, either in travelling or preaching. And I am not conscious of any decay in writing Sermons, which I do as readily and I believe as correctly as ever.
>
> To what cause can I impute this, that I am as I am? First, doubtless to the power of God, fitting me for the work to which I am called, as long as he pleases to continue me therein; and next, subordinately to this, to the prayers of his children.
>
> May we not impute it, as inferior means:
>
> 1. To my constant exercise and change of air?
> 2. To my never having lost a night's sleep, sick or well, at land or at sea, since I was born?
> 3. To my having sleep at command, so that whenever I feel myself almost worn out I call it, and it comes, day or night?
> 4. To my having constantly, for above sixty years, risen at four in the morning?
> 5. To my constant preaching at five in the morning, for above fifty years?
> 6. To my having so little pain in my life, and so little sorrow, or anxious care?
>
> Even now, though I find pain daily, in my eye, or temple, or

arm, yet it is never violent, and seldom lasts many minutes at a time.

Whether or not this is sent to give me warning that I am shortly to quit this tabernacle, I do not know; but, be it one way or the other, I have only to say:

> My remnant of days
> I spend to his praise,
> Who died the whole world to redeem:
> Be they many or few,
> My days are his due,
> And they all are devoted to him.

John Wesley's death in 1791 led to a host of eulogies, followed by a group of biographies prepared too hastily and surrounded by controversy over the handling of his manuscripts. Even then there were a few critics of his views and idiosyncrasies, though the general tone was reverential and protective. The best brief assessment of these and subsequent biographies is by Richard Heitzenrater, in *The Elusive Mr Wesley* (1984), a fascinating and eye-opening two-volume introduction to 'John Wesley his own Biographer' and 'John Wesley as seen by Contemporaries and Biographers'.[20] The well-rounded scholarly full-length biography of Wesley that most of us seek still remains to be written, but its possibility has been drawing nearer almost every decade of this century, with its host of specialist studies, with the growing realization that Wesley was not monolithic either in his theology, his spirituality, or his ecclesiology, and especially with the assistance of a steadily accumulating series of definitive texts in the Oxford/Bicentennial Edition of his works.[21]

Explorations of the many facets of this great churchman whose life touched every decade of the eighteenth century continues to enthral students in many seemingly unrelated fields. This volume attempts to secure the views upon his life and influence of twenty scholars, each of whom has made her or his own mark, but sees Wesley differently from anyone else. Even a score of diverse writers, of course, cannot expect to assess him adequately, let alone produce a definitive biography. Each, however, touches upon something of importance which may help to furnish a more reliable cumulative impression of this many-sided man of God after two hundred and fifty years.

It is into a world of rapidly increasing knowledge about John Wesley that we introduce this series of essays, which come from so many different theological and denominational standpoints. We begin with a special essay about one of the more important aspects of this new knowledge, a study of Wesley's diary by Professor Richard P. Heitzenrater. From this we turn successively to some more general fields in which Wesley's presence has been strongly felt, those of Christian experience, churchmanship, the pastoral office, and evangelism.

With our focal point as the awakening experience which came to John Wesley on 24 May 1738, in the society meeting in Aldersgate, London, and its aftermath, Professor W. P. Stephens of Aberdeen University writes on 'Wesley and the Moravians'; Professor Frances Young of Birmingham University on 'The Significance of John Wesley's Conversion Experience', and Bruce Kent on 'John Wesley: Inspiration', a Roman Catholic's view of Wesley's personal religion. Different aspects of Wesley's churchmanship are discussed by Father Aelred Burrows, OSB, Monk of Ampleforth Abbey, on 'Wesley the Catholic'; Bishop Ole Borgen of Sweden on 'John Wesley: Sacramental Theology. No Ends without the Means'; the Rev. C. Norman R. Wallwork of Keswick on 'Wesley's Legacy in Worship'; Christopher Stell of the Rural Commission of Historical Monuments on 'Wesley's Chapels'; and the Rev. A. Raymond George, Warden of Wesley's New Room at Bristol, on 'John Wesley: The Organizer'. The theme of Wesley's witness as a pastor is expounded in varying ways by Lieutenant-Colonel David Guy, Literary Secretary of the Salvation Army, on 'John Wesley: Apostle of Social Holiness'; the Rev. Dr John A. Newton, Chairman of the Liverpool District of the Methodist Church, on 'Wesley and Women'; Bishop Maddocks of the Church of England on 'Health and Healing in the Ministry of John Wesley'; and the Rev. Wesley A. Chambers of the New Zealand Methodist Church on 'John Wesley and Death'.

The final essays deal with various aspects of Wesley's evangelical message. Professor Melvin E. Dieter of Asbury Theological Seminary, Wilmore, Kentucky, writes on 'Wesley Theology'; the Rev. William R. Davies, President of the British Methodist Conference and former Principal of Cliff College on 'The Relevance of John Wesley's Message for Today'. The Rev. the Lord Soper expounds 'Wesley the Outdoor Preacher', the Rev. Dr A.

Skevington Wood, 'Wesley as a Writer', and Dr Pauline Webb of the BBC Overseas Religious Broadcasting Service, 'Wesley the Communicator'. The symposium is rounded off, and reaches its true climax, with the essay of Dr Joe Hale, General Secretary of the World Methodist Council, on 'Wesley the Evangelist'.

On the occasion of the two hundred and fiftieth anniversary of a great leader's spiritual birthday it is natural that we should take off our hats to the past, but with his example powerfully before us, it is certainly appropriate that we should also take off our coats to the future!

1

Wesley and his Diary

Richard P. Heitzenrater

No single name in the history of our tradition is more familiar to Methodists world-wide than John Wesley. Nevertheless, historians and biographers, as well as painters, have had difficulty for over two centuries in capturing a portrait of Wesley that commands a consensus as being true to life. The picture is usually larger than life, perhaps not unexpectedly so – Wesley was, after all, a significant historical personality. But in the process of depicting his significance, the epic proportions of his traditional public image often overshadow the human, personal aspects of the man. The task before us is not to redraw the portrait completely – that is neither possible nor perhaps necessary. The historian's task is to bring the portrait into the light, review it, and make whatever alterations are appropriate on the basis of new evidence or new interpretations. Wesley's private diary proves to be a very useful resource in this endeavour because it gives us such an close view of the personal side of the man.

Many otherwise unsuspecting Methodists, when they hear of Wesley's multi-volume private diary (many parts of which are as yet unpublished), wonder if these notebooks might reveal more than we would (or should) want to know about Wesley's private life. We can set such apprehensiveness aside at the outset. Only those who forget that Wesley was human will have any problem with these writings. And the Wesley-cultists actually have more to cope with in his letters than in his 'secret' diary.

The well-known stereotype of Wesley is essentially a 'public' image, built upon documents that were published during Wesley's lifetime – journals, sermons, tracts, hymns, and a few letters. This image depicts Wesley as he wanted the public to see him. The present popular image of Wesley still reflects the literary portraits done by his nineteenth-century followers. Most of these arose in the midst of a powerful Methodist triumphalism and were firmly fixed long before any significant study of Wesley's private letters and diary.

The Wesley of the diary is a more candid, spontaneous, searching individual, less concerned about defending himself in the public eye, more pre-occupied with his personal interests and more concerned with tracking his own pilgrimage as a follower of Christ. There is no inherent contradiction between the private and public Mr Wesley; these are two sides of the same man. But a careful look at him through the diary (especially in conjunction with the letters) helps us to develop a more accurate and complete portrait than we can see in the public documents, which tend to support (if not promote) the more stereotypical image.

John Wesley kept a personal, daily diary from the year of his ordination as a deacon at the age of twenty-two in 1725 until just a few days before his death in 1791 – the last three-quarters, or sixty-six years, of the nearly eighty-eight years of his life. The diary is quite different from his *Journal*. The diary, like most of his letters, is a very private document, primarily designed for Wesley's own use, while the *Journal*, like most of his sermons and tracts, is a public, published document. The *Journal* narrative is based in part on events listed in his manuscript diary, but the purpose of the material he published is to provide a description and defence of himself and his movement from 1735 wards. Wesley also had a particular purpose in mind in keeping a diary; it was not simply a nonchalant noting down of main events for the day. He started this daily exercise to measure and record his progress in holy living and, in fact, to promote such progress through the careful management of his time. Wesley's little notebook was a constant companion into which he would, at frequent intervals, carefully enter the activities of the past few hours, occasionally using notes on scrap paper to assist his memory from one writing to the next.

Among several impressions that are obvious throughout the little notebooks that comprise his diary, two are especially fascinating: 1. Wesley developed a coded system of diary entry and 2. his method changed and developed in stages. The so-called 'code' is made up of several elements that change both internally and in their combinations with each other. First is a cipher which is a combination of substitution and transposition ciphers. In the substitution aspect of the cipher, Wesley uses numbers, dots, or symbols for the vowels he wishes to write. In the transposition aspect, he occasionally switches consonants so that when he writes down a letter such as 'd', he may indeed mean the consonant on either side, e.g. for a 'd', he would use a 'c' or an 'f'. To further complicate matters, Wesley at times applies the transposition rule to the substitution aspect of his cipher. That is to say, while 2–4–6–8–10 or 1–3–5–7–9 may in either case substitute for a-e-i-o-u, Wesley occasionally (whether through error or intention) uses a number such as 3 or 4, which would normally indicate an 'e', to mean either an 'a' or an 'i', the vowel on either side of the 'e' (in the usual ordering). One further complication – Wesley occasionally flips the whole scheme over so that the odd or even numbers in *descending* order may also mean a-e-i-o-u.

A second feature of his 'code', evident on almost every page of his diary (especially after 1729), is the persistent and heavy use of abbreviations. These also change and develop as he becomes accustomed to his own use of shortened words. Many words, or even phrases, having become more and more abbreviated, are finally indicated by a single letter. For example, in a typical early morning entry from the early 1730s, Wesley shows that he was asking himself certain 'questions' for the day, proceeding with his self-examination, and then reading the Bible – simply by the letters 'qxb'.

A third aspect of the 'code' is Wesley's use of symbols other than letters or numbers. Besides symbols within the cipher to indicate particular letters, Wesley also uses special symbols to indicate words and phrases. In addition to these, he develops a rather interesting set of symbols to indicate 'degrees of attention'. He uses six variations of the dash, above or below other entries, with or without a tail going up or down, to indicate these 'degrees', six attitudes that range from very negative to very positive: cold, dead, indifferent, attentive, fervent and, best of all – a dash above the entry with the final little tail going up – zealous.

Besides, cipher, abbreviations, and symbols, Welsey also works into his 'code' several number schemes. He uses numbers to indicate a variety of things on the diary page, from the simple notation of the time of day to the rather complicated hourly listing of his resolutions broken and resolutions kept. Simply by entering 't2' under the resolutions-broken column, Wesley indicates that he has failed to measure up to the expectations of the second question for Tuesday, one of a rather long list of questions for hourly self-examination at the front of his diary. The second question for Tuesday is, 'Have I any proud or vain thoughts?' Another use of numbers which occurs in his most complicated scheme of diary-keeping, the 'exacter' diary style of 1734–36, is a rating system whereby he could indicate his 'temper of devotion' by means of numbers from 1 to 9.

A fifth element of his 'code' is the use of eighteenth-century systems of shorthand. Wesley used two different shorthand schemes: Weston's shorthand, starting in 1734, changing to Byrom's shorthand in 1736. Byrom's shorthand predominates in Wesley's diary entries from that point onward to 1791. Although the shorthand appears to be visually baffling and although Wesley's use of it is at times rather imprecise and often abbreviated, it still is probably the simplest part of Wesley's code to decipher.

The second major characteristic of Wesley's diary that I would mention in addition to the 'code' is the fact that the style of diary-keeping goes through stages. Over the first ten years, the system gradually increases in complexity and completeness of daily entry. Over the succeeding few years, it gradually reverts to a simpler format that Wesley then follows for the rest of his life.

Starting in 1725, Wesley uses a rather simple daily entry, sometimes just one line, sometimes two (for morning and afternoon), writing usually in longhand with a few abbreviations, with a few cipher entries scattered among the rest. By 1729, Wesley is writing almost entirely in abbreviations (occasionally using a few special symbols) and expanding his entries to three or four lines per day. He gradually makes more complete notations for each day so that eventually a daily entry takes up half a page.

By 1734, however, this scheme of daily entry has become totally inadequate for his increasingly complex listing of activities. He switches then to what the Oxford Methodists called the 'exacter' diary, one full page for each day and a column format by which he could indicate not only activities for each hour but also the results of his complicated schemes of self-examination. By 1737, he had begun incorporating the shorthand into this format, at the same time making briefer and simpler entries for each hour. By early 1738, he has discarded the column format and has gone back to what we might call the paragraph style, using again half a page for each day's entry. In spite of a gap in the diary from 1742 to 1781 (these volumes having been lost or destroyed after Wesley's death), the only difference in the next extant diary, beginning in 1782, is that the daily entry has shrunk back to about three or four lines per day. The diary, however, is still mostly in shorthand and still rather precise in its indications of time and activities.

A dozen or so of these manuscript volumes have survived, and even the casual observer can tell that they contain a great deal of information. Some of the data from these newly transliterated pages is helping to rewrite the early history of Methodism. The picture of Wesley that emerges from the pages of his diary is overwhelmingly detailed. Over two thousand pages of closely written entries list the activities of Wesley's busy life during those years. The cryptic but extensive notes form a vast data bank about Wesley, some of it *trivia esoteria*, perhaps, but in large part, useful information that helps expand and clarify our understanding of Wesley's life and thought.

Details from the diary

The diary adds a myriad of details to the life story of Wesley – facts about places, people, readings, writings, dates, health, preaching, weather, and a host of other topics. In some cases this information confirms other sources; at other times it corrects misinformation or conjectures.

Some of the facts that we can glean from the diary remind us of Wesley's fascination with the world around him. He tours Blenheim, viewing the tapestries in the newly constructed palace. While travelling near Manchester, he steps into the cavernous darkness of Poole's Hole. Pretending at archaeology, he digs into the hermit's grave at Lindholme Hall. An inquisitive visitor, he steps off the measurements of Lincoln Cathedral. On at least two occasions, he builds a *camera obscura* (a primitive optical gadget). He enjoys the mystery of the *aurora borealis* and the passing of a comet.

We can follow Wesley around England, not only tracing his routes but also noting the names of roadhouses where he ate and slept. Many, like the Red Lodge south of Newark, are still entertaining guests.

We discover some of the tribulations of his travels – his horse falls on a bridge in Daventry and slips into a muddy ditch near Leicester; he loses his way in the woods of Oxfordshire and the swamps of

Georgia; his leg goes lame near Tetsworth. A wall falls out from under him near Coscombe, raising the question of what he was doing walking on the wall to begin with! His purchase of a pistol just before setting out on foot from Oxford to Epworth (a five-day walk) hints at other dangers of eighteenth-century travel.

Some of the entries provide clues to the dates and origins of Wesley's writings – sermons, letters, treatises that have previously been undated. The fire which cancelled a scheduled horse race, mentioned in his sermon, 'On Public Diversions' (No. 143, new edition), is noted in his diary on 1 September 1732, at Epworth, just before he began writing a sermon to preach in his father's church on the following Sunday. Another series of diary entries confirms the fact that a group of sermons, though extant only in Charles Wesley's handwriting, are actually John's sermons, written and preached first by John, then copied and used by Charles.

The diary also mentions other private activities not often evident in the more public accounts of Wesley's life as a young man. He constructs an arbour at Epworth, helps the workmen build his house in Savannah, works in his garden in Georgia, and plants trees at Wroot. He goes fishing with Thomas Hawkins and pares apples with Benjamin Ingham. As a student at Oxford, he exercises with frequent walks around Christ Church meadow and occasional games of tennis.

Wesley notes other leisure activities in his early diary entries that we do not hear about in his own or other accounts of his life, such as going to the races at Port Meadow or playing a variety of games common in the eighteenth century: backgammon, billiards, Pope Joan, brag, ombre, quadrille, loo, quoits, draughts, similies, cross questions and crooked answers.

Some of the activities listed in his diary are similar in nature to some noted in his *Journal*. But without the diary we would not have known that Wesley saw a performance of *Hamlet* at Goodman's Fields Playhouse in London or that he heard Handel direct a performance of the oratorio *Esther* at the theatre in Oxford. He gave Lord Oxford a tour of the Bodleian Library and walked around Lord Aylesford's estate in Meridan. The diary shows Wesley confronting mobs, visiting the House of Commons, and even mending his breeches.

We can also see in the diary an occasional entry that reflects

Wesley's reaction to special events in his life. On a summer day in 1733 he writes: 'Waked by spitting blood. O Eternity!' After viewing the hanging of a horse-thief he notes with some surprise, 'I but little affected!' Upon his first arrival in Savannah he notes at the bottom of a page, 'Beware America; be not as England.' In April 1738 he remarks after having been visited by Peter Böhler, 'Convinced that faith converts at once.' The news that his would-be love Sophy Hopkey was to be married to someone else led him to end his diary entry that day with 'No such day since I first saw the sun! . . . Let me not see such another!'

The diary also contains, for some periods, rather complete financial accounts, whereby we can tell how much he paid to ride the Trent ferry (a penny each way) how much he was paid for preaching in rural Oxfordshire churches (up to a guinea per Sunday), how much he paid to hire a horse for a day (about a shilling), or how much a 'Cromwell shilling' cost him (two shillings). He visits the bookbinder, the printer, the barber and the brazier. He goes to auctions, to markets, to exhibits and to fairs and often records the cost of these excursions to the halfpenny.

The diary also reveals the private side of many of Wesley's public activities. For instance, Wesley spent over fifty hours preparing his sermon, 'Circumcision of the Heart' (three to four times his normal effort at that time) and revised it several times after reading it to friends. In the spring of 1740, he spent twenty to thirty hours during some weeks preparing the first extract of his *Journal* for publication. The diary for January 1783 indicates that Wesley spent over fifty hours preparing the monthly edition of his *Arminian Magazine*.

Such careful indication of time in the diary (usually to the quarter-hour, sometimes to the minute) makes it possible to know how much time Wesley spent daily in prayer, meditation, reading, writing, travelling, talking, eating, worshipping, and other 'necessary business' (as he notes at times). A statistical analysis and comparison of different periods of his life reveals a remarkable degree of consistency (as well as some important changing patterns) in the nature of his busy-ness as well as the course of his daily schedule.

The diary contains not only a record of Wesley's hourly activities, but also on many of the prefatory pages, notes on a variety of miscellaneous concerns. Predominant on these pages are lists – questions for self-examination, resolutions for self-improvement, writings to be done, writings already finished, members of societies and bands, books read, books owned, laundry sent out, money lent, ideas borrowed, even colloquialisms picked up along the way.

Details of this sort, fascinating in themselves, combine to give us a more complete and accurate view of a Wesley whose image at times appeared somewhat elusive. This material also makes possible a more careful examination of the development of Wesley's mind and spirit and of his leadership in the Methodist movement. The sources of Wesley's thought and the context of his writings, both essential to an understanding of his theology, become much more explicit. Once these materials are more widely accessible, biographers and theologians will have a unique resource to help them understand Wesley in a more particular as well as holistic manner.

The portrait in the diary

What sort of Wesley emerges from the pages of the diary? It is not an unfamiliar Wesley, but rather a much more complicated one than we usually see. The diary allows us to paint in some details we find in no other sources, thereby in its own way helping to make his portrait more lifelike. No one would doubt that Wesley was busy, devout, methodical, and resolute, but with the help of some samplings from his diary we can see precisely in what ways his life exhibited these characteristics.

We all know that Wesley was *busy*, but what precisely was the extent and nature of his busy-ness? The statistics of his accomplishments are a well-rehearsed part of the Wesley story: travelling 250,000 miles during his ministry, preaching 40–50,000 times, publishing over 400 separate items, some of them multi-volume works – all adding up to more than one, or perhaps even two, normal lifetimes of productivity.

The diary helps us answer some of the questions that naturally arise. Where did he go? What did he do? Whom did he visit? What did he read? A sampling from his first diary shows him during his Oxford days, reading Horace, *De Arte Poetica*, writing a sermon, going to an auction and visiting friends at a local pub. A sample page from the second diary shows Wesley visiting his lady friends in the Cotswold Hills on his way back to Oxford in the summer of

1729 and reading *Reflections on Learning*, the *Art of Thinking*, and several other works. Once at Oxford he is again visiting friends, on one occasion rowing up the river with some fellow students, as he says 'by water to Ensom', losing more than once while playing cards on the way (his financial accounts for this period tell us that he spent and lost twelve shillings on this little jaunt).

A page from his 'exacter' diary of 1735 shows him again talking with many friends, indicating the nature of their conversation (rt, 'religious talk'; vt, 'various talk'; it, 'idle talk'; lt, learned talk'). In the morning he is studying shorthand; in the evening he is reading the Greek Testament with his Methodist friends. On a page from the Georgia period, the shorthand reveals that he is reading Clement of Rome and spending a great deal of time talking to Sophy Hopkey and her aunt. Another sample page from a weekend in October 1738 shows, among other things, the people he is visiting and the places he is preaching, with two of his preaching texts noted in Greek at the bottom of the page. One of them is especially noteworthy, a favourite text even after Aldersgate: 'And by works was faith made perfect' (James 2.22). His diary just a year or so before his death shows Wesley at the age of eighty-six reading Brevint's works, still writing sermons, editing the *Arminian Magazine*, attending a love-feast, and spending many hours writing letters to friends and associates: a regular activity during the winter months that he spent in London.

These sample pages show every day, every hour, packed with activity. The time is well spent, except perhaps for those infrequent occasions when Wesley notes 'idleness'. These documents tell not only his schedule of rising, singing, fasting and other daily activities, but also the breadth and depth of his reading, the variety of his writing and editing, the scope of his travelling and the nature of his conversations with people, as well as the many regular occasions for personal prayer, Bible study, meditation and other specifically religious practices. In all this busy-ness Wesley was trying to do all for the glory of God. He saw idleness as sinful, along with some other light-hearted activities not conducive to promoting God's glory. The regularity and frequency of his spiritual exercises bring into focus this desire to glorify God in his devotional life.

Wesley was indeed *devout*. Every one of the diary pages is filled with a variety of symbols to indicate periods of prayer: private prayer, public prayers morning an evening, as well as short-sentence prayers (called ejaculatory prayers) at the turn of every hour. On the day he discovered Miss Sophy was to be married he even indicated in his diary his consternation at not being able to pray. Wesley also indicates periods of meditation: in a college garden at Oxford, on his way to preach at Islington, and on other occasions appropriate for reflection.

Two other specific details indicated in Wesley's scheme of diary-keeping help us to see the measure of his devotional stance. One of these is the set of symbols I mentioned earlier, the dashes which show 'degrees of attention' for private prayer, meditation or almost any other activity. Another detail is his hourly rating scheme whereby he indicates his 'temper of devotion' by number. Within this scheme 6 seems to be his most normal entry, so that 7 and 8 are generally better, 4 and 5 a lesser evaluation of his attitude.

From the nature of these details in the diary it quickly becomes evident that Wesley was not only busy and devout, but also *methodical*. The diary itself is a visual illustration of his methodistic tendencies, but these tendencies extended far beyond the method for the diary. Wesley also had a specific method for reading, a method for writing, a method for acquaintance (that is, making new acquaintances), a method for visiting and even a method for deciding important questions. By 1735 he was beginning to question some of his regular practices such as early rising and fasting, and as Wesley's body yearns for more sleep in the morning, the young scholar casts lots to see whether he should stay up or go back to bed. And as breakfast approaches on a fast day and his stomach cries out for food, he again casts lots to see whether he should break the fast. In most of these instances, the drawn lot, determined of course by God's providence, supported his time-tested resolutions more often than his weakening will-power.

Wesley was a methodist not only in his activities, living by method and rule (as the title of an earlier book stated), but also in his theology. Eclectic as it was, his method of theologizing approximated in significant ways to that of some Dutch and English Arminians who had been called 'New Methodists' in the previous century because of their new method of doing theology. That, however, is a full story in its own right.

In all of Wesley's frantic activity he demonstrates yet another attribute: he was *resolute*. He had purpose and direction, with specific expectations for each step of the way. In the early diary entries his resolute attitude is visible in the many lists of resolutions by which he guided his thoughts and activities. The 'exacter' diary during the 1730s is the high point of his systematized approach to score-keeping in this regard. Two columns at the right-hand side of the page indicate 'resolutions broken' and 'resolutions kept', keyed by letter and number to long lists of guidelines he sought to follow. His resolutions usually arose from (and therefore indicate some problem areas in) his attempt to press on toward perfection. Many of his periods of self-examination resulted in the drawing up of new resolutions. We can sympathize with Wesley when he writes, 'Before you sit at a full table, pray for help'. The pervasiveness of his self-inquiry is illustrated by one particularly persistent question over which Wesley frequently stumbled: 'Have I said or done anything without a present or previous perception of its direct or remote tendency to the glory of God?' It is easy to understand Wesley's difficulty in trying to answer that in the affirmative at the end of every hour.

These resolutions and questions gradually evolved into lists of rules for the Methodists. Though none of the later lists were quite so specific and thorough as those he designed for himself, the temper of them all is evident in what came to be known as the 'General Rules', summarized under three simple directives: to avoid evil of every kind, to do good of every possible sort and to attend upon all the ordinances of God. Wesley's own resolute intention is best illustrated in a resolution copied down by his friend, Benjamin Ingham: 'Resolved – to make the salvation of my soul my chief and only concern.'

Certainly Methodism is more than the lengthened shadow of one man, but we cannot fully appreciate the richness of our heritage without recognizing the mark left upon it by the character and personality of John Wesley. Sometimes the halo and tinfoil of well-meaning triumphalists obscure our view of the real person. But these diary records, along with other private materials from his pen such as the letters, help us to recall the failures as well as the triumphs, the tedium as well as the excitement, the struggles as well as the strengths, of Wesley's own personal attempt to press on to perfection. Some observers will find his peculiar interests fascinating. Many will be intrigued by the sheer energy that his life-style exhibits. To some he will seem more than slightly eccentric or compulsive, as he certainly did to many in his own day. To others, the depth of his spirituality and the breadth of his learning will appear overwhelming.

The diary does not alter the broad judgements history has passed on John Wesley's reputation. These records reveal him no less of a hero. They detract not an ounce from our admiration for him. But these valuable little notebooks do take us a bit closer to a more life-like portrait of John Wesley the man.

2

Wesley and the Moravians

W. P. Stephens

The Moravians are inseparable from the decisive events of 24 May 1738.[1] Indeed we can assert that without them there would have been no evangelical conversion on that day. Before his contacts with them Wesley had been searching for salvation through a life of holiness. It was they who helped him to see that he had been trusting in his own righteousness, and through them that he came to trust in the righteousness of Christ (*Journal* I, 465–72).[2]

Wesley first met the Moravians (or Germans, as he also calls them) on his journey to America in 1735. He came to know them more intimately during his time in Georgia. Then in the months after his return in 1738 he received the help which led to his conversion at Aldersgate Street and the visit to Herrnhut which followed it.

His relations with the Moravians changed dramatically in 1739 and never regained that first fine careless rapture of 1735, yet his sense of indebtedness to them never wavered and his esteem for them persisted even in the sharpness of controversy. The sense of indebtedness may be seen in his letter to Mrs Hutton on 22 August 1744, 'I love Calvin a little, Luther more, the Moravians, Mr Law, and Mr Whitfield far more than either' (*Letters* II, 25). The esteem is evident a month earlier on 24 July in the preface to Part Four of his *Journal* in which he presented his disagreements with them.

What unites my heart to you is the excellency (in many respects) of the doctrine taught among you . . . I magnify the grace of God which is in many among you, enabling you to love

Him who hath first loved us . . . I praise God that He hath
delivered, and yet doth deliver, you from those outward sins
that overspread the face of the earth . . . I love and esteem you
for your excellent discipline, scarce inferior to that of the
apostolic age . . . (*Journal* II, 310–11).

This account of Wesley and the Moravians looks at five periods:
the voyage, the time in Georgia, the meetings with Böhler on his
return to England, the visit to Herrnhut, and the controversy with
Molther and Zinzendorf.

(i) The voyage

On Friday, 17 October 1735, three days after boarding the ship
Simmonds as a missionary for America, Wesley refers to his
meeting with them.

I began to learn German, in order to converse a little with the
Moravians, six-and-twenty of whom we have on board, men
who have left all for their Master, and who have indeed learned
of Him, being meek and lowly, dead to the world, full of faith and
of the Holy Ghost (*Journal* I, 110).

Four days later Wesley could write of a regular pattern of life in
which he learned German from nine to twelve (*Journal* I, 112),
while some of the Moravians had begun to learn English. His
contact with them was varied – visiting their sick, studying their
hymns, conversing, and singing and worshipping with them.

They made a profound impression on him by their life and by
their faith. In the ordinary circumstances of life on a ship they
stood out as extraordinary. On Sunday, 25 January 1736, his
journal includes an impressive testimony to them in the midst of a
dramatic account of a storm at sea. It was the third storm during
the voyage, one which he described as 'more violent than any we
had had before'.

At seven I went to the Germans. I had long before observed the
great seriousness of their behaviour. Of their humility they had
given a continual proof, by performing those servile offices for
the other passengers which none of the English would undertake; for which they desired and would receive no pay, saying,
'It was good for their proud hearts', and 'their loving Saviour
had done more for them'. And every day had given them

occasion of showing a meekness which no injury could move. If they were pushed, struck, or thrown down, they rose again and went away; but no complaint was found in their mouth. There was now an opportunity of trying whether they were delivered from the spirit of fear, as well as from that of pride, anger, and revenge. In the midst of the psalm wherewith their service began, wherein we were mentioning the power of God, the sea broke over, split the mainsail in pieces, covered the ship, and poured in between the decks, as if the great deep had already swallowed us up. A terrible screaming began among the English. The Germans looked up and without intermission calmly sang on. I asked one of them afterwards, 'Was you not afraid?' He answered, 'I thank God, no.' I asked, 'But were not your women and children afraid?' He replied mildly, 'No; our women and children are not afraid to die.'

From them I went to their crying, trembling neighbours, and found myself enabled to speak with them in boldness and to point out to them the difference in the hour of trial between him that feareth God and him that feareth Him not. At twelve the wind fell. This was the most glorious day which I have hitherto seen (*Journal* I, 142–3).

Their simple confidence in God searched out the character of Wesley's own faith in God, as their devotion to God and to others challenged one who had for years been given to the pursuit of 'the holiness without which no one will see the Lord'. Here were people who were exemplars of holy living and holy dying. Theirs was not that 'fair summer religion' of which Wesley could accuse himself at the end of his journey back to England in 1738. Then he was to write, 'But in a storm I think, What if the gospel be not true?' 'I can talk well; nay, and believe myself, while no danger is near. But let death look me in the face, and my spirit is troubled' (*Journal* I, 418). Wesley saw in them what he himself lacked: a living faith – and they wakened his longing for it.

(ii) In America

Wesley's intimacy with the Moravians continued after their arrival in America in the first week of February 1736. The day after he 'set foot on American ground' he met Spangenberg, to whom he later referred as 'that good soldier of Jesus Christ'

(*Journal* I, 371). The following day, Sunday 8 February, he recorded a strikingly direct conversation in which he reveals the nature of his own faith at this stage.

> I asked Mr Spangenberg's advice with regard to myself – to my own conduct. He told me he could say nothing till he had asked me two or three questions. 'Do you know yourself? Have you the witness within yourself? Does the Spirit of God bear witness with your spirit that you are a child of God?' I was surprised, and knew not what to answer. He observed it, and asked, 'Do you know Jesus Christ?' I paused and said, 'I know He is the Saviour of the world.' 'True,' replied he; 'but do you know He has saved you?' I answered, 'I hope He has died to save me.' He only added, 'Do you know yourself?' I said, 'I do.' But I fear they were vain words (*Journal* I, 151).

Spangenberg's view of Wesley was less critical than Wesley's later reflection, for he recorded in his diary, 'I noticed that genuine grace dwells and rules in him.' (The later emphasis on the witness of the Spirit can be seen here.)

Just over two weeks later Wesley and Delamotte went to lodge with the Moravians. Once again it was the way they lived that impressed him: their activity, their relations, and the absence of evil.

> We had now an opportunity, day by day, of observing their whole behaviour. For we were in one room with them from morning to night, unless for the little time I spent in walking. They were always employed, always cheerful themselves, and in good humour with one another; they had put away all anger, and strife, and wrath, and bitterness, and clamour, and evil-speaking; they walked worthy of the vocation wherewith they were called, and adorned the gospel of our Lord in all things (*Journal* I, 169).

It is the same concern for holiness that had engaged him for years. But in them there was the holiness of life, not the holiness of books.

The contacts were constant and were both personal and ministerial. Wesley consulted them in matters as diverse as his mission to the Choctaw Indians and his possible marriage to Sophy Hopkey (*Journal* I, 238–9, 315–16), and he also employed their method of discerning God's will in the latter question by the use of lots. They sang and preached together and he also led their worship. (Indeed with his growing command of languages he could be found leading worship in Italian and French as well, *Journal* I, 396–7.) His study of German, which had begun after his first meeting with them, now bore fruit in his translation of German hymns, both Pietist and Moravian. But his translations were not an academic pursuit They were part of a piety in which the singing of hymns had a vital place, so that both the hymns and the singing of hymns were part of his debt to the Moravians.

There was also the appeal of the primitive church which Wesley saw manifested in them in their election and ordination of a bishop, reminding him of an assembly presided over by 'Paul the tent maker or Peter the fisherman' (*Journal* I, 170–1). Others were uneasy about his contacts with the Moravians, as James Hutton was in relation to the validity of their ordinations. For Wesley, however, it was God who had opened the door to the Moravian Church, and the style of that church, as of its bishops, was radically different from that of much of the Church of England as Wesley knew it. Alongside this was the way they ordered their life as a church – all that is embraced in the word discipline. Small intimate groups for Christian fellowship were not wholly new to Wesley any more than a reverence for the early church. What the Moravians did was to set them in a new key and breathe new life into them.

Yet Wesley clearly had a number of reservations about the Moravians and in particular about Zinzendorf, as can be seen for example in some of the questions and answers in his conversation with Spangenberg on 31 July 1737 and the comment for the following day with its reference to the 'Count's exposition of Scripture and method of public prayer'. Wesley was convinced of Zinzendorf 'that he likewise is but a man'. The concern expressed about 'openness and plainness of speech' was one that was often to recur afterwards (*Journal* I, 372–6).

Wesley left America hurriedly at the end of 1737 after the break-up of his friendship with Sophy Hopkey. He returned bereft of the great hopes with which he had gone to America. As he approached Land's End in January 1738 he wrote, 'I went to America, to convert the Indians; but oh, who shall convert me? who, what is he that will deliver me from this evil heart of unbelief?' He sees that what he lacks is a living faith, a faith that is free from sin, fear, and doubt (*Journal* I, 418–20). Yet Wesley is now aware of what he lacks – and the stage is therefore set for the next act.

(iii) England and Peter Böhler

The Moravians are again his companions on this final stage of his journey to Aldersgate Street. Indeed within days of landing came his first meeting with Peter Böhler who was to be the crucial person in his life in the weeks from February to May. Significantly he is the only person to be mentioned by name in Wesley's brief summary of his contacts with the Moravians in a letter to Thomas Church in 1746 (*Letters* II, 179–80).

He met him with others on Tuesday 7 February, 'a day much to be remembered', and took every opportunity 'of conversing with them' (*Journal* I, 436–7). Yet Wesley confesses that he did not understand Böhler, especially when he told him, 'that philosophy of yours must be purged away' (*Journal* I, 440). By Sunday 5 March, however, Wesley was 'clearly convinced of unbelief, of the want of that faith, whereby alone we are saved'. This naturally led him to think he should stop preaching, but Böhler rejected such a thought and, in response to Wesley's question 'But what can I preach?', said 'Preach faith *till* you have it; and then, *because* you have it, you *will* preach faith.' On the following day he records: 'I began preaching this new doctrine, though my soul started back from the work. The first person to whom I offered salvation by faith alone was a prisoner under sentence of death' (*Journal* I, 442). The task was doubly difficult as for years he had asserted the impossibility of a deathbed repentance. It is but one example of Wesley's obedience to his spiritual counsellors and his putting matters to the test – both of scripture and of experience. Three weeks later a condemned man (perhaps the same person) came to an assurance of faith and the enjoyment of perfect peace through prayer and preaching (*Journal* I, 448).

It was from this period that Wesley was himself increasingly persuaded from scripture of the nature of saving faith, of the happiness and holiness that are its fruits (from Romans 8 and 1 John 5 with their reference to the witness of the Spirit, and from 1 John 3 with its reference to the person born of God not committing sin), and of the instantaneous way in which it is given (from the Acts of the Apostles). But still Wesley could not believe that God

acted in his day as he did in the apostolic age until Böhler produced
for him living witnesses who testified that God had given them 'in a
moment such a faith in the blood of His Son as translated them out of
darkness into light, out of sin and fear into holiness and happiness.
Here ended my disputing. I could now only cry out, "Lord, help
Thou my unbelief!"' Again Wesley thought he should stop teaching
others, but Böhler's response was 'No; do not hide in the earth the
talent God hath given you.' Accordingly ten days later, Tuesday 25
April, he spoke 'clearly and fully' to others, including his brother,
'of the nature and fruits of faith' (*Journal* I, 455–6). With Böhler's
encouragement he continued to teach 'the faith as it is in Jesus'.
Others found it strange, as did Charles, who was 'strongly averse
from what he called "the new faith"' (*Journal* I, 457–8) (Charles
stated that the issue was not the nature of faith but whether
conversion was gradual or instantaneous.) But this preaching led –
on each of the three Sundays before 24 May – to the closing of
churches to him (*Journal* I, 460, 462, 464) On 24 May he came
himself to that living faith – a trust in Christ 'as *my* Christ, as *my* sole
justification, sanctification, and redemption'. This faith involved 'a
sense of pardon for all past and freedom from all present sins'
(*Journal* I, 472).

In his account of his life up to that point Wesley spoke of how he
had lived under law and not under grace and how it had been the
Moravians who had first endeavoured to show him 'a more
excellent way'. But although 24 May may have been the climax in
Wesley's search for a living faith in Christ, it was not the end of the
way. The days that followed showed a man much buffeted. He had
peace, but not joy. There was victory, but there were also fear,
temptation, doubt, and heaviness. On Friday 26 May he was
consulting a Moravian, John Töltschig, and it is not surprising that
he decided soon after that the time had come to 'retire for a short
time to Germany', something he had determined to do while still in
America. As he put it in his journal on 7 June:

> My weak mind could not bear to be thus sawn asunder. And I
> hoped the conversing with those holy men who were themselves
> living witnesses of the full power of faith, and yet able to bear with
> those that are weak, would be a means, under God, of so
> establishing my soul, that I might go on from faith to faith and
> 'from strength to strength' (*Journal* I, 482–3).

In a way this was to be the last stage of his pilgrimage towards a living faith.

(iv) In Germany

The journey through Holland and Germany lasted six weeks. Wesley, however, was no ordinary tourist, for when asked in Weimar why he was going as far as Herrnhut, he replied, 'To see the place where the Christians live'. On the way there Cologne struck him as 'the ugliest dirtiest city I ever yet saw with my eyes' and its cathedral as 'a huge mis-shapen thing', whereas the Orphan House in Halle was 'so conveniently contrived, and so exactly clean, as I have never seen any before' (*Journal* II, 7–8, 17; cf.*Letters* II, 249). It was supported in part by the selling of books and medicines – and was in more ways than one an example to Wesley. After three weeks the party reached Marienborn where Wesley met Zinzendorf and where the sight of a multinational community of ninety people provoked the cry, 'Oh how pleasant a thing it is for brethren to dwell together in unity!' (*Journal* II, 11), and – in a letter to his mother – the comment: 'I now understand those words of poor Julian, "See how these Christians love one another!"' (*Letters* I, 250).

In Germany he found what he was searching for: 'living proofs of the power of faith', people saved from inward and outward sin and from doubt and fear. (*Journal* II, 13). That is where the emphasis lay in the conversations he recorded (*Journal* II, 28–56). The people he talked with were continued evidence that what God had done in the first century in giving holiness and happiness, and peace and joy in the Holy Spirit, he could do in the eighteenth, and that the only way to this was faith in Christ crucified for us (*Letters* I, 254). Although at Marienborn he had alluded to certain reservations, yet they were 'smaller points that touch not the essence of Christianity'. He would not concern himself with them but rather with those who are witnesses that 'Every one that believeth hath peace with God and is freed from sin, and is in Christ a new creature.' For what had impressed Wesley was that young and old 'breathe nothing but faith and love at all times and in all places' (*Letters* I, 250–1).

In a letter to his mother on 6 July he had compared Zinzendorf's behaviour with that of Christ in the gospels (*Letters* I, 250), and his letter to Zinzendorf after the visit was warm and appreciative, although it also voiced his concerns (*Letters* I, 265–6). In a letter sent much later, though begun in September 1738, he raised these points, including the personality cult of Zinzendorf (*Letters* I, 257–8). Another criticism, that was also to persist was the lack of 'plainness of speech', something which Wesley was certainly not lacking, as his earlier letters to William Law testify. (His letter to Hutton from Herrnhut implies a concern here.) For him there is the dominical command to tell someone his fault directly (*Letters* I, 256).

The record that Wesley made of personal testimonies and Moravian history show divergences among the Moravians, some of which were to surface later in Wesley's dealing with them, such as the emphasis on either Christ in us or Christ for us, the relation between holy communion and a person's faith and between justifying faith and the assurance of faith, and the possiblility of agreement on the foundation while differing on some points of doctrine (*Journal* II, 28–56).

The visit to Marienborn and Herrnhut helped to complete theologically and experientially the process that had reached its climax for Wesley on 24 May. He had the evidence of that living faith in Christ in which the love of God is shed abroad in the heart and in which the Spirit bears witness with our spirit. He continued to think about the nature of faith and consulted the Moravians on this, as his letter to Charles on 28 June testifies (*Letters* I, 248). But his return from Germany marks in a way his independence of the Moravians. The visit perhaps had done for him something of what Paul's visit to Jerusalem and his time in Arabia had done for him. They had led him to faith. They had given him a host of witnesses to a living faith whose testimony could lead to the sharing of that faith with others. They had shown how men, women, and children could be built up in faith and love with forms of pastoral care that were both individual and corporate. They had expressed their faith in ways that were social as well as spiritual, above all with the orphan house in Halle. It is not surprising therefore that the critical letter of September 1738 should begin:

> I cannot but rejoice in your steadfast faith, in your love to our blessed Redeemer, your deadness to the world, your meekness, temperance, chastity, and love of one another. I greatly approve of your conferences and bands, of your method of instructing

children, and in general of your great care of the souls
committed to your charge' (*Letters* I, 257).

There is a sense in which his farewell words on 14 August show
just this: that Herrnhut marked an end and a beginning. 'I would
gladly have spent my life here; but my Master calling me to labour
in another part of His vineyard . . . I was constrained to take my
leave of this happy place . . .' (*Journal* II, 28).

(v) Controversy

A commemoration of 1738 leaves the relations of Wesley and the
Moravians at a high point. There were the seeds of disagreement
between them but no division and no conflict. In 1739 and 1740
the situation changed with the arrival of Philip Molther in
October 1739.[3] With it a period of controversy began, that was to
cloud relations for decades.

Wesley describes the development of his conflict with Molther,
Spangenberg, Zinzendorf, and others, in the fourth part of the
Journal (*Journal* II, 307–500), in the period from 1 November 1739
to 3 September 1741. Among the many issues raised, two stand
out: quietism (or stillness) and antinominianism, both issues that
can trouble revival movements.[4]

Molther encouraged those who did not have true faith, that is
who doubted, who did not have the free assurance of faith, to be
still (that is to abstain from the means of grace). They were to wait
for God to act and not to use outward means, as there is no other
means than Christ, and using them would be putting their faith in
them rather than in Christ. Outward works were also discouraged
for the same reason. As a result those whom Wesley regarded as
'strong in faith and zealous of good works' considered themselves
as needing faith, with the consequence that they must abstain
from good works (*Journal* II, 312–13; cf.*Letters* I, 347).

For Wesley this teaching worked havoc with those in his
pastoral care. He spoke of people as 'in great confusion', of their
being 'cold, weary, heartless, dead' (*Journal* II, 343). He and his
brother Charles, except when Charles was also under the sway of
stillness, used every available means to win back those who had
succumbed and overcome those who had persuaded them. There
were private conversations and public disputes (*Journal* II, 316,
343, 345). There were the letters and tracts in which both the

Moravians and their views were attacked. There was the explaining of 'true stillness' (*Journal* II, 331, 464). There was the exposition of scripture (*Journal* II, 354–62), with sermons on appropriate texts such as 'Do this in remembrance of me' against stillness and the use of the Epistle of James, 'the great antidote against this poison' (*Journal* II, 349), against antinomianism. There were hymns on the means of grace. There was the witness of those whose experience supported him, whether in their degrees of faith or their receiving of faith in the Lord's Supper (*Journal* II, 315, 345, 349), though some testified on the other side (*Journal* II, 366). There was the dramatic intervention in the meeting of the Fetter Lane society on Sunday 20 July, unanimously agreed on two days earlier, when John read a prepared text and invited those who agreed with him to leave.

The sum of what you asserted is this:

1. That there is no such thing as *weak faith*: That there is no justifying faith where there is ever any doubt or fear, or where there is not, in the full sense, a new, a clean heart.

2. That a man ought not to use those ordinances of God which our Church terms 'means of grace', before he has such a faith as excludes all doubt and fear, and implies a new, a clean heart.

You have often affirmed that to search the Scriptures, to pray, or to communicate before we have his faith is to seek salvation by works; and that till these works are laid aside no man can receive faith.

I believe these assertions to be flatly contrary to the Word of God. I have warned you hereof again and again, and besought you to turn back to the Law and the Testimony. I have borne with you long, hoping you would turn. But as I find you more and more confirmed in the error of your ways, nothing now remains but that I should give you up to God. You that are of the same judgement, follow me' (*Journal* II, 370).

The controversy shows that there were elements in Wesley's theology which antedated his contact with the Moravians and which persisted after that contact. The Articles, the Homilies, the Prayer Book and the writings of Anglican divines, not least William Law, had all contributed to his formation and left their mark, and they account in part for his opposition to stillness and antinomianism. Ironically the question of stillness showed Wesley as more Lutheran than the Moravians. His insistence on the means of grace was in keeping with Luther in his attack on the spirituals, although Wesley drew on his Anglican tradition rather than on Luther. Molther, with his urging of those who did not have true faith to be still and wait for God to act, ignoring the means that God had appointed, was closer to the spirituals.

The question of antinomianism (in doctrine rather than in practice) showed Wesley as the critic of Luther, whom he saw as 'the real spring of the grand error of the Moravians' (*Journal* II, 467). (Already in 1738 he had written of 'some Lutheran and Calvinist authors, whose confused and indigested accounts magnified faith to such an amazing size that it quite hid all the rest of the commandments', *Journal* I, 419.) The insistence on faith alone, and the describing of the law as something from which the Christian is freed, and the virtual rejection of the Epistle of James, conflicted with another part of Wesley's Anglican background: that insistence on the whole law of God, on 'the holiness without which no one will see the Lord'. The influence of William Law and others did not disappear, for all Wesley's criticism of Law in 1738, for not pointing him to the one thing needful: faith in Christ's death for our sins (*Letters* I, 239–44).

Once joined, the controversy developed. There were sharp, not to say, bitter expressions on both sides. Wesley referred to the Moravians as 'the German wolves' in contrast to Christ, the great shepherd (*Journal* III, 499), and Zinzendorf and the Moravians spoke with equal vigour. There were reasons for this. Wesley held that in many places the Moravians had 'well nigh destroyed the work of God' (*Letters* IV, 36), and that their views both went beyond scripture and were contrary to scripture (*Journal* II, 419–20). The Moravians also had their serious concerns. They were troubled by the sighing and groaning in Methodist meetings, regarding as animal spirits what Wesley considered the joy given by God. They considered Wesley's stress on the law as legalism and his stress on perfection as a denial of Christ as our sole perfection.

The controversy sharpened the differences, though it sometimes brought moments where the positions seemed close to each other, a difference of words or of emphasis rather than of substance. This seems the case in *A Second Dialogue between an*

Antinomian and his Friend in 1745 with the reference to 'a liberty to walk in the Spirit and not fulfil the lust (or desire) of the flesh' (*Works* X, 271).

Wesley's criticism was usually of some Moravians and some of their teaching or practice, not of all, and it must be set alongside his continuing sense of indebtedness and his desire for unity. He experienced pain in the separation, and a longing to be with them (*Journal* II, 441–2) and could recognize 'how much holier some of them were than me, or any people I had yet known' (*Journal* II, 378). He wrote on 8 December 1745 to the Synod of the Moravian Brethren at Marienborn asking whether they might not 'in a free and brotherly conference . . . 3. Settle how far we might unite . . . even if there should be some points wherein we cannot avoid speaking contrary to each other?' (*Letters* II, 54). And while Böhler was dying in 1775 he wrote to him, 'By the grace of God I shall go on . . . loving your Brethren beyond any body of men upon earth except the Methodists' (*Letters* VI, 141). To Hutton he had written 'If we do not think alike, we may at least love alike' (*Letters* V, 294).

The main debt of Wesley to the Moravians is their role in his coming to a living faith, a faith marked by the love of God shed abroad in the heart and the witness of the Spirit with our spirit. Through them he moved from formal to vital religion. Others influenced him before and after, but without that contribution the influence of the others would have borne little fruit. The Moravians also helped to shape the development of the Methodist movement in the whole pattern of fellowship, devotion, and oversight that was to be found in the bands. Wesley had already learnt from this in Georgia, but his visit to Germany extended this experience. However, Wesley did not simply copy what he saw, and so he did not establish communities of those who lived together as in Marienborn and Herrnhut but created societies of those who met together, although they lived separate from each other in the world. In Professor Rupp's words, 'it was to the Moravians more than to any other single source that Methodism owed its pattern of devotion and discipline, of bands, societies, conference, of vigils, love-feasts – within the sacramental and liturgical frame of the Church of England'.[5]

Yet with many things it is not a question of direct dependence (as perhaps in the use of the lot) but rather a sense of family likeness – in matters as diverse as the orphan home, the singing of hymns, the admission of children to holy communion, the response to physical hostility, and the being a society or church within the church.

3

The Significance of John Wesley's Conversion Experience

Frances Young

When I was growing up in the Methodist Church, teenagers were from time to time presented with the Gospel message in highly emotional terms, and invited to repent and give their lives to Christ. An evangelical tradition of the 'conversion experience' was well established, the once-for-all challenge and change in a person's orientation. John Wesley's warmed heart on 24 May 1738 was an influential model.

I do not wish to suggest that this belongs solely to the past, though it does seem to me that in Methodism this kind of thing has, for better or for worse, been weakened. William James' book *The Varieties of Religious Experience* had long since taught people to recognize two kinds of believer – the 'once-born' and the 'twice-born' – and there was considerable concern to avoid the implication that one kind of experience was superior to another: some simply 'grew up' as Christians, and not everyone should expect to have a conversion experience. People had also long been concerned that the converted so often got stuck there and never matured in the Christian life, always going back to the experience of the past. But for many the final nail in the coffin was probably the controversial book by William Sargent, *Battle for the Mind*: uneasiness about manipulating people into the Kingdom emotionally was increased by the realization that the procedures were psychologically analogous to brain-washing.

It seems to me that the consequent nervousness about 'conversion experiences' is really rather unfortunate. Throughout Christian history we find examples of people for whom dramatic moments have been profoundly significant for their future: Paul of Tarsus, Augustine of Hippo, John Wesley. The problems arise when the complexity of their experience is reduced to a kind of reproducible formula, and assimilated to what has become a kind of liturgical practice. Neither Paul nor Augustine nor John Wesley were subjected to the group dynamics of a mass evangelistic rally, and none came to Christianity exclusively through an emotional experience. In each case the experience was the end-product of a long search, and the past was not so much rejected as taken up in a new way. So attempts to explain away what happened to them in terms of psychological and emotional manipulation have never been entirely successful and certainly fall short of accounting for the 'fruits' produced by the experience in each case. We should not dismiss John Wesley's warmed heart, not should we denigrate the power of the story. Rather we should resist the temptation to think that that was all it was!

What was the significance of 24 May for John Wesley's life and development?

Let's begin by hearing again what John Wesley himself said about the experience:

> In the evening, I went very unwillingly to a society in Aldersgate Street, where one was reading Luther's Preface to the Epistle to the Romans. About a quarter before nine, while he was describing the change which God works in the heart through faith in Christ, I felt my heart strangely warmed. I felt I did trust in Christ, Christ alone for salvation; and an assurance was given me that he had taken away *my* sins, even *mine*, and saved *me* from the law of sin and death.
>
> I began to pray with all my might for those who had in a more especial manner despitefully used me and persecuted me. I then testified openly to all there what I now first felt in my heart. But it was not long before the enemy suggested, 'This cannot be faith, for where is thy joy?' Then was I taught that 'peace and victory over sin are essential to faith in the Captain of our salvation but that, as to the transports of joy – that usually attend the beginning of it especially in those who have mourned deeply – God sometimes giveth, sometimes withholdest them, according to the counsels of his own will.'

There are a number of things to notice here. First, the emotional element was far less central than the 'myth' has suggested. John Wesley's desire for 'faith' had been born of long conversations about the interpretation of Paul with his Moravian friend Peter Böhler, and he had only been convinced that the 'faith' his friend spoke of was something real and something he lacked when it had been proved from scripture and evidenced in the lives of people he actually met. He then began to pray for this gift. The gift came when he was engaged with a 'study group' in reading Luther's Preface to the Epistle to the Romans. It was confirmed later by his rediscovery of the Anglican Homilies dating from the time of the Reformation. It was as much an intellectual conviction as an emotional experience: he felt he did trust in Christ for his salvation, and his heart was strangely warmed. Whose wouldn't be? Afterwards he doubted whether it was the real thing, since he 'felt no joy'. The emotional element was rather cooler than we might expect, and certainly not the most important thing about it.

The second thing we notice about Wesley's account of it is that the immediate effect was that he began to pray for his enemies: in other words it was far from a self-indulgent experience, as seem to be so many of the experiences that people claim are religious. He did not wallow in his feelings, but his whole being was released from self-concern and turned outwards to others. For Wesley this was surely fundamental. All his life he had been concerned about his 'holiness' or lack of it, had done 'good works' aplenty, and undertaken spiritual disciplines that put most of us to shame. The great change was loss of concern about his own salvation, and indeed about his own respectability: this alone could open the way a little while later to his submitting 'to be more vile' and preach in the open air. In a sense his 'conversion' was not for himself but for others.

The third surprising thing about it is that apart from the famous *Journal* entry, Wesley hardly ever refers to this experience. What has seemed to the 'myth-makers' of Methodism the most important thing about Wesley does not seem to have been regarded in that light by himself. On the other hand, the manner of his reporting it suggests that at the time he regarded it as of peculiar significance: he led up to it by a review of his past life, and seemed to present this as the climax. His later estimate of the experience is right in the sense that it was one element in a period of profound development, and as others have pointed out, it was not his only 'conversion'. But the estimate of the observers is also right. Had Wesley's deepest drives and feelings not been taken up into his changing ideas, had he not begun to be liberated from concern with his own spiritual temperature, there could not have been the remarkable fruits which ensued. Before this period, Wesley was an ineffective campaigner for a more whole-hearted Christian profession in the midst of the complacency and indifference of the eighteenth-century church, a prickly Pelagian, over-moral and over-religious. Afterwards things began to happen.

And yet can we really describe the change that took place? It can hardly be called a conversion from being a non-Christian, even though at first Wesley himself could almost regard it in that light. Like all converts to a new perspective, to begin with Wesley was a rather belligerent advocate of his new ideas; but gradually his past was reclaimed in the face of extremist followers. In the case of all the great names we have mentioned, Paul and Augustine as well as Wesley, there is an amazing blend of the new and the old in their mature Christianity. Paul remained a Jew, and despite his attacks on the 'Law', he never rejected his Jewish past which he saw taken up and fulfilled in Christ. There was continuity as well as change. Similarly Augustine and Wesley consciously and unconsciously took their past into the new present and into their future. To some extent this is humanly inevitable, but it also points to something deeper – the recognition that 'the child is father of the man', and in some mysterious way discernible by hindsight alone, the future is prepared in the past. Wesley's change is best described in his own terms: he left behind the relationship of slave to master, and entered by adoption into the relationship of son and heir. Duty remained, but the sense of obligation was infused with an altogether different spirit. The change was born of a long search, and yet was experienced as gift, as sheer undeserved grace. Thanksgiving rather than fear became the hallmark of devotion. What happened was that things long known, things Wesley himself had preached, became meaningful to him in a new way, and therefore his communication of them became the more powerful.

Clearly the experience was significant for Wesley's career, even if it was not quite what the pious legend has passed down.

Does it remain significant for us? Is it worth remembering?

There are, I think, at least three reasons why it is:

1. Our culture is hungry for 'religious experience'. This is partly because its popular 'empiricism' will only believe what has been experienced. But its popular empiricism is also deeply sceptical about experiences which cannot be 'tested'. When David Hay (*Exploring Inner Space: Scientists and Religious Experience*, Penguin Books 1982) proves by research and statistics that lots of people have experiences which are out of the ordinary, and it is not just people who are mad or obsessed and ought to be in mental hospitals, many people feel relieved, as if this provides some kind of reassuring 'proof'. But if it does, it only proves a very watered down and vague sort of thing; and raises profound questions about the criteria for deciding what are truly 'religious' experiences. Why should we regard Wesley's experience as any different from a woman who came to see me once with her story of a revelatory experience years before which no-one would take seriously, despite her visits to archbishops. . . ?

Wesley stood for personal experience of the Gospel in a very different age, an age in which religion was thought to be founded on reason, and 'enthusiasm' was frowned upon. Their religion founded on reason was as vague as our religion founded on experience. Neither will do without a profound earthing in the corporate experience of the Christian tradition, something which relieves the narrowness of individualism, and provides a way of 'testing the spirits whether they be of God'. The process of discernment cannot be reduced to formulae or objective criteria that can be spelt out and applied, but the New Testament points to a fundamental principle: 'by their fruits you shall know them'. Nothing came of that woman's 'experience' because she was stuck with it, obsessed by it, and no fruit was born of it. Much came of John Wesley's experience, because it arose in the context of a search for the truth, particularly the truth of scripture, and so it was a 'scripture-shaped' experience; besides that, it was formed out of active engagement with Christian tradition, in its Protestant forms and also through Anglicanism in its more catholic and ecumenical forms; above all it was not something he got stuck with – it was something that released him in such a way that it became significant on a far broader canvass. In the end it was more significant for others than it was for him personally. It proved to be more a 'call' than a 'conversion'.

The 'fruits' of religious experience and the 'graces' in a person's life are more often discernible by others than by the individual. The complex relationship of 'change' and 'continuity' will hardly be fully analysable, by the self or by the observer. But the reality of a religious experience will emerge as the recipient 'grows' in response and obedience, or not emerge as the individual keeps trying self-indulgently to have the same kind of experience again. Wesley's experience is a challenge to our expectations. It is a challenge to those who have foregone conclusions about the pattern of religious experience; and it is a challenge to those who are wary of untestable claims to communication with God. We desperately need to reclaim in the life of the Church the tradition of 'conversion experiences', of Wesley's 'doctrine of assurance' that holds out to people the possibility of really knowing that God so loves them that their spiritual struggles and moral anxieties are as nothing compared with the sheer grace and the riches of Christ's gift of salvation. But we need to do so without reverting to an individualism and subjectivity that focusses on the experience rather than its fruits, and without manipulating people into thinking that religion is only genuine if it issues in emotional 'highs'. Nothing is so deceptive as 'feelings'; nothing so creative as a love that captures the whole person, mind and will as well as heart, and issues in a transforming commitment. John Wesley demonstrates what that kind of experience can produce.

2. One of the fruits of Wesley's conversion was the emergence of a new 'mind' as well as a new heart. Increasingly he forged a new integration of many perennial tensions within the Christian tradition, and it is here that his significance as a theologian really rests. Since the Reformation, faith and works had been dialectical opposites, with Lutherans particularly tending to emphasize the idea that humanity on its own can do nothing good, that human nature is totally depraved, that only God in Christ can save, and all you need is faith, over against the tendency to see Christianity as a God-given morality. Once John Wesley had embraced the need for faith and faith alone, he was able to create that very special integration which we know as the doctrine of Christian Perfection. Faith does not take away from good works, it gives works a new spirit. Faith does not undermine obedience, it means

that obedience is the willing response of one who is loved to one loved in return. Perfect love casts out fear; and perfect love is a possibility for the one who receives it from God. Like 'humility', it is scarcely something one can claim for oneself without paradox; but for Wesley it was something to be sought actively in the hope and belief that even in this life it could be realized. Wesley translated from Greek for his followers the Homilies attributed to the fourth-century monk Macarius, so bringing together the ancient ascetic search for perfection and the faith of the Reformation. Both aimed to cultivate 'the real life of God in the heart and soul, that kingdom of God which consists in righteousness, and peace, and joy in the Holy Ghost', to kindle the ambition 'to recover the divine image we were made in', to fulfil the Law by faith working through love.

This was not the only area in which he managed to maintain the balances: providence and freewill, the gift of grace and free response, those paradoxical tensions over which Augustine and Pelagius had struggled – John Wesley contrived to hold together. He affirmed both the universal call of God and his particular election, of a people, of individuals. His emphasis on personal experience and commitment was married with the requirement of fellowship and community; his emphasis on the Word was balanced by a renewed sacramental focus – it is often forgotten that early Methodism anticipated the Oxford Movement as a eucharistic movement in the Anglican Church. The individual and the community, the personal and the corporate, like Law and Gospel, Old Testament and New Testament, rationalism and emotionalism, were welded inseparably together. And in each case, Wesley's experience informed the integration, and made it plausible rather than contradictory.

Now this too seems particularly significant for our generation. Methodism anticipated liberation theology with its social gospel, and has often become a religion of good works. 'Mission alongside the poor' is a practical emphasis we know very well. So is mission in the more evangelical sense. Sometimes it seems that those who emphasize one are at loggerheads with those who emphasize the other. The evangelical emphasis suggests that the only way to change the world is to change people's hearts, minds and lives; the social emphasis insists that people are bound by social structures, and change can only take place through political action to free people from oppression. Truth, of course, lies on both sides, and Wesley's ability to hold together such tensions was born of the commitment to charity which preceded his conversion, and was transmuted by it. And this is not the only tension which lives on in the contemporary Church. We need the catholic spirit among Methodists, as well as on the ecumenical scene – not least when we struggle to balance word and sacrament, individual and community, heart and head, the culture of the old and the culture of the young, the role of the laity and the role of the ordained, the claims of order and the claims of spontaneity . . . 'Conversion' involves an enlargement of the spirit, not a narrowing down, an opening of the heart and mind.

3. The experience of the Wesleys created a real sense of 'chiming' between their lives and the biblical story. Charles Wesley's hymns are a brilliant expression of this, and the conversion of Charles, a few days before John, must not be forgotten. Many of these hymns have shaped Methodist self-understanding, and they are a treasure to be reclaimed over and over again, and passed on into the great treasury of the whole Christian heritage.

There is a mood in the Church which prefers to focus on the new rather than reclaim the old and traditional. But in many ways the new songs of charismatic renewal, at their best, are in the same tradition. It is not just musical fashion, but the sense of 'chiming' with the language and experience of scripture that gives the singing vitality. But how much deeper it goes when the language of scripture is not simply repeated, but re-minted into sustained theological expression and interpretation by the mind and experience of such as the Wesleys! We need the fruit of their experience to save ours from frothy superficiality.

There is another tendency in the Church these days, the 'liberal' tendency to reduce the 'scandal' of particular providence, and promulgate a rather generalized utopian ideal of peace which easily becomes a kind of tolerant 'niceness'. Here more than anywhere else has the personal note of the Wesleys' biblical spirituality been eroded. Even the approved liturgies, like the form of Covenant Service in the new Service Book, seem shy of the particularizing expressions of the old thanksgivings:

> . . . we give Thee thanks for thy loving kindness which has filled our days and brought us to this time and place . . . Thou hast

comforted us with kindred and friends, and ministered to us through the hands and minds of our fellows . . . Thou hast set in our hearts a hunger for Thee, and given us Thy peace . . . In darkness Thou hast been our light; in adversity and temptation a rock of strength; in our joys the very spirit of joy; in our labours the all-sufficient reward . . . Thou hast remembered us when we have forgotten Thee, followed us even when we fled from Thee, met us with forgiveness when we turned back to Thee. For all Thy long-suffering and the abundance of Thy grace, *We praise Thy holy Name, O Lord.*

The experience of the Wesleys and the great hymns of the Wesleys will not let us water down the particular claim of Christ upon each individual, who is elected and destined to be what he or she was meant to be, and over whose life hangs a mysterious providence. We need to face up to this 'scandal of particularity'. It is difficult philosophically, not just for a sophisticated philosophy but for the 'man in the street' with his common sense. But here the experience of the Wesleys enabled them to appropriate boldly a feature of the biblical story which will not go away, and which alone draws out those deeper levels of spirituality and commitment which we need to rediscover. It was no more comfortable a doctrine in those days of rational deism in which the Wesleys lived, and certainly contributed to the charges of 'enthusiasm'. But for all the mockery, because of their experience and because of its 'chiming' with scripture, the Wesleys would not let it go, not even in the interests of resisting predestination and hanging on to the universal love of God. We need to learn from that. There are some mysteries that will not go away. And the significance of an event like John Wesley's conversion is that its recollection and celebration cannot help but remind us that they will not go away. Everyone of us is a 'called' person. That is the glory of it, and the obligation of it, and the wonder of it.

> And can it be that I should gain
> An interest in the Saviour's blood?
> Died he for me who caused his pain,
> For me, who him to death pursued?
> Amazing love! How can it be
> That thou, my God, shouldst die for me?

Behold the servant of the Lord!
I wait thy guiding eye to feel,
To hear and keep thy every word,
To prove and do thy perfect will,
Joyful from my own works to cease,
Glad to fulfil all righteousness.

All praise to our redeeming Lord,
Who joins us by his grace,
And bids us, each to each restored,
Together seek his face.
We all partake the joy of one,
The common peace we feel,
A peace to sensual minds unknown,
A joy unspeakable.

Finish then thy new creation,
Pure and spotless let us be;
Let us see thy great salvation,
Perfectly restored in thee:
Changed from glory into glory,
Till in heaven we take our place,
Till we cast our crowns before thee,
Lost in wonder, love and praise!

4

John Wesley: Inspiration

Bruce Kent

The invitation to write this short essay came as something of a
surprise. I have preached in a few Methodist churches, and as a
university chaplain and parish priest I have been on good terms
with many a Methodist counterpart. Lord Soper has always been
a Christian witness much admired and Dr Kenneth Greet a friend
in whom administrative ability and prophetic vision can and do go
happily hand in hand. Since I met the Methodists I have liked and
admired them. There is of course a lot of significance in that
'since'. If there was a word said about Methodists in six long
seminary years I do not remember it, and in the late 1950s and
early 1960s we were told to keep to our clerical selves when
suggestions about joint Christian initiatives were proposed.
Ecumenism as an industry had not yet been invented. It was not
until the late 1960s as a university chaplain that I learned a little
more about Methodism and its class groups system, which I found
most impressive. As Wesley envisaged it, every Methodist would
be part of a small support group. My young Catholics were full of
interest and life, but for most of them the idea of a holy evening of
any sort in addition to Sunday Mass would have been taking
loyalty into the realm of fanaticism. Since university days I have
come to admire even more the commitment of many a Methodist
congregation and have most especially been impressed by the
sense of shared responsibility. No Methodist church is a one-man
band.

So this invitation to write about John Wesley was not only an
honour – it was also an eye-opener. Of course one does not become
an expert on anyone by reading a few books in as many months.
Those like me who are not experts but are trying to be Christians

in a confusing world have much to learn from the life of this astonishing man. By any standards he was exceptional. His energy would make most people tired just to read about it. Books, pamphlets, letters, diaries, journals, were all grist to his productive mill. All this written work was undertaken in a life of endless travel in most difficult circumstances. The physical effort involved simply amazed me. Twenty miles a day on good roads would be quite enough for most reasonably athletic people today. In Wesley's *Journal* for 18 March 1747 a snow storm is described which filled up the roads making the way to Grantham, his next stop, almost impassable. 'At least we can walk twenty miles a day with our horses in our hands,' wrote Wesley, and so, despite such daunting conditions, the group reached Grantham.

Wesley's various interests were almost Churchillian in range. He had opinions on everything from tea to landscape gardening, from electricity to sanitation. This was a lively, energetic human being who despite a rigid religious discipline – or because of it – did not find anything human outside his sphere of interest. It was indeed a rigid discipline. It was entirely normal in his eyes to rise at 4 a.m. for fifty years, turn to prayer for nearly an hour and then preach a first outdoor sermon at 5 a.m. If Wesley felt himself 'strangely warmed' in 1738, two hundred years and more have not ended his power to communicate that warmth. The man lived as he did because he actually believed, not in some notional way but fully, demandingly and inspiringly. What an obvious thing it is, after all, if you have some news to impart, not just to provide a building and expect the public to come to you to hear it but to go out to them. Open-air preaching is something most of us would now find rather bizarre: embarrassing in fact. It was, too, for Wesley when he first started on it, but it became his bread and butter – an essential way of taking the Gospel to the people. It took considerable courage on his part and some loss of what was thought to be dignity to get started on that apostolate, but a very important one it was.

In short, to write about John Wesley is not just to produce a bit of history. It is to be challenged all the time with the reflection: what about me? How we compare to this quite extraordinary person and what meaning his life has now are questions that do not go away. Methodists today must have just the same problems as those affecting dozens of religious orders and communities. An inspiring figure arrives and blazes across his or her age and the rest of us are left to try to make the machinery work after he or she is gone. Perhaps the Wesley blueprint no longer fits exactly into the world of Concorde, television and computer. But some things, I think, remain constant. His was a reaction against a Christianity of the head but not of the heart, of form without personal conversion, of getting by rather than the struggle for perfection. Things haven't changed too much. The house churches and basic communities of today sound remarkably like a considerably less organized and rather less demanding class structure. The official churches still find enthusiasm rather embarrassing and the vexed question of religion and politics remains unresolved.

Our worlds are, of course, in many personal ways very different. I shuddered when I learned how Susanna Wesley thought it right to bring up her children. She told John in 1732 that 'when turned a year old (and some before) they were taught to fear the rod and to cry softly . . . that most odious noise of the crying of children was rarely heard in the house. . . .' That régime cannot have done much for John Wesley's understanding of women, which was the one disaster area of his life. But then someone who travelled on foot, horse and boat some five thousand miles a year, with every detail of an ever-growing Methodist community under his eye, was not an ideal marriage partner. The laconic entry in his *Journal* for 12 October 1781: 'I came to London and was informed that my wife had died on Monday. This evening she was buried though I was not informed of it till a day or two after . . .' leaves something to be desired when it comes to the most human of human relationships.

Nevertheless, this is not the place to go into a lengthy discussion of eighteenth-century attitudes to the upbringing of children and the disciplines that ought to be involved or the emotional consequences. Most ages look rather odd to those which follow. One day someone will wonder how it was that we in our time have come to accept a culture of personal and national violence as if a dozen TV murders a night and a booming national arms industry was a normal world for a Christian to live in, while divorce has become almost a regular end to marriages.

From his parents Wesley certainly learned about prayer, but it would be a mistake to discuss his spiritual life as if that could be separated from his ordinary existence. Those very early Oxford dons and undergraduates who earned for themselves the sarcastic 'Holy Club' description did not make such a division. Concern for the poor, the uneducated, the orphan, the prisoner, flowed from their response to the Gospel. Quite right too. St Matthew's Gospel Chapter 25 is still the only yardstick which we were given for self-measurement. But all this came from a spiritual search. 'I began to aim at and pray for inward holiness', he says in his *Journal* at an early stage. 'My one aim in life is to secure personal holiness for without being holy myself I cannot promote real holiness in others.' He was a reformer, not a revolutionary, when it came to the Church. The purpose was not to found a new church, though history managed that for him. It was to inspire fellow Christians 'to have the mind that was in Christ and walk as he walked.'

It is only honest to admit that the endless soul-searching that went on amongst Wesley and his companions is not a process with which most of us can empathize. It all gets a bit tedious. Perhaps this might be because we do not take the presence of God as seriously as he did. Certainly few monks in monasteries could claim to lead today the single-minded, regulated life of prayer, scriptural reading and reflection that was meat and drink to John Wesley throughout his active life. Perhaps we ought to become a little more disciplined. Perhaps a spot of communal examination of conscience on a regular basis would be no bad thing. Perhaps an active daily awareness of the existence of God in our lives as the sustainer of all creation would help us on the road to real religion. Certainly such belief changed the lives of tens of thousands of ordinary working people in the eighteenth century and gave Britain a new force for social change whose effects have lasted until this day. Lord Soper comes from a long and convincing tradition.

The encouraging feature of Wesley's religion was the conviction that sanctity, holiness, perfection and with it joy, were not objectives for the religious specialist alone. This was and is the result of God's grace. A positive awareness of both the call to holiness and the possibility of achieving it was open to all. Indeed, no Methodist could join one of the Bands, or spiritual sub-circles, unless such an awareness was there and tested. Wesley's *A Plain Account of Christian Perfection* is a very encouraging booklet. It challenges mediocrity and pessimism. It does not suggest that falling by the wayside is impossible. Freedom and even the freedom to fall is there. But so is the possibility of holiness for everybody.

This message is a challenge of a very positive sort to those of us brought up in an 'officers and other ranks' understanding of religion. We Catholics somehow came to accept that the counsels of perfection, as they were called, were for the chosen few. For the rest, half standards were more or less accepted. The concentration was on avoiding sin: mortal catastrophic, venial undesirable but open to correction. Holiness – usually expressed as poverty, chastity and obedience – was for those with a real vocation. Wesley's genius was to offer such a real vocation to everyone. All become spiritual A-level candidates. 'Be ye perfect as your heavenly Father is perfect' is an instruction to everyone, which takes us back to the days of the Acts of the Apostles and to the generations of Christians trying to renew themselves in the spirit of the Gospel. It presents radical challenges to all Christians, not only in relation to prayer but especially in relation to money, power and service.

Oddly enough, or so it seems to me, as a consequence Wesley became much more radical about church structures than he did about state structures. His commitment to the poor is beyond question. He took the Gospel to places where more established churchmen would not go. That the world was his parish was his answer to those who told him that he had no licence to preach. He had far-reaching things to say about taxation and pensions, poverty and prison. But it all falls short in a strange way of a head-on collision with Caesar. On the contrary. He certainly opposed war and wrote an essay (*Works*, Vol. X I I) about it which sounds like Erasmus: 'How shocking, how inconceivable . . . utter degeneracy of all nations from the plainest principles of reason and virtue. . . .' Nevertheless, when it came to the threat of a possible invasion in 1756 he was quick to offer the Government a two-hundred-strong volunteer force to be self-funding and entirely at the disposal of His Majesty. His support for the Monarchy when Bonnie Prince Charlie was moving south was almost servile.

Despite an initial sympathy for the American Revolutionaries, he came quickly to explain that their activities were wholly unreasonable. Universal suffrage was not at all his political aim. In his 1772 *Thoughts upon Liberty* he described Britain as a society in terms which only the middle and upper classes could have recognized. That there might even be a need for Catholic emancipation as evidence of all this British liberty which he championed so loudly does not occur at all. Wesley's political spirit was very much that of Romans 13. Authority came from God and not from the people. Early radicals like John Wilkes got no sympathy at all.

This is not to deny the enormous worth and Christian logic of his many social concerns. These followed naturally from belief in the one Father to whose family all belong. Christ suffers in the poor and the prisoner, the widow and the orphan. So Wesley went out to find him there. The marvel is not that he did these things, but that so many Christians, then as now, can still see 'good works' as an optional extra rather than the main course of Christian living. Nevertheless we look in vain for a radical reappraisal of the norms of society itself. I'm not sure that Wesley would have understood the sentence in the 1971 Rome Synod on Justice which said that the Gospel is not just good news to set us free from sin 'but from what sin has done to our society'. Wesley was not out of the Leveller stable. Indeed, I wonder what he would have said of the Tolpuddle Martyrs, very much his children, if they could have asked him not about the right to a decent wage, but about the right to withdraw labour in an organized way as a means of putting pressure on landowners and farmers.

He was at his most radical when it came to his judgment on the slave trade. This was very much part of the national economic system, and his base in Bristol made him very much aware of it. He hated it and condemned it in appeal after appeal. His own experiences in America must have made it impossible for him to think of Africans as sub-human creatures, not even fit for baptism, as some churchmen of his day maintained. He was outraged by the institution and by its dreadful attendant cruelties. Of all his many letters and instructions (how on earth did he find the time?) that last letter to William Wilberforce, written the day after his last sermon and a week before he died, is a blast of encouragement for anyone struggling for social change. He had heard that Wilberforce was becoming despondent. 'But if God be for you who can be against you . . . go on in the name of God and in the power of his might till even American slavery (the vilest that ever saw the sun) shall vanish away before it.' So cheer up nuclear disarmers, Amnesty workers, Oxfamites and all that breed. Wesley has a message for you, too!

I suppose that he might well have denied that he was in our terms radical when it came to the Church. Perhaps he intended not to be so. All his life he saw himself as a communicating priest of the Church of England. Though church doors were often closed to him and his Methodist chapels were seen as a threat not an inspiration, it was never his intention to found a different church. But he did. It is almost impossible for a Roman Catholic to understand the free-wheeling priesthood which Wesley claimed for himself. He certainly did not see himself as being responsible to any bishop. As time went on he began to see priesthood and episcopacy as two sides of the same coin and not very different at that. His American ordinations were, he judged, entirely orthodox.

Like many contemporary charismatics, in any event, he thought the Spirit for more important than the structures. Yet he survived. No excommunication, no defrocking and no feeling on his part that loyalties had been stretched so far that he ought to resign. His ecumenism, of course, advanced with the years. In 1747 he patronizingly wrote of the Trappists that God makes allowances 'for invincible ignorance', but nevertheless he acknowledged in them 'deep experience of the inward work of God'. He could recognize holiness when he saw it. By 1773 he had become more generous. On a trip through 'dreary' Galway, he noted twenty thousand Papists and five hundred Protestants. 'But which of them are Christians, have the mind that was in Christ and walk as he walked? And without this how little does it avail whether they are called Protestants or Papists?' Just seven years before the Gordon Riots that was generous indeed. If Wesley managed to avoid an irrevocable rupture with the authorities of his own English Church, he certainly managed, towards the end, an ecumenism before its time.

5

Wesley the Catholic

Aelred Burrows OSB

The Provost (breaking in with some heat): You will all see, Mr Wesley will finish up a papist. I knew his father a little, that was a bad husband of his own affairs, and has wrote up very bitterly against the Nonconformists. And as for the son, it is true what Mr Shillett has told you, that he is become a dangerous sort of enthusiast; and there is no other way of it, but such enthusiasm will carry a man to Rome; which is what I anticipate for Mr Wesley, and other the like coxcombs with him.

Ronald A. Knox, *Let Dons Delight*, Chapter 5

Without commenting one way or the other on the spiritual logic proposed by Fr Knox's provost, it is still the usual reaction among many, especially perhaps of the Roman Catholic communion, to assume the innate Protestantism of John Wesley. This is surmised on the grounds that he founded a community of Christians, the Methodists, who eventually broke away from the Church of England in a generally non-episcopal, anti-ritualist direction. Just how true, however, is this assumption about Wesley? Is there a real sense in which Wesley's religion is more 'Catholic' than 'Protestant'? Is it possible for Christians of all the major denominations to see in Wesley a figure of considerable ecumenical importance, whose religious journey has ultimately assisted rather than hindered the healing of Christian disunity?

It might be of profit, therefore, to take a look at Wesley's life and teaching to see just how far he remained grounded in the traditional 'marks' of the Church: viz., one, holy, catholic and apostolic. His life as well as his teaching should be our subject of study because Catholicism involves orthopraxis – the living-out of a Catholic life style – as well as orthodoxy, the adherence to correct teaching.

Wesley the unifier

The dearest aspiration in the heart of John Wesley was the unity in love of all those who have received and responded to the grace of Christ. He rightly saw this unity of love as fundamental to the oneness of the body of Christ; Christians manifested disunity primarily because they did not love one another. For Wesley, the root of this unifying love was the apprehension by the individual Christian within himself that God genuinely loves him; an apprehension which is primarily in the will, an acceptance of the heart (in the biblical sense of the seat of intelligence and decision), which may (as in the case of Wesley's 1738 conversion) or may not be accompanied by a certain emotional uplift.

To love and forgive others, then, is central to the Christian calling. Wesley in a remarkable passage in his *Journal* speaks with an impressive humility of this gift within himself:

> I cannot but stand amazed at the goodness of God. Others are most assaulted in the weak side of their soul; but with me it is quite otherwise; if I have any strength at all (and I have none but what I have received) it is in forgiving injuries; and on this very side am I assaulted more frequently than any other. Yet leave me not here one hour to myself, or I shall betray myself and Thee (29 October 1752).

For example, throughout his difficult relationship with George Whitefield, an awkward and touchy ally in the Gospel, whose sincere commitment to Calvinistic predestination he could in no way share, Wesley made real efforts at reconciliation. Thus on 5 November 1755: 'Mr Whitefield called upon me. Disputings are now no more; we love one another and join hand in hand to promote the cause of our common Master.'

Much more remarkable is Wesley's attitude to Roman Catholics. Although he inherited the common anti-Popery tradition of early modern England, he gradually developed an openness and a truly eirenic mind towards the adherents of the old religion. This is all the more remarkable given the state of Catholicism in the mid-eighteenth century. The Popes, with the outstanding exception of Benedict XIV, were politically and personally unimpressive and weak men, who eventually, under political pressure, suppressed the Jesuits, who had been the most loyal and effective instruments of Catholic missionary and educational advance. In its doctrine, liturgy and devotion, the Catholic Church was in the full flowering of Baroque forms and expression, a style which, despite Wren, Gibbs and Vanbrugh, was not naturally appealing to Protestant Englishmen. The English Catholics, the local representatives of this tradition, were not an impressive lot, despite the personality of Bishop Challoner. They were a tiny remnant, suspect in their allegiance, and politically tarred by the Irish connection.

Wesley would have come across very few Catholics in England in the normal course of his apostolate, though in Ireland he inevitably met very many. Often his outdoor congregations there largely consisted of Catholics who frequently made a good impression on him by their quiet attention. Wesley could, nevertheless, give vent to his inherited prejudices, as on the occasion in 1761 when upon reading an unimpressive life of St Catherine of Genoa he wrote that, 'We seldom find a saint of God's making sainted by the Bishop of Rome.' None of this therefore prepares us for the remarkable 'Letter to a Roman Catholic' penned in July 1749. This letter is ecumenical love in action, and is a remarkable anticipation of the best fruits of the ecumenical movement of our own time. Here the centrality of the 'religion of love' as the dynamic which unites the Church is most clearly expressed.

Wesley begins his letter by regretting the bad image Protestants and Catholics have of each other, leading to 'both sides less willing to help one another, and more ready to hurt each other'. He then appeals to the common following of Christ which Catholics share with Protestants, as a basis for mutual love and respect: 'I think you deserve the tenderest regard I can show, were it only because the same God has raised you and me from the dust of the earth, and has made us both capable of loving and enjoying him to eternity; were it only because the Son of God has bought you and me with his own blood. 'Wesley then proceeds to outline the doctrinal and ethical agreement which already exists between Catholics and Protestants. 'Are we not thus far agreed? Let us thank God for this and receive it as a fresh token of his love. But if God loveth us, we ought also to love one another. . . .

O brethren, let us not still fall out by the way. I hope to see you in heaven.'

As a conclusion to his letter, Wesley suggests four resolutions for separated Christians. First, 'not to hurt one another' but rather to behave in as kind and friendly a way as we can towards each other. Secondly, 'to speak nothing harsh or unkind of each other' and to look for opportunities to speak good of each other. Thirdly, getting to the internal roots of prejudice by resolving 'to harbour no unkind thoughts, no unfriendly temper towards each other'. Finally, to offer each other mutual help in 'whatever we are agreed leads to the Kingdom . . . to strengthen each other's hands in God'. John Wesley clearly understands that the heart of the unity of the Church lies in the love of Christ made manifest in mutual Christian love: 'If we cannot as yet think alike in all things, at least we may love alike.' Maybe only in our century are we beginning to take seriously Wesley's programme for healing our divisions.

It is not only, however, in relation to the Church that John Wesley is a man of 'unity'. He was also, in a very traditional Catholic way, aware of the unity of *all* knowledge, natural and revealed, humane and scientific. His search was for a wholeness, an integrity of knowledge. This is seen not only in his absorption in the things of God but also in his wide breath of interest in natural phenomena and their causes, and in his imaginative curiosity. His *Journal* records this immense breadth of imaginative interest, whether it is in waterspouts which surprisingly move on to land (September 1760); the beneficial effects of electricity (January 1768); the *History of Charles the Fifth* by Dr Robertson, which Wesley found disappointing; the most unusual summer-house in the gardens of the Duke of Athol (April 1772); or the effect of music upon animal behaviour (December 1764). Wesley, unlike Luther, refused to despise reason; he was, after all, a man born into the 'Age of Reason'. Although no Deist (Wesley registers his distaste at finding this phenomenon at provincial Matlock – 'a gentleman-like man asked me, "Why do you talk thus of faith? Stuff, nonsense!" Upon enquiry, I found he was an eminent deist. What, has the plague crept into the Peak of Derbyshire?'), Wesley always valued the role of logic and reason in Christian and natural enquiry. In the great tradition of the Christian Fathers, and his English predecessor, the Venerable Bede, he saw all knowledge as one, ancillary to the study of theology, and centred on the Holy Scriptures.

Wesley the sanctifier

'. . . being as tenacious of inward holiness as any mystic, and of outward, as any Pharisee'. Thus Wesley at the age of eighty-four expressed the Methodist concern for sanctification. John Wesley throughout his life was as zealous as any Catholic should be for the holiness of the Church in each and all its members. As with most Christians, Wesley owed his first apprehension of the love of Jesus Christ, and his first steps in holiness, to his family. He inherited an instinct to be true to his conscience, whatever the family pressure, from both his father and his mother's family. His own mother, Susanna, clearly a woman of conscientious principle, for a long time refused to answer 'Amen' to the public prayers for the 'usurper' William III, which must have caused certain tensions for her husband. It was also from his parents that Wesley became familiar with that eighteenth-century High Church breadth of mind in things of the Spirit which received its nourishment not only from the devout Puritan tradition, and the Caroline and Non-Juring divines, but also from the French and Spanish Catholic Counter-Reformation writers.

This blend of piety gave its colour to the whole of Wesley's life. The truths he fed on, the spiritual values he most pursued, were those found in the great overlap (always more than is often imagined) between Roman Catholic and Protestant spirituality. He came to esteem very highly the *Imitation of Christ*, the writings of St Francis de Sales, the works of Archbishop Fénelon, the insights of Pascal, and the life and reflections of that simple and attractive Carmelite lay-brother, Br Lawrence. All of these writings bear witness to the great Catholic tradition of 'sanctification', centred in the awareness of the presence of Christ with us, and living in that presence in simplicity and holiness, in response to Christ's grace. Wesley brought this 'Catholic' stress on sanctification into his 'Protestant' life of justification by faith; in fact he found himself at times unhappy with Luther when the latter seems to belittle or deny the need for sanctification:

> I set out for London, and read over on the way that celebrated book, Martin Luther's '*Comment on the Epistle to the Galatians*'. I was utterly ashamed. How have I esteemed this book, only because I heard it so commended by others. How blasphemously does he speak of good works and of the law of God –

constantly coupling the law with sin, death, hell, or the devil; and teaching that Christ delivers us from them alike. Whereas it can be no more proved by Scripture that Christ delivers us from the law of God than that he delivers us from holiness or heaven (15 June 1741).

Wesley saw our sanctification as a process, suited to our organic nature; it was not necessarily complete when a man came to an adult faith, to a 'conversion'; such might only be the beginning of 'working out our salvation'. This doctrine of Wesley is above all optimistic; he is confident that God will fulfil his promises and never abandon the souls that he loves. For Wesley, this faith and trust is bound up with his belief in God's abiding presence in all the circumstances of life – at Church, at home, at rest, or on horseback – a belief which he expressed on his deathbed, 'the best of all is, God is with us'. Hence his willingness to believe in 'providences', those divine 'coincidences' in which the believer can occasionally discern the will of God who is always present to us and in charge of all our ways. Thus he saw the direct hand of God in his remarkable escape from being dashed to pieces in the chaise on the road to Burslem (20 July 1763), and in the quiet attention which an ass gave to his sermon at Rotherham (31 March 1764). The way Wesley records such 'providences' links him firmly with the seventeenth-century Puritan tradition, but the underlying awareness that man is always living in God's presence links him with a much more ancient spiritual source, the Rule of St Benedict. There in the chapter on 'Humility', St Benedict reminds his monks that all the actions of their life are known, seen and watched over by God; hence the need to do everything as well as we can. After one thousand years this teaching reached simple Br Lawrence in his Carmelite monastery in Paris, and it is his teaching on *The Practice of the Presence of God* which was probably the means by which the Benedictine teaching reached John Wesley.

Wesley therefore saw the need for the Christian to live in the present moment, to grow towards Christian perfection by accepting and obeying God's will in each passing moment of time ('redeeming the time', Eph. 5.16). Wesley in fact refers directly to Ephesians 5.16 in his *Journal* on 22 August 1743. During his difficulties in trying to leave London that day he had been presented with several opportunities to talk with people. So he writes: 'I mention these little circumstances to show how easy it is to redeem every fragment of time (if I may so speak), when we feel any love to those souls for which Christ died.' Twenty years later, Wesley notes: '. . . believers grow dead or cold. Nor can this be prevented but by keeping up in them an hourly expectation of being perfected in love. I say an hourly expectation; for to expect it at death, or some time hence, is much the same as not expecting it at all' (15 September 1762). The same sense of sanctification in time is seen in a later reflection of Wesley's; 'Today I entered on my eighty-second year and found myself just as strong to labour and as fit for any exercise of body or mind as I was forty years ago. I do not impute this to secondary causes, but the Sovereign Lord of all. . . . We can only say, "The Lord reigneth!" While we live, let us live to Him!' (28 June 1784).

Wesley the catholicizer

Driving Wesley on like a dynamo was his deep personal love of Christ, a heartfelt devotion which fed everything else, and everybody else, he had to do with. Here again Wesley is feeding on the ancient Catholic tradition stretching from the *nihil amori Christi praeponere* of the scripturally-rooted St Benedict, to the sublime chapters of the *Imitation of Christ* on the 'Love of Jesus above all things' and 'Of Familiar Friendship with Jesus'. This christocentric spirituality found expression in Wesley's appreciation of the traditional means of Christian holiness: prayer, fasting, spiritual reading, personal discipline and the sacraments.

The practice of personal spiritual discipline on a daily basis was with Wesley as early as (if not before) his days in the 'Holy Club' at Oxford from 1729 to 1735. The value of such a discipline he found in the great tradition represented by Thomas à Kempis, Jeremy Taylor and William Law. He saw the need to structure and regulate the day in such a way that the priority of the things of God remained uppermost. Each day was an opportunity to give a practical daily gift of himself by regular prayer times, by systematic reading of the Scriptures and other spiritual reading, by living frugally, by detailed regular examinations of his daily life into how he spent his time. His criterion always was: does my life-style tend to the glory of God? This was happily reminiscent of the *Ad Majorem Dei Gloriam* motto of the sons of St Ignatius Loyola. It is often said with some justice that had Wesley been reared in the Church of Rome, he would have ended up as the founder of a religious order, with a large probability of posthumous beatification.

That Wesley loved reading and solitude was partly forced on him by his itinerant way of life. In old age he noted: 'I generally travel alone in my carriage and so consequently am as retired ten hours a day as if I were in a wilderness . . . I never spend less than three hours (frequently ten or twelve) in the day alone'. This element of quiet and recollection was complemented by his constant devotion to the public prayer of the Church, the liturgy of praise and sacraments. He was aware that the Cranmerian two-fold daily office of the Church of England was rooted in the more frequent prayer times of the Patristic period – a frequency represented by the ancient Roman and Monastic breviaries. Thus in October 1760, as part of a day of fasting and prayer for God's blessing on the new King's reign, we find that, 'we met at five, at nine, at one, and at half-past eight'. He clearly regarded the traditional discipline of fasting (of both Catholic and Protestant provenance) very highly in these mature years of his life. Three years later, after advising his society at Barnard Castle 'to observe every Friday with fasting and prayer', he proceeds to reflect: 'Is not the neglect of this plain duty (I mean fasting ranked by Our Lord with almsgiving and prayer) one general occasion of deadness among Christians? Can anyone willingly neglect it and be guiltless?' (7 June 1763).

However, for one who claims to be a Catholic it is always the sacramental and specifically Eucharistic piety of John Wesley which impresses and even surprises. There is no question of any acceptance by Wesley of the Roman teaching on transubstantiation; in so far as he thought he understood it – as a belief in a 'local deity', as a material physical presence – he rejected it. But his teaching is far from a Zwinglian memorialism. He talks of the Eucharist as one of the indispensable 'means of grace', an awesome ordinance given by Christ to his Church, a real sacrament, a token or pledge, conveying a real grace. Hence, his life-long insistence upon the value of 'constant communion', i.e. considerably more frequent than the eighteenth-century Anglican norm. In 1787, towards the end of his life, he republished in *The Arminian Magazine* a sermon which fifty-five years before he had written on the subject 'that it is the duty of every Christian to receive the Lord's Supper as often as he can'. He thanks God that over all those years since 1732 'I have not yet seen any cause to alter my sentiments in any point which is therein delivered'.

In discussing the duty of constant Communion, Wesley expands the idea of the Eucharist as a means of grace:

> This is the food of our souls: this gives strength to perform our duty and leads us on to perfection. If therefore, we have any regard for the plain command of Christ; if we desire the pardon of our sins, if we wish for strength to believe, to love and obey God, then we should neglect no opportunity of receiving the Lord's Supper. Then we must never turn our backs on the feast which the Lord has prepared for us.

He was as aware as the later Pope Pius X – Roman Catholics would have to wait another century for this – of how venerable was the tradition of daily Communion. Wesley refers to 'the first Christians, with whom the Christian sacrifice was a constant part of the Lord's day service. And for several centuries they received it almost every day: four times a week always, and every saint's day besides. Accordingly those who joined in the prayers of the faithful never failed to partake of the blessed sacrament.' The impression given here of the essential 'Catholicism' of Wesley's thought is borne out by the theological tone of *Hymns on the Lord's Supper*, written by himself and his brother Charles in 1745, and by the incidental references to his Eucharistic practice in his *Journal*. For example, we find him in August 1762 reflecting upon the Holy Communion both as a focus of reconciliation and as eschatological pledge:

> At the cathedral (Exeter) we had a useful sermon, and the whole service was performed with great seriousness and dignity. . . . I was well pleased to partake of the Lord's Supper with my old opponent Bishop Lavington. Oh, may we sit down together in the kingdom of our Father!

In his outlook on worship and spirituality, therefore, it seems that Wesley was no individualist; he has an ecclesial dimension which permeates both his heart and intellect. Just as St Paul went first to the synagogues on his missions, so John Wesley gravitated towards the parish church; only when he encountered rejection there did he move out to the fields and hedgerows. Indeed, Wesley felt very uncomfortable, in March 1739, when he began his outdoor preaching. It went right against his conservative grain:

> I could scarcely reconcile myself at first to this strange way of preaching in the fields, of which he (Whitefield) set me an example on Sunday; I had been all my life, till very lately, so tenacious of every point relating to decency and order that I should have thought the saving of souls almost a sin if it had not been done in a church.

Throughout his life he remained attached to the Prayer Book, the Liturgy, and the ancient feast days of the Church of England. It distressed him when worship was conducted in a slovenly or negligent fashion; instance his comments on the morning service in the English Church in Aberdeen on Sunday 3 May 1772:

> I could not but admire the exemplary decency of the congregation. This was the more remarkable, because so miserable a reader I never heard before; listening with all attention, I understood but one single word, Balak, in the first lesson; and one more, begat, was all I could possibly distinguish in the second. . . . Why is such a burlesque upon public worship suffered? Would it not be far better to pay this gentleman for doing nothing, than for doing mischief and for bringing scandal upon religion?

Wesley the apostolic

> It is clear that missionary activity flows immediately from the very nature of the Church. Missionary activity extends the saving faith of the Church, it expands and perfects its Catholic unity. . . and bears witness to its sanctity. . . . The Holy Spirit. . . implants in the hearts of individuals a missionary vocation . . . and they take on the duty of evangelization, which pertains to the whole Church, and make it, as it were, their own special task (Vatican II, *Decree on Missionary Activity*, 6 & 23).

In the case of John Wesley this Catholic pattern also holds true, that his spirit of fervent evangelism flowed out of his participation in Christ's life in the Church. It was his faith and love, and his commitment to Christian orthodoxy, which overflowed into apostolic mission. His apostolic zeal is a remarkable example of a truly caring 'episcope', of pastoral oversight. As befits an apostle of the one who identified with the poor and simple, Wesley made mission to the spiritually and materially deprived his special vocation. It was the tin-miners of Cornwall and the colliers of Newcastle whom he found more open to the Gospel than those fashionable ladies of Bath at whom he fired the sharp observation: 'I do not expect that the rich and the great should want either to speak to me or to hear me; for I speak the plain truth – a thing you little hear of, and do not desire to hear' (5 June 1739).

A major feature of Wesley's apostolate was his possession of the virtue of courage in a high degree. He certainly needed it when he faced frequent indifference or hostility from the establishment, and initial incomprehension or even mob violence in the de-christianized, virtually pagan, industrial towns: 'I came to Leeds, preached at five, and at eight met the society; after which the mob pelted us with dirt and stones a great part of the way home' (12 September 1745); 'As soon as ever we entered the town (Roch-dale) we found the streets lined on both sides with multitudes of people, shouting, cursing, blaspheming, and gnashing upon us with their teeth' (18 October 1749). Wesley faced scenes such as these time and time again with a calmness and serenity stemming from his complete trust in God. Linked with this was his perseverance, his refusal to let up on the Lord's work, to be put off by problems and difficulties. Despite the problems of eighteenth-century travel, of the English weather, and of local hostility, he gave himself to the work of missionary follow-up well into his eighties. And all the time he put the credit for his gifts, his stamina, his successes, down to God. He was aware of his growing measure of success. Yet, as the following extract shows, he saw it all as due to God's doing:

> From a deep sense of the amazing work which God has of late years wrought in England, I preached in the evening on those words, 'He has not dealt so with any nation'; no, not even with Scotland or New England. In both these God had indeed made bare his arm; yet not in so astonishing a manner as among us (19 June 1755).

Without therefore trespassing further on the area to be covered by others in this volume, it is sufficient here to note that Wesley exemplified in his own life and activity that inner drive and those specific virtues associated with a true Christian apostle. In short, John Wesley eminently fulfils the criteria of a Catholic missioner so admirably described by the Second Vatican Council:

> Those people who are endowed with the proper natural temperament, have the necessary qualities and outlook, and are ready to undertake the work of mission, have a special vocation . . . they go forth in faith and obedience to those who are far from Christ. . . . When God calls, a man must reply without taking counsel with flesh and blood (cf. Gal. 1.16) and give himself fully to the work of the Gospel. . . . He enters upon the life and mission of Him 'who emptied himself, taking the nature of a slave' (Phil. 2.7). Therefore he must be prepared to renounce himself and everything that up to this he possessed as his own, and 'to make himself all things to all men' (1 Cor. 9.22) (*Decree on Missionary Activity*, 23–24).

'There can be no ecumenism worthy of the name without interior conversion.' So teaches this same Catholic Council; and the interior conversion of John Wesley to his beloved Lord and Saviour set him on the path to that 'ecumenism', that reconciling of all men to Christ, and that reconciling of all Christ's followers with one another, which drove him to take the whole world as his parish, and to pen such a seminal document as his *Letter to a Roman Catholic*. The phrase 'Wesley the Catholic' may still sound surprising, especially to members of my communion. It is true that for all sorts of understandable historical reasons, Wesley remained deficient in appreciating, even perhaps unaware of, the primacy and spiritual role of the Petrine Office within the church; for all his love of, respect for, and frequent reception of Holy Communion, Roman Catholics would feel that it needed the completion of a fuller Catholic teaching both on presence and sacrifice.

Yet, without letting the side down, one must also admit within John Wesley, the presence of the essential substance of Catholic faith, life and worship, in and through which he was baptized, he lived and became holy. This essay has concentrated on 'Wesley, the one who *lived* a Catholic life', but we should remember too that his *doctrine* also was essentially that of Catholic orthodoxy. His rootedness in the great patristic truths of the Trinity, the Incarnation and Christology; his almost Tridentine orthodoxy concerning the relationship between justification and sanctification; his doctrine of 'assurance' which, when carefully scrutinized, seems extremely close to the Catholic tradition of expected consolation, and grace-reliant optimism, found in Romans 8.28, or in Julian of Norwich ('but all shall be well, and all shall be well and all manner of things shall be well'); his rejection of the Calvinist teaching on absolute predestination and limited atonement; his deep appreciation of the Gospel sacraments of Baptism and the Lord's Supper – in all these ways, Wesley was a man of undoubtedly Catholic spirit. Who could deny that Wesley belonged by intention, heart and soul to the one, holy, catholic and apostolic Church? During his visit to Ireland in May 1748, Wesley was addressing a mixed congregation in Dublin when 'one of them, after listening some time, cried out, shaking his head, "Ay, he is a Jesuit, that's plain." To which a popish priest who happened to be near replied aloud, "No, he is not; I would to God he was."' In so far as a genuine compliment was implied – and abstracting from its back-handed nature and unecumenical wording! – I would wholeheartedly agree with the anonymous priest.

6

John Wesley: Sacramental Theology
No Ends without the Means

Ole E. Borgen

The teachings of John Wesley on the sacraments, their presuppositions, their content and consequences, are rather extensive. However, the space available here will only allow a survey-type presentation, where only some of the main points can be taken up. It is hoped, however, that in spite of these limitations some of Wesley's rich theology may be revealed.[1]

Wesley's theology, and thus also his sacramental theology, is unitive and systematic and not incidental or disconnected. However, the theological and practical importance of the sacraments for John Wesley lies in their functions: within the framework of the *via salutis*, they function as 1. effective signs, 2. effective means of grace, and 3. effective pledges of glory to come, conjoined with the added aspect of sacrifice.[2]

Wesley operates with a threefold doctrine of sin: first, original sin, involving guilt and loss of the image of God; secondly, involuntary sin, sins of infirmity, ignorance and error; thirdly, actual wilful sin against a known law (including the 'law of love'), which in essence is a rebellion against God.[3] All of these need the atonement of Christ, but man is only responsible and condemned for the latter, unless they are repented of and forgiven. Thus it is clear that the atonement plays an essential and decisive role in Wesley's understanding of God's saving work for man.[4] Christ is the author and efficient cause of all our salvation, and the sole meritorious cause both of our justification and sanctification.[5] By virtue of the atonement, prevenient grace (which includes 'natural conscience') is given to all men.[6] By virtue of the atonement every one who receives is justified, born again and made a believer. By virtue of the same atonement, the believer gradually grows in holiness until he is perfected in love. And by virtue of this atonement all sins of omission, all mistakes and shortcomings are covered, until, on the basis of the same atoning work of Christ, he shall be received in glory.[7] Such is the basis of all grace, also the grace conveyed through the means of grace, including the sacraments.

The Holy Spirit's function as agent bringing God's grace to men is central in Wesley's thought.[8] Whenever Wesley speaks of the means of grace, and the sacraments in particular, he unhesitatingly affirms that whatever is, or becomes, or happens in, with, or through any means whatever, or any action or words connected therewith, is done by God through his Holy Spirit. He would not accept any automatic or *ex opere operato* effect of any means or sacraments.[9] At the same time he rejects the opposite error of a 'stillness' doctrine. For him there exists no difference between 'immediate' and 'mediate' in God's economy of salvation: '. . . every Christian grace is properly supernatural, is an *immediate* gift of God, which He commonly gives in the use of such means as He hath ordained'.[10]

When faced with the question of a definition of a sacrament, Wesley turns to the Church of England *Catechism* and directly adopts its Augustinian distinction of *signum* (the sign) and *res* (the thing signified): '. . . our own Church, which directs us to bless God both for the means of grace and hope of glory; and teaches us, that a sacrament is "and outward sign of inward grace, and means whereby we receive the same".'[11]

The definition Wesley adopts clearly demands of a sign that it be 'outward' and 'visible', and ordained by Christ.[12] God has ordained outward and visible signs to aid us in overcoming our weaknesses.[13] The cleansing and purifying qualities of water, the matter of baptism, symbolize analogically the inward washing of the Holy Spirit.[14] Likewise, as bread and wine nourish our bodies, so the partakers of the Lord's Supper will be fed with the Body and Blood of Christ.[15]

The second part of a sacrament is the thing signified, the 'inward and spiritual grace'. In baptism it is 'A death unto sin, and a new birth unto righteousness.'[16] Baptism is a means of grace. The thing signified in the Lord's Supper is the 'food of our souls . . . that Inward Grace, which is the Body and Blood of Christ, which are verily and indeed taken and received by the Faithful in the Lord's Supper.'[17] The inward grace of the Lord's Supper is 'His bleeding Love and Mercy'.[18]

However, the sign and the thing signified are not identical or the same.[19] Wesley allows for no confusion of the *signum* with the *res*: the one is outward, material, and visible; the other is inward, spiritual, and invisible. This view can be traced back beyond the Reformers to Augustine.[20] There is a carrying over from one to the other, in baptism as well as in the Lord's Supper. Thus both parts are required.[21]

Wesley asserts: 'Transubstantiation, or the change of the substance of bread and wine in the supper of the Lord, cannot be proved by holy writ; but is repugnant to the plain words of Scripture, overthroweth the nature of a sacrament, and hath given occasion to many superstitions.'[22] Likewise, he also rejects the Lutheran doctrines of consubstantiation and ubiquity which require a communication of the properties of the divine nature to the human.[23] Wesley holds a view of the 'Real Presence' of Christ which may properly be called 'dynamic' or 'living presence': where God acts, there he is.[24]

Wesley never uses the term 'visible word' and refuses to apply it to the sacraments. They must not be subsumed under the word. For Wesley, the Lord's Supper is the foremost of the means of grace.[25] The validity of the sacraments is thus not constituted by the 'word', although the word is a part of the sacramental celebration. Formal validity is for Wesley dependent upon three factors. First, the proper material elements (water, bread and wine) must be employed. Secondly, baptism is to be administered in the name of the Father, Son and Holy Spirit. For the Lord's Supper the pronouncing of Christ's words of institution together with an invocation are required. Thirdly, an ordained minister is necessary.[26] But formal validity must not be confused with efficacy: the former is related to the work of men; the latter wholly to God's gracious work of salvation.

(i) Effective sign. The atonement remembered

Wesley holds that there are three aspects to the Lord's Supper as a sacrament. He says:

THE LORD'S Supper was chiefly ordained for a sacrament,

1. To *represent* the Sufferings of CHRIST, which are *past*, whereof it is a Memorial; 2. To *convey* the First Fruits of the Sufferings, in *Present Graces*, whereof it is a *Means*; and 3. To assure us of *Glory to come*, whereof it is an infallible *Pledge*.[27]

The concept 'memorial' is nothing new in sacramental theology: it has largely been connected with a 'memorialist' conception of the Lord's Supper and, consequently, with a doctrine of what is very aptly called 'real absence'. On the other hand, the 'memorial' Wesley presents is a dynamic drama of worship in which both the believer and the Holy Spirit are actively involved. The memorial has, of course, a direct connection with 'remember', in the sense of 'calling to mind'. But Wesley proceeds beyond the mere level of memory. He operates with the existential and personal question of meaning. The meaning of the sacrament is the 'setting before our eyes Christ's death and suffering', and the fact that he sacrificed himself to atone for our sins: that is, the Lord's Supper *shows forth* Christ's death. God appointed the sacrament, and it was his express design to *revive* his *sufferings* and expose them to *all our senses* as if they were present now. Not only our mind or memory is involved, but all our senses as well.

Thus the sacrament as a memorial involves a total and vital experience of worship, which is expressed in what is called the three degrees of devotion or worship.[28] On the first level, the worshipper begins by meditating upon 'the Great and dreadful Passages' of Scripture which the ordinance sets before him. When looking at the consecrated elements he says in his heart, '. . . I observe on this Altar somewhat very like the sacrifice of my Saviour'. Employing the powerful means of analogy and similitude, the worshipper, with his whole being, empathically enters into the sufferings of Christ. Thus the Bread of Life was broken: 'My LORD and my GOD, I behold in this Bread, made of Corn that was cut down, beaten, ground and bruised by Men, all the heavy Blows and Plagues and Pains; which thou didst suffer from thy Murderers.'[29] But the path of analogy leads further; the whole drama of the atonement enters in: 'I behold in this Bread dried up and baked with Fire, the fiery Wrath which thou didst suffer from above. My GOD, my GOD, why hast thou forsaken him?'[30] Quoting Augustine, Wesley declares, '. . . this Sacrament duly received, makes the thing which it represents, as really present for our Use, as if it were newly done'.[31] Having thus existentially appropriated the message conveyed analogically through the consecrated elements, the worshipper naturally enters the second stage: 'Ought he not also to reverence and adore, when he looks toward that Good Hand, which has appointed for the Use of the Church, the Memorial of these great Things?'[32] The eye of meditation and worship penetrates beyond the elements to the giver of all mercy, God himself. The first two 'degrees of devotion' fit, of course, perfectly into a memorialist conception of the sacrament. The memorialist operates exactly within the framework of meditation, analogy and attitudes of praise and prayer. However, the memorialist is unable to follow Wesley into the third and essential stage. It is here that we meet with what I have called Wesley's doctrine of the 'Eternal Now': 'The main Intention of CHRIST herein was not the bare *Remembrance* of his Passion; but over and above, to *invite* us to his Sacrifice . . .' — to a 'Soul-transporting Feast':

> Oh what a Soul-transporting Feast
> doth this Communion yield!
> Remembering here thy Passion past
> We with thy Love are filled.[33]

Christ invites us to his sacrifice, but he alone can give the 'dreadful Power':

> PRINCE of life, for Sinners slain,
> Grant us Fellowship with Thee,
> Fain we would partake thy Pain
> Share thy mortal Agony,
> Give us now the dreadful Power,
> Now bring back thy dying Hour![34]

The whole economy of salvation is brought to bear upon this awesome event: looking with the eyes of faith, by the power of the Holy Spirit, the worshipper transcends both time and space, and finds himself, as it were, at the foot of the cross, and realizes it is for *him* Christ dies. As one who has seen and experienced, Wesley cries out:

> HEARTS of Stone, relent, relent,
> Break by JESU's Cross subdued,

See his Body mangled, rent,
Cover'd with a gore of Blood!
Sinful Soul, what hast Thou done?
Murther'd G O D's eternal Son![35]

Thus there is a two-way suspension of time and place: Christ is crucified now and here; and *my* sins drive the nails through his hands on Calvary, then and there. But as the believer repents, almost crushed under the burden of acknowledged guilt, he also realizes the full importance for him now: Christ invites him to his sacrifice '. . . not as done and gone many Years since, but as to Grace and Mercy, still lasting, still *new*, still the same as when it was first offer'd for us'.[36] Christ himself is present here and now to save and uphold. And his presence is as real as God is real, and, as a means, the sacrament actually conveys what it shows.

(ii) Effective means of grace. The atonement applied

(a) *The means of grace in general*   In his sermon 'The Means of Grace' Wesley clearly defines his topic: 'By *Means of Grace* I understand Outward Signs, Words or Actions, ordain'd of G O D, and appointed for this End, to be the *Ordinary* Channels whereby he might convey to Men, preventing, justifying or sanctifying Grace.'[37] The means are given as aids to men, who should 'wait upon God in all his ordinances'.[38] Writing to William Law, Wesley flatly rejects any quietist doctrine of an inward, purely mystical way to holiness: '*There is but one scriptural way wherein we receive inward grace – through the outward means which God hath appointed.*'[39] Thus, the outward means are indispensable and a necessity for all who desire God's grace, because God has so ordained. But God is above all means. 'He can convey his Grace, either in or out of any of the Means which he hath appointed. Perhaps he will.'[40] But Wesley definitely warns of any *ex opere operato* effect.[41] All means are nothing but channels or instruments in God's hand. Their only value lies in their being actually *used* by him.[42]

There are two misconceptions concerning the place of the means of grace in God's plan of salvation against which Wesley fights a continuous battle most of his life. One is the pitfall of 'enthusiasm'. He fights this problem in his own society in Fetter

Lane, from which he and his brother Charles consequently feel compelled to withdraw. After that he firmly asserts: 'Enthusiasts observe this. Expect no ends without the means.'[43] On the other hand, Wesley also attacks the opposite error of putting the means in the place of their end, of 'trusting in the means'.

> But I of *Means* have made my Boast,
> Of *Means* and Idol made;
> The Spirit in the Letter lost,
> The Substance in the Shade.

The solution for this misuse is not non-use, but the proper use:

> I do the thing thy Laws enjoin,
> and *then* the Strife give o'er:
> To Thee I *then* the whole resign:
> I *trust* in Means no more.[44]

Without God's grace added to the means, these are useless.[45]

Wesley operates with three kinds of means of grace. First, the general means: 'How should we wait for the fulfilling of this promise? A. In universal obedience; in keeping all the commandments; in denying ourselves, and taking up our cross daily. These are the general means which God hath ordained for our receiving his sanctifying grace.'[46] Secondly, there are the prudential means. They may vary according to the person's needs and circumstances. These means can be almost anything. Whatever is conducive to holiness and love becomes to that extent a means of grace. But the third kind, the instituted means of grace, are of the greatest importance for Wesley. For him there are five *chief*, instituted means of grace: prayer, the Word, fasting, Christian conference (the Christian fellowship) and the Lord's Supper.[47]

'. . . all who desire the grace of God are to wait for it in the way of prayer'. 'Prayer may be said to be the breath of our spiritual life. He that lives cannot possibly cease breathing.'[48] A Christian prays always, at all times, and in all places and 'with all sorts of prayer, public, private, mental, vocal'.[49] There are four parts of all prayers: deprecation (pleading for forgiveness and mercy), petition (asking), intercession (praying for others) and thanksgiving. Prayer prepares and enables him who prays to receive God's blessings.[50] No man is under the necessity of falling from grace, but the possibility is always present. Wesley, therefore, exhorts, 'Watch, that ye may pray, and pray, that ye may watch.'[51]

The greatest efficacy of fasting, as Wesley sees it, is in connection with prayer.

> And it is chiefly as it is a help to prayer, that it has so frequently been found a means in the hand of God, of confirming and increasing, not one virtue, not chastity only . . . but also seriousness of spirit, earnestness, sensibility and tenderness of conscience, deadness to the world, and consequently the love of God, and every holy and heavenly affection.[52]

Through fasting our bodies are 'kept under', and a spiritual strength from God is graciously bestowed.[53]

Christian fellowship as Wesley understands it has two aspects, 'Christian conference' or 'conversation' and the 'assembling together'. The matter of conversation is never an indifferent matter. It may tear down or build up.[54]

The other aspect of this ordinance is the assembling together. Attending church, the public worship of God and sharing in Christian fellowship have been shown to be essential in growing in grace.[55] Christian fellowship and conversation are truly efficacious means for all who desire God and his salvation.

'All who desire the grace of God are to wait for it in searching the Scriptures.'[56] The Word, through the Holy Spirit, convicts of sin; faith is given by hearing the same Word preached; and believers grow in holiness. Although private reading and meditation are important aids to a life of faith, hearing the Word preached has always remained central in Methodism. It should be preached both as law and Gospel, '. . . duly mixing both, in every place, if not in every sermon'.[57] God's Word appears as a complete means of grace, conveying severally to each person God's grace according to his needs.

How, then, are the means related to one another? If fasting and prayer are *preparatory* and, as such, indispensable, then God's Word, preached, heard, read and meditated upon, may be termed a convicting, converting and confirming ordinance. At Wesley's time the Lord's Supper was considered the chief and superior *confirming* ordinance. But Wesley affirms it to be a converting ordinance as well. 'I showed at large: 1. That the Lord's Supper was ordained by God to be a means of conveying to men either preventing, or justifying, or sanctifying grace, according to their several necessities.'[58] And, finally, the 'Christian fellowship' and 'Conference' provide the proper environmental context within which all the other instituted means, as well as other prudential means, may be exercised.

The Word plays an important role in God's plan of salvation. But for Wesley, the Lord's Supper always remains the means of grace *par exellence*. Such conceptions seem only natural when it is remembered that, in a service of the Lord's Supper, *all* instituted means are involved: the Word of God is read, preached, and meditated upon; prayers of several kinds are central to the whole sacrament; there issues communion and fellowship with God and fellow worshippers, all woven together into a mighty symphony of blessings.[59]

(b) *Baptism*

> By water, then, *as a means*, the water of baptism, we are regenerated or born again; whence it is also called by the Apostle, 'the washing of regeneration'. Our Church therefore ascribes no greater virtue to baptism than Christ himself has done.[60]

Baptism parallels closely the various aspects of the Lord's Supper, with the main distinction that baptism is initiatory; its function is to *commence* what the Lord's Supper (with other means of grace as well) is basically ordained to *preserve* and *develop*: a life in faith and holiness. We are obliged to make use of baptism, to which God has tied us, although he is free to bestow his grace with or without means.[61]

In Wesley's teaching on the way of salvation the doctrine of total corruption is a necessary presupposition for God's grace:

> *This*, then, *is the foundation of the new birth – the entire corruption of our nature.* Hence it is that being born in sin, we must be 'born again'. Hence every one that is born of a woman must be born of the Spirit of God.[62]

So far Wesley follows the Calvinist position. That the guilt of Adam's sin is imputed to all men, he allows. 'But,' he asserts, 'that any one will be damned for this alone, I allow not, till you show me where it is written.'

No dire decree of thine did seal
or fix th'unalterable doom;
Consign my unborn soul to hell,
Or damn me from my mother's womb.

'And none ever was or can be a loser but *by his own choice*.'[63] By virtue of Christ's atonement, prevenient grace is given to all men.[64] Thus no person is lost because he has not received grace, but because he has not used the grace he has received.

But man sins and stands guilty and condemned before God. He needs forgiveness and finding favour with God, that is, justifying grace.[65]

Baptism, as Wesley sees it, generally, in an *ordinary* way, *is* necessary to salvation, but not in the *absolute* sense: 'I hold nothing to be (strictly speaking) necessary to salvation but the mind which was in Christ.'[66]

But Wesley's conception of baptismal grace consequently includes also the second 'grand branch of salvation', namely sanctification, here expressed in terms of its inception, the new birth. The new birth implies a radical, inward change effectuated by the workings of the Holy Spirit. Wesley states, 'By water then, as a *means*, the *water of baptism, we are regenerated or born again*; whence it is also called by the Apostle, "the washing of regeneration". Our Church of England ascribes no greater virtue to baptism than Christ himself has done.'[67] He goes on to clarify what he means, in order to prevent a splitting up of the sacrament into its two parts by emphasizing the one or the other: 'Nor does she ascribe it to the outward washing, but to the inward grace, which added thereto, makes it a sacrament.'[68] The Spirit brings the cleansing of the soul, and effectuates the new birth.

'By baptism we are admitted into the Church, and consequently made members of Christ, its Head. The Jews were admitted into the Church by circumcision, so are the Christians by baptism.'[69] This does not only mean becoming a member of the Church as an institution. It involves a union with Christ:

> For 'as many as are baptized in Christ', in his name, 'have' thereby 'put on Christ' (Gal. 3.27); that is, are mystically united to Christ, and made one with him. For 'by one Spirit we are all baptized into one body' (I Cor. 12.13) namely, the Church, 'the body of Christ' (Eph. 4.12).[70]

Thus, although baptism admits into the visible and organizational church as well as the church as the mystical Body of Christ, nevertheless it is possible to be a member of the former and not of the latter, because membership in the mystical Body is not a formal, but a spiritual matter.

'The Baptism of young children is to be retained in the Church.'[71] With this simple sentence Wesley affirms his preference for infant baptism.[72] He argues on several levels. First, on the basis of the infant's need: 'If infants are guilty of original sin, then they are proper subjects of baptism; seeing in the ordinary way, they cannot be saved, unless this be washed away by baptism.'[73]

Secondly, infants ought to come to Christ, be admitted into the church, and dedicated to God. Wesley understands this aspect of baptism to include the parents' willingness to give their child to God by bringing him to be baptized, as well as their taking a twofold vow: on behalf of the child they promise to take up the obligation as well as the privileges of the covenant; and on their own behalf they promise to teach the child the ways of the Lord.[74]

Wesley next argues from apostolic practice. There are no explicit examples in Scripture of baptism of infants. But Wesley argues: 'If infants were to be excluded from baptism, Jesus must have expressly forbidden them. He also argues on the basis of probabilities: '*She was baptized, and her family.* Who can believe that in so many families there was no infant? or that the Jews, who were so long accustomed to circumcise their children, would not now devote them to God by baptism?'[75] Wesley also refers to several church fathers.[76]

But Wesley's main argument in support of baptizing infants is based upon the continuity of the covenant of grace established with Abraham. Baptism is now the 'circumcision of Christ' and the New Testament seal of the covenant. He asserts: 'Now, if infants were capable of being circumcised, notwithstanding that repentance and faith were to go before circumcision in grown persons, they are just as capable of being baptized; notwithstanding that repentance and faith are, in grown persons, to go before baptism.' 'They may be saved, and may be baptized too, notwithstanding they are not Believers.'[77]

It is clear that Wesley accepts a doctrine of new birth through the means of baptism, and that this suffices for those who die in their infancy. This grace may properly be termed 'objective' in that its origin is found outside the subject, in this case an infant. It must not be considered objective, however, in the sense of being impersonal and formal only: Wesley teaches that something new is *born*, comes into being, a 'principle of grace is infused', the Holy Spirit is given, and the baptized is 'mystically united to Christ'. 'From which *spiritual*, vital union with *him*, proceeds the *influence* of his grace on those that are baptized.'[78] A fact which is often overlooked is that Wesley firmly believes that adults are 'born again' through the means of baptism. He only makes, with the Church of England, two conditions: that they repent and believe the Gospel. 'Baptism, administered to *real penitents*, is both a means and a seal of pardon. Nor did God ordinarily in the primitive Church bestow this on any, unless through this means.'[79] Actually, for adults baptism may function in one of two ways. If a person is already converted, he should also be 'born of the water'. On the other hand, if he is not, he should be baptized that he may be 'born again' through that means.[80] In his *Journal* Wesley gives many examples of adults who were baptized and who found that God poured out his grace, according to the person's need.[81]

All grace, also baptismal grace, may be lost, although it is never necessary. Wesley speaks of 'baptized heathens' or 'baptized infidels'.[82] If this grace were lost they could still receive God's grace anew; it is therefore extremely important that the children be taught in order to counteract the natural corruption and make it possible for them to grow in grace.[83]

(c) *The Lord's Supper*

> Receiving the Bread
> On JESUS we feed,
> It doth not appear
> His manner of working;
> but JESUS is here.[84]

'At the Holy Table the People meet to worship GOD, and GOD is present to meet and bless his people. . . . And GOD offers to us the Body and Blood of his SON, and all the other blessings we have to receive.'[85] The sacrament, therefore, conveys to men, first, Christ's death and sacrifice, and, secondly, all the fruits or benefits flowing from this sacrifice as 'present Graces'. Through the sacrament the communicant receives; Christ's sacrifice is *conveyed* to him. Communion, therefore, in this sense, becomes *communication*: 'And by this means it conveys to me the *Communion of his Sufferings*, which leads to a Communion in all his Graces and Glories.'[86] Christ there feeds our souls with the constant supply of his mercies, as really as he feeds our bodies with bread and wine.[87] The Lord's Supper is an efficacious means of grace:

> Is not the eating of that bread, and the drinking of that cup, the outward, visible means, whereby God conveys into our souls all that spiritual grace, that righteousness, and peace, and joy in the Holy Ghost, which were purchased by the body of Christ once broken and the blood of Christ once shed for us? Let all, therefore, who truly desire the grace of God, eat of that bread, and drink of that cup.[88]

As for the direct content of the grace conveyed through the Lord's Supper Wesley is definite and clear. 'I showed at large: 1 That the Lord's Supper was ordained by God to be a means of conveying to men either preventing, or justifying or sanctifying grace according to their several necessities.'[89] In his *Dictionary* Wesley defines 'prevent' as 'to come or go before': in this context it would then refer to grace 'coming before' the saving grace of justification and the new birth.[90]

The second great branch of the sacramental grace is justification. Since justification means forgiveness of sins and finding favour before God, it must follow that the Lord's Supper is also a converting ordinance. Wesley had seen this happen. In a versified epitaph for his mother, Charles Wesley speaks of 'A Legal night of seventy years', until

> The Father there revealed His Son
> Him in the broken bread made known;
> She knew and felt her sins forgiven,
> And found the earnest of her heaven.[91]

Therefore, unbelievers ought to communicate: 'Ought every unbeliever to pray and communicate? Yes! "Ask and it (faith) shall be given you." And if you believe Christ died for guilty, helpless sinners, then eat that Bread and drink of that Cup.'[92]

Thirdly, the Lord's Supper conveys the grace of sanctification. 'When we are born again, then our sanctification, our inward and outward holiness begins: and thenceforward we are gradually to "grow up into Him who is our Head." '[93] God not only sustains the new life in the soul of man, he makes him grow up into the full stature of Christ.[94]

Not only is the Lord's Supper a communion with Christ. It is a communion of all believers, a union of love, holiness and perfection: '*We being many are* yet, as it were, but different parts of *one* and the same broken bread, which we receive to unite us in *one body*.'

> One with the Living Bread Divine,
> Which now by Faith we eat,
> Our Hearts, and Minds, and Spirits join,
> And all in Jesus meet.[95]

(iii) *Effective pledge of heaven. The atonement: possession of its purchase assured*

As a pledge, the Lord's Supper functions on two levels. First, the right and the title to the inheritance is actually made over to the communicant through the sacrament. Secondly, the holy sacrament is a plege from the Lord that he will give to the believers his glory, that he will 'faithfully render to us the Purchase'.[96] The Lord's Supper is a pledge and assurance that God will, as it were, keep *his* side of the covenantal agreement. But this does not mean that Wesley indirectly accepts the Calvinistic doctrine of the perseverance of the saints. The possibility of falling out of grace is always present. But God's promise is sure. In this sense only can the sacrament be considered an 'infallible pledge'.[97] There is one use of the idea of assurance by means of a pledge which Wesley clearly rejects. 'No outward form or action is a guarantee that I am in a state of grace, or born again *now*. Even if a person is baptized, partakes regularly in prayers, worship and the Lord's Supper, he may still not be a Christian.'[98] As quoted above, Wesley witnessed: 'I trust in means no more.' The distinction between a pledge and an earnest is crucial here:

> A *Pledge* and an *Earnest* differ in this, That an Earnest may be allow'd upon *Account*, for part of that Payment which is promised, whereas *Pledges* are taken back. Thus for Example, Zeal, Love and those Degrees of Holiness which G O D bestows us in the Use of his Sacraments, will remain with us when we are in Heaven and there make Part of Our Happiness. But the

Sacraments themselves shall be taken back and shall no more appear in Heaven than did the Cloudy Pillar in *Canaan*. We shall have no Need of these sacred Figures of C H R I S T, when we shall actually possess it. But till that Day, the Holy Sacrament hath that Third Use, of being a *Pledge* from the L O R D that he will give us that Glory.[99]

The sacrament, therefore, is not an earnest, The content of the earnest is love, zeal and holiness, even Christ the Redeemer himself. It is heaven here.

> Thee in thy glorious Realm they praise,
> and bow before thy Throne,
> We in the Kingdom of thy Grace,
> The Kingdoms are but One.[100]

Again Wesley's doctrine of the 'Eternal Now' clearly becomes visible. The efficacy of the sacrament is proven by the inner witness of the Holy Spirit. The ultimate test of the efficacy and, consequently, assurance is that God actually bestows the earnest. Although both past and future, salvation is always and essentially a present salvation.[101]

(iv) *Effective sacrifice. The atonement appropriated*

For Wesley there are two main branches of the Lord's Supper: a sacrament, the functions of which are 'memorial', 'means of grace' and 'pledge of heaven', and a sacrifice. The content of sacrifice for Wesley is the offering up by the believer of his body, soul and whatever he can give.[102] Wesley understands Christ's 'Priestly Office' as consisting of two parts: first, his life, death and suffering upon the cross, i.e. the atonement, his dying in our place; secondly, Christ's continuing high-priestly office as constantly interceding at the throne of God the Father. However, although Christ's atoning work is continual and ongoing, it must not be implied that Christ's sacrifice can be repeated. Wesley rejects the sacrifice of the Roman Mass, whether that is said to be 'bloody' or 'unbloody'; if they are both propitiatory, then they are of the same virtue and serve the same end.[103] For Wesley the sacramental sacrifice is neither propitiatory nor expiatory. The Lord's Supper is a means of conveying Christ's sacrifice *both ways*. First, Christ's sacrifice is received and feasted upon.[104] Secondly, it is this sacrifice, already received, which is 'set forth' before the Father as a pleading sacrifice together with the offering up of 'self'.[105]

Thus the second part of the sacrament as it is a sacrifice is 'the sacrifice of ourselves'. The believer offers up to God all his thoughts, words, and actions, 'through the Son of his love, as a sacrifice of praise and thanksgiving'.[106] But the believer does not only share in the benefits of Christ's sacrifice. He also bears the Cross of Christ and dies with him in sacrifice.[107] 'Prepare for the Cross; welcome it; bear it triumphantly, live Christ's Cross, whether scoffs, mockings, contempt, imprisonments. But see it be Christ's cross, not thine own.'[108]

In conclusion, it seems only appropriate to close with the words which Wesley concludes his preface to the sacramental hymns, and pray with him:

> Forgive, I beseech Thee, my Sins, deliver me from my Sorrows, and accept of this my Sacrifice: or rather look in my Behalf, on that only true Sacrifice, whereof here is a sacrament; the Sacrifice of thy wellbeloved Son, proceeding from Thee, to die for me. O let Him come unto me now, as the only-begotten of the Father, full of Grace and Truth![109]

7

Wesley's Legacy in Worship

C. Norman R. Wallwork

John Wesley's legacy to the modern worshipping Methodist community consists of the principles that he established and the types of services that he introduced. It does not lie in the forms that he used, for, as we shall see, these have either been greatly revised, or have fallen into disuse.

Wesley, for instance, insisted on only two hymns in a preaching service and, even with the abolition of the 'lining out' of the hymns by a precentor, he would surely have jibbed at the standard British five. Similarly he would have wondered why modern Methodists sit in fidgety silence waiting for their turn to move to the communion rail, when they could be singing their way through the one hundred and sixty-six hymns provided for just that purpose. Not only did Methodists subsequently employ the Wesley hymnody according to different principles, but their response to Wesley's revision of the *Book of Common Prayer* never worked out as he envisaged it. Similarly, in its modern counterpart, Wesley's Covenant Service is only traceable in a couple of paragraphs. Love-feasts have virtually disappeared, and the survival of Wesley's watch-night services is very patchy. Even Wesley's preaching service, the most enduring of his weekly innovations, has changed both in its form and its purpose.

Broadly speaking, Wesley gave the Methodist movement a revision of the *Book of Common Prayer* (with a set of optimistic instructions about its use on Sundays), and a number of supplementary services for weekly or occasional use. Most of the latter he borrowed from other Christian traditions, either from the Moravians or from the Puritan tradition.

Wesley was quite unwilling to separate evangelism from liturgy, or from the sacramental life of the church, or from social revolution. He stubbornly refused to let his societies secede from the Church of England – even when, as at times, he was almost single-handed in such a refusal – because he knew that evangelism outside a context of the sacramental means of grace is as finally invalid for the converted as are the means of grace for the unconverted.[1]

Once it was clear to John Wesley that the Methodist preachers and people in the American colonies were permanently independent of the British crown, and had become the fastest-growing and most vibrant section of the Methodist family, he resolved to settle upon his followers both a three-fold ministry of Superintendent, Elder and Deacon, and a revision of the *Book of Common Prayer*, which he entitled the *Sunday Service*. These decisive steps he took in September 1784.

Two years later, it also became clear to John Wesley that, despite his wishes to the contrary, perhaps the majority of Methodists in England were intent on finding their Sunday home in the Methodist preaching house, and not in the parish church.

In what cases do we allow of service in Church hours?
I answer,
1. When the minister is a notoriously wicked man.
2. When he preaches Arian, or any equally pernicious doctrine.
3. When there are not churches in the town sufficient to contain half the people. And,
4. When there is no Church at all within two or three miles. And we advise everyone who preaches in the Church-hours, to read the Psalms and Lessons, with part of the Church prayers: because we apprehend this will endear the Church Service to our brethren, who probably would be prejudiced against it, if they heard none but extemporary prayer.[2]

Against this background, Wesley published his 1784 American *Sunday Service* in an English edition in 1786.

In the parish churches the principal service of the day consisted of Morning Prayer, followed immediately by the Litany, which was then followed by the first part of the Communion Service up to and including the sermon and intercessions. Most of the congregation could not read, would not have been provided with copies of the service, and would simply have listened to the parish priest reading the service and the parish clerk making the responses. Such prayers as the General Confession in Morning Prayer and in the Communion Service would have been repeated after the parson or clerk, line by line.

John Wesley's proposals for the shortening of The Service of the Lord's Day included a reduction in the amount of psalmody per service; the omission of the Litany on Sundays, and a shortening of the Communion Service by the omission of the longer exhortations and the Creed. However, Wesley clearly intended the communion office to include the Lord's Supper, and not to end immediately after the sermon and intercessions.

> I have prepared a liturgy little differing from that of the church of England (I think, the best constituted national church in the world) which I advise all the travelling-preachers to use, on the Lord's day, in all their congregations, reading the litany only on Wednesdays and Fridays, and praying extempore on all other days. I also advise the elders to administer the supper of the Lord on every Lord's day.[3]

Wesley's detailed alterations to the *Book of Common Prayer* include minor doctrinal amendments in a Puritan direction. Among his deviations Wesley omits almost all references to the Apocrypha; he prefers 'minister' to 'priest' (except in the Communion Service, where he substitutes 'elder' for 'priest'); he replaces the absolution with a collect in Morning and Evening Prayer; and removes the declaratory pronouns from the absolution in the Communion Service. He omits a third of the Psalter (882 verses out of 2507) on grounds of brevity and unsuitable sentiments, and substitutes whole phrases and verses with the text of the Authorized Version. Most of the references to baptismal regeneration are removed from the service for the Baptism of Infants, and there is no reference to the ring in the service for the Solemnization of Matrimony. Private Baptism, Confirmation, The Visitation of the Sick, Churching, The Commination, The State Services and The Sea Service are also omitted. The service for the Communion of the Sick is retained. In the ordination services the threefold ordinal is retained both for America (1784) and for Britain (1786), but Superintendants (*sic*), Elders and Deacons replace Bishops, Priests and Deacons, and the texts have been carefully amended.

Few of the expectations surrounding Wesley's *Sunday Service* were realized. In America, only the second part of the Communion Service was retained for use at the close of a preaching service, along with such occasional offices as ordinations, baptisms, weddings and burials. In Britain, those Wesleyan chapels which opted for Morning Prayer almost invariably used the form in the *Book of Common Prayer*, and in 1882 and 1936 the British Methodists opted to continue this custom. However, most British Methodists, including the Wesleyans, never accepted Morning Prayer, though it had an honoured place in some chapels. Evening Prayer was a non-starter.

Wesley's revision of the Prayer Book communion service fared somewhat better, for it has been in continuous use in many Methodist chapels in Britain and has been included in the 1975 *Methodist Service Book* as an alternative order. However, the shortage of ordained travelling-preachers and, immediately after Wesley's death, questions of church order, meant that his ideal of a weekly eucharist was never realized.

Perhaps only three principles of Wesley's prayer-book abridgement have survived among the Methodists. In the first instance, British Methodists, by and large, have inherited a basically Anglican approach to the communion service and the occasional offices. (In the case of the communion service, this means that many congregations now have copies of the service, join in the responsive sections and move to the rail for communion.) In the second instance, British Methodists tend to adapt their printed services rather than abandon them. Thirdly, Methodists have retained and often have taken full advantage of the rubrics which provide for extempore prayer as an alternative to the printed forms at certain points in the text.

Outside the forms for Sunday and occasional services which Wesley included in the *Sunday Service*, his other legacy to the Methodists was a series of supplementary acts of worship designed, like the whole of the movement, to spread scriptural holiness.

The most well-known of Wesley's supplementary services was The Renewal of the Covenant. David Tripp has demonstrated that here Wesley was influenced to some degree by the covenanting theology of scripture, by the covenanting principle of the Puritans, of the Laudian Anglicans, of his own family and of the Moravians.

From 1755 or slightly earlier, Wesley urged his followers to make an express and solemn Covenant with God. He adopted for use on such occasions, a form of prayer composed by the Puritan minister, Joseph Alleine, in the late 1650s, and to it were added lengthy directions composed to accompany the prayer. These directions were compiled by Joseph Alleine's father-in-law, Richard. Wesley published the directions and the prayer in a form of his own as *Directions for Renewing our Covenant with God*, in 1780. At first Wesley held his Covenant Services at various times, but finally settled on the first Sunday of the New Year. It was Wesley's practice to include in these services the celebration of the Lord's Supper.

Wesley's Covenant Service was very different from the highly praised version that came into general Methodist and ecumenical use after the publication of the *Book of Offices* of 1936. Four portions of Wesley's original text which have more or less survived in the present Covenant Service demonstrate something of the power and depth which the service has retained. In the section bidding the worshippers to know that Christ has appointed them both their work and station there is a solemn reminder:

> Christ hath many services to be done, some are easy and honourable, others more difficult and disgraceful; some are suitable to our inclinations and interests, others are contrary to both: in some we may please Christ and please ourselves . . . but then there are other works, wherein we cannot please Christ, but by denying ourselves.

And a solemn promise is to be made:

> I put myself wholly into thy hands: put me to what thou wilt, rank me with whom thou wilt; put me to doing, put me to suffering, let me be employed for thee, or trodden under foot for thee; let me be full, let me be empty, let me have all things, let me have nothing, I freely and heartily resign all to thy pleasure and disposal.

In the third and tenth sections of Wesley's publication of the Covenant Prayer we read:

I call heaven and earth to record this day, that I do solemnly avouch thee for the Lord my God; and with all veneration bowing the neck of my soul under the feet of thy most sacred Majesty, I do here take Thee the Lord Jehovah, Father, Son and Holy Ghost, for my portion; and do give up myself, body and soul, for thy Servant, promising and vowing to serve Thee in holiness and righteousness, all the days of my life . . . O dreadful Jehovah, the Lord God Omnipotent, Father, Son and Holy Ghost, thou art now become my Covenant-Friend, and I, through thy infinite grace, am become thy Covenant-Servant. Amen. And the Covenant which I have made on earth, let it be ratified in heaven.[4]

Wesley clearly believed that it was not enough for the early Methodists to respond to the preaching of the law and the gospel, nor even to be set in the nurture house of the local Methodist band and class meetings. Once each year they were to commit themselves anew to their pilgrim journey. They were to lay hold again on the grace of their covenant God, and this they were summoned to do in the presence of their fellow Methodists. Year by year Wesley's followers were exhorted to renew their covenant in the preaching service at the turn of the year, and then, kneeling down, the travelling preacher would read the covenant directions and the prayer over their bowed heads. More often than not the Renewal of the Covenant ended with the singing of Charles Wesley's Covenant hymn, with its final verse:

> To us the covenant blood apply,
> Which takes our sins away;
> And register our names on high,
> And keep us to that day.[5]

In 1727, into his Moravian community at Herrnhut, Count Zinzendorf spontaneously introduced the agape or love-feast, which had held such an honoured place in the early centuries of the Christian church. This service was a common meal, with token food and drink, held for prayer, praise and fellowship, with the emphasis on testimony and thanksgiving. Sometimes the elements were identical with those of the Eucharist, but more often than not bread and wine were replaced by cake or special biscuits and water, in order to avoid any confusion between the love-feast and the Lord's Supper. Ten years after the introduction of the love-feast at Herrnhut, the Moravian settlers in Georgia had brought the service with them to Savannah. It was here that Wesley encountered the service in the summer of 1737.

> After evening prayers, we joined with the Germans in one of their love-feasts. It was begun and ended with thanksgiving and prayer, and celebrated in so decent and solemn a manner as a Christian of the apostolic age would have allowed to be worthy of Christ.[6]

Following his Aldersgate experience Wesley spent mid-June to mid-September 1738 with the Moravians in Germany, and again shared in their love-feast celebrations. On his return Wesley described the introduction of the love-feast to the Fetter Lane Religious Society in London, and a love-feast which he shared on New Year's Day 1739 with (among others) six of his fellow clergyman – all original Oxford Methodists.

> Mr Hall, Kinchin, Ingham, Whitefield, Hutchins, and my brother Charles were present at our love-feast in Fetter Lane, with about sixty of our brethren. About three in the morning as we were continuing instant in prayer, the power of God came mightily upon us, insomuch that many cried out for exceeding joy, and many fell to the ground. As soon as we were recovered a little from that awe and amazement at the presence of His majesty we broke out with one voice: 'We praise Thee, O God; we acknowledge Thee to be the Lord.'[7]

When the London Methodists seceded from the Fetter Lane Society and set up their own headquarters at the Foundery in Moorfields, they took the love-feast with them. Sometimes the celebration would be held fortnightly, alternating between a gathering for the men and one for the women, but eventually the 'general love-feast' predominated. Wesley's intention, both for his preachers in Conference and for his poeple in the Methodist societies, bands and classes, was to deepen their fellowship and increase their joy. For Wesley, the New Testament knew nothing of solitary religion.

> In order to increase in them a grateful sense of all His mercies, I desired that, one evening in a quarter, all the men in band, on a

second all the women, would meet, and on a third both men and women together; that we might together 'eat bread', as the ancient Christians did, 'with gladness and singleness of heart'. At these love-feasts (so we termed them, retaining the name as well as the thing which was in use from the beginning) our food is only a little plain cake and water. But we seldom return from them without being fed, not only with the 'meat which perisheth', but with 'that which endureth to everlasting life'.[8]

Wesley presided at love-feasts throughout his ministry, and they continued to be celebrated in all branches of Methodism, on both sides of the Atlantic well into the nineteenth century. Leslie Church testified to their ministry in the following terms:

The supreme value of the love-feast lay in its frank fellowship and its Christian expression of freedom, equality, and brother-hood . . . It was not the material elements of the love-feast that were important, nor even the order of the proceedings – but rather the sense of prayer and expectation with which the people came, and the satisfaction of their spiritual hunger as they fed on the Bread of Life.[9]

Charles Wesley wrote an eight-verse hymn for the love-feast, published in his *Hymns and Sacred Poems* of 1740, which captures the spirit and the blessing which attended the first Methodist celebrations:

> Come, and let us sweetly join
> Christ to praise in hymns divine;
> Give we all, with one accord,
> Glory to our common Lord:
> Hands and hearts and voices raise;
> Sing as in the ancient days;
> Antedate the joys above,
> Celebrate the feast of love.

In Germany Wesley also attended Moravian watch-night ser-vices; but the Methodist watch-night services began with Wesley's approval of the spontaneous watch-night held by the Methodists at Kingswood, Bristol.

About this time, I was informed that several persons in Kingswood frequently met together at the school; and, when they could spare the time, spent the greater part of the night in prayer, and praise and thanksgiving. Some advised me to put an end to this; but, upon weighing the thing thoroughly, and comparing it with the practice of the ancient Christians, I could see no cause to forbid it. Rather, I believed it might be made of more general use. So I sent word, I designed to watch with them on the Friday nearest the full moon, that we might have light thither and back again . . . On Friday abundance of people came. I began preaching between eight and nine; and we continued till a little beyond the noon of night, singing, praying, and praising God.[10]

Once established, Methodist watch-nights were held monthly in Bristol, London and Newcastle.

On 8 June 1750, Wesley prepared a long letter of defence to John Baily, Rector of Kilcully, Cork, in which among many other matters he justified watch-night services as follows:

You charge me . . . with holding 'midnight assemblies'. Sir, did you never see the word 'Vigil' in your Common Prayer Book? Do you know what it means? If not, permit me to tell you that it was customary with the ancient Christians to spend whole nights in prayer, and that these were termed *Vigiliae*, or Vigils. Therefore, for spending a part of some nights in this manner, in public and solemn prayer, we have not only the authority of our own national Church, but of the universal Church in the earliest ages.[11]

Methodists ultimately abandoned regular monthly watch-nights in favour of an annual service on New Year's Eve. The latter custom has survived in many places, and has been adopted by other Christian traditions outside Methodism.

The least documented but most universal of Wesley's innovative and supplementary services was his Sunday and mid-week preaching service. Although this service has not survived anywhere in its original form, it became the basis of the Methodist weekly worship in all the chapels and preaching-houses which declined the use of Wesley's *Sunday Service* or the *Book of Common Prayer* for non-Eucharistic services. Even at communion services, for most of Methodist history, the Lord's Supper has been celebrated at the close of an extempore preaching service.

In his summary of the customs and practices of early Methodism, Wesley, writing in the third person, recalls the early preaching services at the Foundery in Moorfields:

> In November (1739), a large building, the Foundery, being offered him, he began preaching therein, morning and evening, that the people's labour might not be hindered.
>
> From the beginning the men and women sat apart, as they always did in the primitive church; and none were suffered to call any place their own, but the first comers sat down first. They had no pews; and all the benches for rich and poor were of the same construction.
>
> Mr Wesley began the service with a short prayer; then sung a hymn and preached, (usually about an hour), then sang a few verses of another hymn, and concluded with prayer, preceded by repentance and followed by holiness.[12]

The Foundery preaching service ran thus: short prayer, hymn, sermon, hymn, and prayer. Mr Silas Told describes a Methodist preaching service of 1740, also conducted by John Wesley:

> Exactly at five o'clock a whisper ran through the congregation, 'Here he comes! here he comes!' I had a curiosity to see his person, which, when I beheld, I much despised. The enemy of souls suggested, that he was some farmer's son, who, not able to support himself, was making a penny in this low manner. He passed through the congregation into the pulpit, and, having his robes on, I expected he would have begun with the Church service: but, to my astonishment, he began with singing a hymn, with which I was almost enraptured; but his extempore prayer was quite unpleasant, as I thought it favoured too much of the Dissenter. After this, he took his text in the second chapter of St John, 12, 13, 'I write unto you, little children, because your sins are forgiven you, etc.' The enemy now suggested he was a Papist, as he dwelt much on forgiveness of sins . . .[13]

In 1766 Wesley urged the Methodist Conference and the societies to ponder the strengths, weaknesses and limited purpose of their preaching services:

> But some say, 'Our own service is public worship.' Yes, in a sense: but not such as supersedes the Church Service. We never

designed it should. We have a hundred times professed to the contrary. It pre-supposes public prayer, like the sermons at the University. Therefore I have over and over advised, Use no long prayer, either before or after the sermon. Therefore I myself frequently use only a collect, and never enlarge in prayer, unless at intercession, or on a watch-night, or on some extra-ordinary occasion.

If it were designed to be instead of the Church Service, it would be essentially defective. For it seldom has the four grand parts of public prayer; deprecation, petition, intercession, and thanksgiving. Neither is it, even on the Lord's day, concluded with the Lord's Supper.

The hour for it on that day, unless where there is some peculiar reason for a variation, should be five in the morning, as well as five in the evening.[14]

In 1785 Wesley was still insisting that the 'lining-out' of two hymns in the preaching service was quite sufficient:

I desire that none of our preachers would sing oftener than twice at one service. We need nothing to fill up the hour . . .[15]

Wesley's preaching service was the primary vehicle for the three grand dimensions of Methodist weekly worship – extempore prayer, extempore preaching, and the singing of hymns composed or selected by the Wesleys.

Though Wesley attended at least one Moravian preaching service at Herrnhut, it is most likely that the early Methodist preaching service was based on the Bidding Prayer and Sermon. This was, after all, the only legitimate extra-liturgical public service available to a canonically-minded Anglican clergyman. Love-feasts and Covenant services were not open to the public, and the watch-night was a preaching service.

The Bidding Prayer and Sermon, though formalized at the universities, at the assizes and at charity sermons, was orginally a people's service. Its origins, via the fifty-fifth Canon of the Church of England, lay in the vernacular intercessions and sermon, which French, German and English Catholics had re-introduced into the Mass in the early Middle Ages. Known as the Prone or the Bidding of the Bedes, this service was utilized by Calvin and Zwingli on the continent, and by the Puritans within the Church of England throughout the sixteenth and seventeenth centuries. Both Thomas Coke and John Fletcher employed models of the Bidding Prayer when they combined their roles as clergymen and Methodist preachers in the preaching houses.

When it became obvious that the early Methodists were not attending the parish churches Sunday by Sunday, and that the travelling preachers dare not introduce either the *Book of Common Prayer* or Wesley's *Abridgement* for Methodist Sunday worship, the preaching service with two hymns, a prayer and a sermon became the norm. Both before and after Wesley's death the Conference realized the need for the reading of at least one chapter of scripture at those preaching services held in church hours. The scene was now set for the filling out of the service with more hymns, more prayers, and later with introits, anthems, and a psalm or canticle, so that up-and-coming Methodist congregations could own a service which bore the atmosphere, if not the form, of worship in the parish churches and in the 'better' dissenting chapels. In the village chapels at least four hymns, a long prayer and the Lord's Prayer, two readings and a sermon, became standard practice. In most cases the preaching service also took the place of the pre-communion service at the Lord's Supper.

Every one of Wesley's supplementary services, and indeed his crowded and frequent celebrations of the Lord's Supper were brought alive, not only by extempore prayer and extempore preaching, but also by the integral place which each assembly for prayer and praise assigned to the use of hymns.

During the fifty years that the Wesley brothers presided over the Methodist movement, they published something like sixty hymn books. Some of these collections were small pamphlets containing less than a dozen hymns, while others contained perhaps thirty or forty items. Some of the publications were for general occasions, but many collections were designed for specific seasons of the year, or celebrated particular Christian themes or stages of evangelical Arminian experience, under such titles as: *Hymns on God's Everlasting Love* (1741–2); *Hymns for the Nativity of our Lord* (1745); *Funeral Hymns* (c.1746) *Hymns for the Watchnight* (c.1746); *Hymns for those to whom Christ is all in all* (1761); *A Collection of Hymns for the Lord's Day* (1784).

Of all the hymn-books published in the Wesleys' life-time, the greater part either bore the name of both John and Charles (John's name always coming first), or no name at all, on the title page. There are only three which were published by Charles alone, on two of which John remarks that as he had not seen them before publication, there were expressions of which he could not approve. Charles has left no reference to the editing of books which they published together.[16]

The most definitive of the Wesleys' hymn books was the volume of 1780, containing some 525 items and entitled *A Collection of Hymns, for the use of the People called Methodists*. Cecil Northcott wrote of this definitive volume:

The 1780 Methodist hymn book is a spiritual biography, a kind of hymnodic Pilgrim's Progress beginning with the exhortation to the sinner to return to God, and leading him through the great facts of religious experience in this life to the final confrontation with Death, Judgement, Heaven and Hell . . . From repentance the Wesley hymns guide the believer through the phases of human life as one who will rejoice, fight, pray, watch, work, suffer and intercede for the world. Only after the individual experience has been fully provided for come the hymns of the corporate life of 'the Methodist Society' in its meetings, thanksgivings, praying and parting.[17]

John Bishop maintains that:

Charles Wesley sets forth the whole range of the evangelical faith. It is a remarkable feat. Methodists have learned their doctrines from hymns. By singing them they have not only got to know them, but to receive and approve them.[18]

Leslie Church makes the perceptive observation:

Through all the formative years, when the Societies were divided on ecclesiastical or theological issues, the hymns helped those who sang them towards a deeper unity than Conference or Trustees meetings could effect . . . for it was not the commentary on the shelf but the song in the heart which inspired and continually instructed the first Methodists. When the travelling preacher had ridden away on his round, and his closely-reasoned sermon was forgotten, the people in the cottage meeting went on singing.[19]

A similar point is made by Frank Baker:

> It was the profound conviction of the Wesleys that . . . salvation
> must be 'free', but it must also be 'for all', otherwise it was
> hardly a gospel. Both became key-notes of Methodist preaching
> and Methodist singing. As a result the theological atmosphere
> of English religion changed from the rigid Calvinism of the
> seventeenth century to the Arminianism and modified Calvin-
> ism of the nineteenth century. In this theological revolution no
> two men played a greater part than the brothers Wesley, and it
> seems that the hymns of Charles were even more influential
> than the sermons of John.[20]

What then are the permanent contributions of John Wesley to
contemporary Methodist and ecumenical liturgical faith and
practice?

Foremost is the Wesley commitment to the main diet of worship
on the Lord's day. This is to be drawn from the accumulated
wisdom and custom of the universal church and should include
the Lord's Supper every week.

Secondly, no set of liturgical texts, however treasured and
venerable, is beyond adaptation and revision, and such a process
is a constant necessity in the life of the church.

Thirdly, at least once a year the Lord's people should be
summoned to a renewal of their commitment to God. For the
Methodists this summons is to the Covenant Service. For other
Christians the summons may be to the renewal of baptismal vows
in the Easter Vigil.

Fourthly, provision must be made for the recurring needs of
prayer, praise and fellowship which occur outside the formal
liturgical life of the local church. This need Wesley met in the
celebration of the love-feast, but, as with the Lord's Supper,
admission was by membership ticket because the language and
experience of believers could confuse the enquirer. Much of the
extra-liturgical worship that has grown out of the charismatic
movement bears witness to this recurring need to which Wesley
responded.

Fifthly, public worship based on the choir offices of *Morning and
Evening Prayer* and the *Eucharistic Liturgy* cannot express the full
range of the instrument in the soul of the evangelical Christian.
Hence John Wesley's preaching service with hymns, extempore

prayer and extempore preaching entered into the very life-blood of the Methodist community. In other words, the people's service may never totally coincide with the hopes and aspirations of liturgical scholars. The people's service will re-emerge, however much it is overlaid or suppressed.

Sixthly, the singing of hymns in the Methodist tradition has not only offered to the universal church an addition to its canon of hymns, but has introduced the concept of a hymn as an integral text in the liturgy and not just a linking item, an introit, a gradual in the Eucharist or an office hymn in the services of Morning and Evening Prayer. At the same time the Wesleys employed the hymn as a vehicle both to teach the faith and to stir up and express the depths of Christian experience in the human spirit.

Bibliography

1. Wesley's Abridgement of the Book of Common Prayer

Frank Baker, *John Wesley and the Church of England*, Epworth Press 1970
G. J. Cuming, *A History of Anglican Liturgy*, Macmillan 1969
A. Raymond George, 'The Sunday Service of the Methodists', *In Communio Sanctorum. Mélanges offerts à Jean-Jacques von Allmen*, Geneva 1982
A. Raymond George, *The Sunday Service 1784*, Friends of Wesley's Chapel Lecture 1983
James F. White, *John Wesley's Sunday Service of the Methodists in North America*, Quarterly Review Bicentennial Reprint, United Methodist Publishing House 1984

2. Wesley's Covenant Service

David Tripp, *The Renewal of the Covenant in the Methodist Tradition*, Epworth Press 1969

3. The Love-Feast

Frank Baker, *Methodism and the Love-Feast*, Epworth Press 1957
Adrian Burdon, *Epworth Review*, 15.2, May 1988
Leslie Church, *More About the Early Methodist People*, Epworth Press 1949
Clifford Towlson, *Moravian and Methodist*, Epworth Press 1957

4. The Watch-night Service

Leslie Church, *More About the Early Methodist People*, Epworth Press 1949
John Bishop, *Methodist Worship in Relation to Free Church Worship*, Scholars Press 1975

5. The Preaching Service

A. Raymond George, 'The Means of Grace', in *A History of the Methodist Church in Great Britain*, ed. Rupert Davies and E. G. Rupp, Vol. 1, Epworth Press 1965

C. Norman R. Wallwork, *Origins and Development of the Methodist Preaching Service*, Birmingham University M A Thesis 1984

Trevor Dearing, *Wesleyan and Tractarian Worship*, Epworth Press 1962

6. The Hymns of Methodism

Frank Baker and George Walton Williams, *John Wesley's First Hymn Book. A Collection of Psalms and Hymns* (Charlestown 1737), The Dalcho Historical Society and the Wesley Historical Society 1964

Frank Baker, *Representative Verse of Charles Wesley* Epworth Press 1962, *Charles Wesley's Verse*, Epworth Press 1988

Henry Bett, *The Hymns of Methodism* Epworth Press 1913, 1945

George H. Findlay, *Christ's Standard Bearer – A Study in the Hymns of Charles Wesley*, Epworth Press 1956

R. Newton Flew, *The Hymns of Charles Wesley. A Study of their Structure*, Epworth Press 1953

A. S. Gregory, *Praises with Understanding*, Epworth Press 1936

Franz Hildebrandt and O. A. Beckerlegge, *The Works of John Wesley*, Vol. 7, *A Collection of Hymns for the Use of the People called Methodists*, Clarendon Press 1984

H. A. Hodges and A. M. Allchin, *A Rapture of Praise. Hymns of John and Charles Wesley*, Hodder and Stoughton 1966

John Lawson, *A Thousand Tongues. The Wesley Hymns as a Guide to Scriptural Teaching*, Paternoster Press 1987

Bernard Lord Manning, *The Hymns of Wesley and Watts* Epworth Press 1942, 1988

J. Ernest Rattenbury, *The Evangelical Doctrines of Charles Wesley's Hymns*, Epworth Press 1941

J. Ernest Rattenbury, *The Eucharistic Hymns of John and Charles Wesley*, Epworth Press 1948

Erik Routley, *The Musical Wesleys*, Herbert Jenkins 1968

8

Wesley's Chapels

Christopher Stell

Nothing could have been further from the mind of John Wesley as he set out on his mission than that there should ever exist such a class of buildings as 'Mr Wesley's chapels'. Professing a continued loyalty to the church within which he had been ordained, he saw his societies as auxiliary to the established religion, meeting for mutual support and instruction while maintaining a regular attendance at the public services within their respective parishes. Clerical fears of enthusiasm and insistence on the maintenance of hierarchical discipline and privileges soon combined to close many London pulpits against the episcopally ordained Methodist preachers, with the result that chapels such as West Street were acquired in which they felt free to conduct the services of the church and to administer the sacrament. A rapid rise in the number of Methodist societies throughout the country due to the energetic work of many itinerant preachers led to a corresponding demand for 'preaching-houses'; though seen at first as but an elaboration of the society rooms, these soon took on a more positive role as centres of worship and, in popular parlance, became 'chapels' where increasingly towards the end of Wesley's life the right to hold sacramental services was being sought. Few of these chapels or preaching-houses can properly be described as Wesley's in architectural terms, his concern being principally to maintain his right to the appointment of preachers free from the whims of local trustees, but he was by no means without views on their design or hesitant to give advice when that was called for.

Little of architectural quality can have existed in the first of the society rooms to be set up in London when, in November 1739, Wesley was persuaded, with some reluctance, to preach in what

New Room, Bristol. 1739-48   Colliers' Chapel, Kingswood. 1739

Orphan House, Newcastle. 1742   Rotherham. 1761

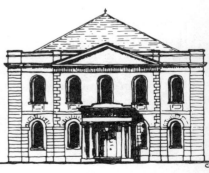

Netherthong. 1769   City Road, London. 1776

The Old Methodist Chapel, Eccleshill. 1775

remained of an old foundry building in Windmill Street, its walls shattered by an explosion many years before. Nothing daunted, he bought the lease, repaired the walls and early in the following year it became the home of a new society, distinct from that in Fetter Lane, later to become Moravian, to which Wesley earlier belonged. There the principal London society remained until 1776 and there in the adjoining house Wesley lodged on his many visits, and there, too, his mother passed her closing years. It was a plain building which by 1763 required further major repairs, but it was large, having three galleries and seating fifteen hundred people, mainly on backless benches, the sexes being rigorously segregated.

Even before the Foundery was brought into use the Religious Societies in Bristol, of which there were several, were in need of more suitable premises than the hired rooms in which they met. Wesley had travelled to Bristol in April 1739 to take over from George Whitefield the superintendence of these societies; on 9 May he entered into possession of a piece of ground lying hidden behind houses at the back of the Horsefair and on 12 May he laid the foundation stone for the new Society Room – Wesley's New Room in the Horsefair. The original appearance of this building is still very much a matter of conjecture following much rebuilding and enlargement in 1748. Perhaps the walls of the 'little tenement or lodge' which stood there were incorporated into it or their materials were re-used, for the contract 'to pay the workmen about 160 pounds as soon as it is finished' left little scope for extravagance. The room served many purposes including that of a day school, its main adornments were a desk covered with a piece of green cloth and a modest pair of eight-branch chandeliers, and its ancillary rooms comprised a small vestry and a garret furnished with a bed. By 1742 concern was being felt over the condition of the building and for the repayment of the debt; the latter was overcome by the introduction of the Class system, the former only by rebuilding. The enlarged room which fortunately survives was much more a preaching-house than was its predecessor and, though still hidden and without the need for external show, it has sufficient internal grandeur, with its six imposing stone columns carrying the upper floor and the all-embracing galleries, to make its ascription to the architect George Tully a distinct possibility. As in the Friends' meeting-house nearby on which Tully was also engaged, additional light is obtained from a central lantern in the roof, while the former garret has blossomed into a full suite of rooms for the 'family' of circuit preachers for whom this was home.

A northern counterpart to the New Room was to be found in Newcastle-upon-Tyne, where a society formed in 1742 met first in a hired room known as 'the Tabernacle'. Again Wesley suffered no delay, by December he had acquired not one but two adjacent pieces of ground on which was built the 'Orphan House'. Its name indicated an intention which was never achieved that it should house orphan children as well as serve as a preaching-house, school and accommodation for preachers. The building survived until 1857 although superseded in its principal function in 1821 by the erection of Brunswick Chapel. It comprised a large preaching room with pulpit and forms, to which galleries were later added, over which were various society rooms; on the top floor were the preacher's apartments and on the roof 'a wooden erection, about eleven feet square, with tiled covering, generally known as "Mr Wesley's Study".'

Of greater architectural prominence was the Colliers' school-chapel at Kingswood where, on his departure from Bristol in 1739, Whitefield laid a foundation stone. Shortly afterwards Wesley took the work in hand with his accustomed vigour on a new site 'between the London and Bath roads'. He describes the schoolhouse as a large room with four small rooms at each end for the schoolmasters. This was a building very much in the meeting-house tradition with a broad front and steeply hipped roof which, although demolished about 1917, survives in the design of the front of Whitefield's Tabernacle, Kingswood, built by John Cennick after his break with Wesley.

One of the few preaching-houses to remain from the first two decades of Methodism and one which still exhibits evidence of modest architectural pretensions is at Bradford on Avon. There, hidden behind other buildings in Market Street, is the former chapel believed to have been opened in 1756. The valleys of its triple roof were evidently supported by four wooden columns standing on stone piers, a gallery extended around three sides and at the end of the longer axis is a Venetian window high above the site of the pulpit. It was registered of necessity, though doubtless to John Wesley's displeasure, in accordance with the Act of Toleration as a meeting-house for Protestant Dissenters and described as 'a house or edifice lately erected adjoining the dwellinghouse of John Silby'.

In the following year Wesley's attention was drawn to a novel design in chapel building which for the next twenty years found considerable favour. This began in 1757 with his visit to 'Dr Taylor's new meeting-house' in Norwich which, in fulsome though guarded praise, he describes as 'perhaps the most elegant one in Europe'. The Presbyterian octagon, even then the seat of questionable orthodoxy, being 'finished in the highest taste' and 'as clean as any nobleman's saloon' was dismissed as unlikely to admit 'the old coarse gospel'. It is interesting to note that the first polygonal Methodist chapel to be built after this visit of which we have any record was not octagonal: the new house in Colchester of 1759 is described by Wesley as 'twelve square' and 'the best building, of the size, for the voice that I know in England'. Its quality as a preaching-house was what mattered, its architectural elegance, if any, receives no mention. The first of his octagon chapels came two years later, at Rotherham, where in July 1761 Wesley preached 'in the shell of the new house' adding the comment: 'Pity our houses, when the ground will admit of it, should be built in any other form'.

The earliest surviving Methodist octagon is at Stroud, built in 1763 and now used by the Salvation Army. This illustrates one of the main problems of the style, subsequent enlargement requiring much more costly construction than in a simple rectangular building. The same problem was subsequently faced at Hepton-stall in the chapel of 1764. Also of that date is the oldest unextended octagon, at Yarm; 'by far the most elegant in England', says Wesley, who two years later contrasts it with one at Thirsk. 'Almost equal to that at Yarm', he says, 'and why not quite, seeing they had the model before their eyes and had nothing to do but to copy after it? Is it not an amazing weakness that, when they have the most beautiful pattern before them, all builders will affect to mend something? So the *je ne sais quoi* is lost, and the second building scarce ever equals the first.' But some improvement was still possible; also in 1766 at Bradford 'the largest octagon we have in England' is described as 'the first of the kind where the roof is built with common sense, rising only a third of its breadth'. No wonder then that the Canterbury polygon, then but two years old, with its ten or twelve sides and its steep roof, was known as the 'pepper box chapel'.

Enthusiasm for the octagon did not last; its limitations and its complexities of construction were soon apparent and, while occasional later examples such as those still remaining at Arbroath, of 1772, and Taunton, of 1776, are known, another and more lasting exemplar was about to appear. The octagon was well suited to its purpose as a preaching-house, and its use was not confined to Methodists. Other denominations, too, even the established Church, had their octagonal churches and chapels. But to Wesley the ideal place of worship was the parish church as built or modified in the eighteenth century, with its communion table at the east end and a tall three-decker pulpit prominently sited centrally in front of it. This was not only the most convenient position for preaching but it preserved to the sacrament something of the mystery which is lacking in other arrangements.

When, in 1775, the time came to replace the Foundery, then threatened by the possibility of redevelopment by the City Corporation, the New Foundery, or the New Chapel as it soon came to be called, built on a nearby site in City Road, was designed in strict conformity to accepted taste. This was Wesley's ideal chapel of which, as having more responsibility for its appearance than many over which he enthused, he modestly wrote on the day of opening in 1776; 'it is perfectly neat, but not fine'. The finery and the elaboration followed later as loving care broke the bounds of discretion and sought to gild a lily which is sufficiently honoured in bearing the name of Wesley's Chapel. Here the full liturgical services of the church to which the Wesleys professed adherence could be maintained free from episcopal restraint, and to this pattern the Methodist societies looked increasingly for guidance as they came to acknowledge their independence as a unique and powerful denomination. A few years later, in 1779, when Wesley opened the new chapel at Bath he observed that 'it is about half as large as that at London, and built nearly upon the same model'. So effective did this prove that in 1790 the Conference decreed that 'all preaching-houses are to be built in future upon the same plan as the London or Bath chapel'.

With the design of most of the innumerable chapels and preaching-houses built during his lifetime John Wesley can have had little direct concern. He and his fellow preachers sowed the seeds of the new societies, he frequently preached 'in the shell of the new house' even before completion and often records a few brief words of admiration. The new house at St Just in Cornwall was, in 1757, 'the largest and most commodious in the county'. The new room in Salisbury, of 1759, was declared to be 'the most complete in England'; Doncaster, of 1776, was 'one of the most elegant houses in England', while at Bolton the new house opened in 1777 was 'the most beautiful in the country'. Advice would occasionally be given on more detailed matters as it was in 1757 over the building of the Peaseholme Green preaching-house in York when he wrote: 'I believe each window may stand eight foot (the bottom of it) from the ground, and be four foot broad and six or seven high, arched at the top', but this was exceptional, and more often the builders would be free to exercise their own judgement in the light of local building traditions.

The little chapel at Whittlebury, Northamptonshire, commenced in 1763 by 'a truly loving and simple people', but not completed until many years later, was hardly more than a simple cottage probably once hidden behind other buildings. The same might be said of the former cob-built preaching-house at Cubert in Cornwall, again a plain building in the local vernacular style. The chapel at Crich in Derbyshire, built in 1765, is more distinctive with its windows 'arched at the top', as was the contemporary preaching-house in St Michael's Lane, Derby, buildings respectively in stone and brick and each with two doorways as a visual reminder of Wesley's remark that 'we make no distinction but between men and women', a separation which he long attempted to enforce. Some Yorkshire preaching-houses follow a pattern which served equally well for other denominations, with two tall windows flanking a front pulpit. One of the best of these is at Eccleshill near Bradford where Wesley preached in 1776 and where, twelve years later, he spent some hours in fruitless discussion with the trustees in an attempt to persuade them to revise the trust deed. A similar, though slightly more elaborate, chapel had been built at Netherthong about 1769 after Methodist preachers had been discouraged for some time from visiting Huddersfield in deference to the wishes of the vicar, the Rev. Henry Venn. Both these buildings survive, though no longer in Methodist hands, as worthy reminders of the ever-declining number of preaching-houses in which the father of Methodism once expounded the word of God. Fewer than fifty of these now remain, some greatly altered, others only recognizable, if at all, with the eye of faith, and yet all possessing not the '*je ne sais quoi*' of which Thirsk was found wanting but a *genius loci* which transcends the glories of architecture. The New Room and the New Chapel in City Road are not the only significant examples of Wesley's chapels. They are the architectural extremes. Between them lie High House and Newbiggin in the north, the hidden gem of Raithby, the little cottage chapel at Winchelsea, the octagons and many others whose walls bear silent but moving witness to the faith which raised them and the spark whence it arose.

Bibliography

N. Curnock (ed.), *The Journal of the Rev. John Wesley, A.M.*, 1909–16.

G. W. Dolbey, *The Architectural Expression of Methodism*, 1964.

G. Eayrs, *Wesley and Kingswood and its Free Churches*, 1911.

F. C. Gill, *In the Steps of John Wesley*, 1962.

C. Dean Little, 'Early Methodist Octagons', *Proceedings of the Wesley Historical Society*, XXV, 1945–46, 81–86.

W. W. Stamp, *The Orphan-house of Wesley . . .*, 1863.

J. Telford (ed.), *The Letters of the Rev. John Wesley, A.M.*, 1931.

J. Vickers and Betty Young, *A Methodist Guide to London and the South-East*, 1980.

M. W. Woodward, *One at London: Some Account of Mr Wesley's Chapel and London House*, 1966.

9

John Wesley: The Organizer

A. *Raymond George*

John Wesley had the gift of being a good organizer. This was no doubt one of the reasons why he, rather than his brother Charles or George Whitefield, became the acknowledged leader of the Methodists and in some sense the founder of a new branch of the Christian Church. Whitefield was a more popular, though less profound, preacher. Whitefield and Charles Wesley both experienced an assurance of God's forgiveness before John did, but John emerged as the leader.

Yet John Wesley was not attempting to found a fresh branch of the Church, or, as we should now say, a denomination. He was, as we all know, a clergyman of the Church of England who urged attendance at the church service and opposed separation from the Church. What he wrote about the Church was not intended as an ecclesiology for a fresh denomination. Yet bit by bit the Methodist system came into being. First came the Societies. There were Societies in London, especially the Fetter Lane Society, and one of its sub-divisions, the Society in Aldersgate, but these were not under Wesley's control, even though in December 1738 he drew up rules for the Band-Societies connected with them. Whitefield's appeal to Wesley to come and help him, indeed to take over his work, in Bristol included the quaint expression that the Societies there were 'ripe for hands'. Wesley in response to this invitation to Bristol preached for the first time in the open air in a Brickfield adjoining the city on 2 April 1739; this led to an immediate increase in the Societies in Nicholas Street and Baldwin Street, and in order to expound the Scripture to these Societies Wesley arranged the building of 'our New Room in the Horsefair', the oldest building in the world erected for purely Methodist purposes. When on 11 July Wesley and Whitefield, who had for a while returned to Bristol, 'united the two leading Societies together', as Whitefield put it, in effect they began the first Society fully under Wesley's control, apart from the Holy Club, which, interesting as it is a forerunner of Methodism, and cause of the nickname 'Methodist', preceded the Aldersgate experience. This seems to have led to the first use of the term 'United Society', which was later employed also elsewhere. In December of the same year a Society was established at the Foundery, London, a building which Wesley leased, and this Society eventually came to be regarded as in some sense the parent Society.

Soon Wesley was employing laymen as preachers. John Cennick seems to have been the first, but when in 1740–41 Thomas Maxfield, one of his first converts in Bristol, began preaching in London at the Foundery, Wesley hastened to forbid him. His mother Susanna, however, said: 'Take care what you do with respect to that young man', and by permitting him to continue Wesley took a decisive step towards the establishment of what would eventually be the Methodist ministry.

In Bristol in 1744 a ship-captain called Foy, in order to pay the debt on the New Room, divided the Society into classes of twelve members, each of whom was to pay, if able to do so, a penny a week to a leader; he thus instituted a system which Wesley perceived to be useful, not merely financially, but also pastorally. The whole membership, and not merely a select few, was thus divided into classes, under the pastoral care of a class leader. Through the next century conservatives fought a losing battle trying to insist on attendance at class as essential to Methodist membership; but to this day Methodism, at least in Great Britain, has its whole membership divided into classes, under the pastoral care of a leader or, nowadays, if they do not actually meet, of a pastoral visitor. The bands have died out, though some chapels, especially in the North of England, still have a band-room, but the division into classes continues.

But it was not only at Bristol or through the initiative of Bristolians that innovations occurred. The first Conference of preachers was held in London in 1744, at which six Anglican clergymen invited four laymen to join them. There followed later the division of the preachers into travelling preachers and local preachers; the institution of the circuits or rounds, the quarterly meetings.¹ What emerged was a Connexion, a term probably derived from the phrase 'preachers in connexion with the Rev. Mr John Wesley', and always spelt with an x.

This was not yet a church, but it was not surprising that some Church of England clergymen saw the intrusion of unordained preachers into their parishes as a breach of church order; and thus the way was prepared for the more decisive breach, namely Wesley's ordinations in 1784 for America, and later for other places, and finally for England.² Well might Joseph Beaumont say at the Wesleyan Conference of 1834: 'Wesley, like a strong and skilful rower, looked one way while every stroke of his oar took him in an opposite direction.'³

Such groups are not uncommon in the history of the Church. They often exist uneasily within the larger church and then either fade away or break away; while such a group still remains within the larger church, it may be called a little church within a church, *ecclesiola in ecclesia*, but like many other writers I use instead the terms society and church to describe, perhaps in an oversimplified way, the contrasting styles of the two bodies in Wesley's lifetime. The preachers, however, have been described as resembling a religious order; the fact that, except for a very small number of Church of England clergymen such as Charles Wesley, they were all laymen until finally Wesley ordained a few of them, does not invalidate this comparison, for some of the historic religious orders did and indeed still do include many laypeople.

Entry to the Church was by baptism, which was usually of infants and, at least theoretically, was followed later by confirmation; entrance to a society was of adults or adolescents by the receipt of a class-ticket on the basis of a desire to flee from the wrath to come. Bishops, priests and deacons ministered in the Church; travelling and local preachers in the societies.

The Church had Morning Prayer in the latter part of the morning and Evening Prayer in the afternoon; the societies had simple preaching services at 5 a.m. and 5 p.m. The Church had Holy Communion; the societies had love-feasts. The Church was established, clearly linked with the state, and largely governed by the bishops; the societies were free from state control and governed by the Conference, which in effect meant by Mr Wesley. The Church had amorphous congregations with virtually no ecclesiastical discipline; the societies were rigorously disciplined bodies with intimate fellowship in society meeting and class meeting. In the Church one might expect a variety of theological, ethical and political views; in the societies, considerable uniformity. The Church, theoretically at least, was the church of the majority of the population; a society is likely to appeal only to a minority.

In 1784 all that changed for America. After Wesley had ordained preachers for America, giving his reasons in a letter from Bristol dated 10 September 1784, the Christmas Conference at Baltimore decided to constitute an episcopal Church, and the Methodist Episcopal Church sprang fully-armed, as it were, from the head of Zeus. It was this action of ordaining preachers and sending them to America which justifies the statement that Wesley was in a sense the founder of a denomination, and the system devised for a connexion was immediately modified to form the constitution of a denomination.

In Britain no such event as the Baltimore Conference occurred. The statement that the Methodist Church existed in America before it existed in Britain sometimes startles British Methodists, but it is undeniably true. Nor did Wesley's actions after 1784 in ordaining a few preachers for Scotland and later England make much real difference. I leave aside the somewhat different case of Scotland, and ask: when did the establishment of the Methodist Church of Great Britain or the separation of Methodism from the Church of England occur? It is impossible to give a definite answer to these questions, for they occurred by a gradual process. The whole subsequent history of British Methodism may be regarded as an evolution from society to church, which has been completed only in our own day. With hindsight we can see that it was inevitable, but that was not obvious to all Methodists in the turbulent years after Wesley's death in 1791, when there was much confusion, not least in Bristol. It was the adherents of the 'Old Plan' who claimed to be loyal churchmen, showing a proper regard for the sacraments and customs of the Church of England. What John Bowmer calls by contrast the Providential Way was to make the people called Methodists into a Church or a denomination.[4] The compromise reached in 1795, with the gloomy name of Plan of Pacification, was not explicitly the establishment of a church, but it marked the point of no return. If any definite date can be given for the separation, this must be it.

From a technical point of view the next great step was the decision of the Wesleyan Conference of 1836 that the Preachers to be publicly admitted into full connexion should be ordained by (interestingly not 'with') the imposition of hands. But this was only one step in a process which recurred after Wesley's death. The whole development of Methodist ecclesiology can be seen as development from society to Church, and cannot be traced here.[5] The point is that Wesley's organizing ability had produced, whether by accident or design, whether by chance or by providence, a system easily adaptable for the purposes of a Church. Of course the system alone was not enough; much had to be added to it from the traditional institutions of a Church. The travelling preachers had to be ordained as well as received into full connexion. The reception of people into membership of Society had to be related to baptism and confirmation. The love-feast was no substitute for the Lord's Supper. The Lord's Supper survived, and the love-feast virtually died out. The simple preaching-services had never been meant to supersede the church service,[6] and when Methodism began holding its own services in church hours, as indeed it had done in some places in Wesley's lifetime, a fuller form of worship was needed.

The point is, however, that the connexional structure which Wesley had developed was fairly easily susceptible of such alterations. The Methodist Church today, though clearly recognized as what is called a mainstream denomination, bears clear marks, both in its terminology and in its ethos, of its societary origin. Is it right to do so, or should these marks, perhaps in the interests of ecumenism, be eliminated?

Some further development may indeed be possible. The continual discussion of episcopacy has led to the use of the term *episkope*, supervision, oversight. It is now almost universally recognized that *episkopoi* or bishops and presbyters or elders were not merely, as Wesley said about the early Church, of the same order, but were in New Testament times identical, different terms to describe the same people. Nevertheless *episkope* is now a useful term to describe an oversight somewhat wider than that of the pastor of a congregation, in other words the pastoral care of a number of pastors and their congregations. It is then customary and proper to say that in British Methodism *episkope* resides, not in *episkopoi*, but in the Conference, though also, by derivation from the Conference, in chairmen of districts and superintendents of circuits. Even in the United Methodist Church of America, the main constituent part of which has had bishops ever since it became a church in 1784, a considerable degree of oversight still resides in the General Conference and in the Annual conferences. But the British style of *episkope* is capable of further development. In accordance with the principle of the Lima document *Baptism, Eucharist, Ministry* that ordained ministry should be exercised in a personal, collegial and communal way, one can envisage further developments which may themselves be an improvement of our system as well as facilitating relations with churches which have what might be called personal bishops.

After all, the switch from a Conference dominated by a Wesley to a Conference presided over by an annual President was itself a considerable change in the style of *episkope*, and Methodism is not tied to any particular style of it, though it has certainly come to share the general Free Church conviction that the Church's leaders should be appointed by the Church, and not by the Crown. Indeed the British Methodist Church has twice in recent years by a substantial majority approved proposals working towards church unity which have involved the acceptance of personal bishops, but these proposals did not carry a sufficient majority with the proposed partner.

Such matters are to some extent controversial and open to discussion, as are other possible developments, which are being discussed by other churches also, such as initiation and the related problem of children at Communion, and non-stipendiary ministry. But such developments should take care to respect the essential ethos of Methodism. Thus, for instance, the disciplined style of our ministry, somewhat reminiscent of a religious order, is one of Methodism's contributions to ecclesiology, and similarly the system of pastoral care and discipline of members, though somewhat weakened in our day, is an equally valuable contribution. Such a development was indeed envisaged by the international bilateral dialogue of Methodists with Roman Catholics, which suggested as an element for a model of organic unity the idea of a religious order. Just as Benedictines or Franciscans have their own traditions but are within the Roman Catholic Church, so might Methodists retain some at least of their traditions within the church of the future.[7]

Churches can be divided into gathered churches and territorial or parochial churches. Each style has something to teach us. Wesley indeed was far from being a Dissenter, and only with great reluctance secured in 1748 for the New Room at Bristol a Dissenting meeting-house licence, against which his brother protested, but Methodism, having ceased to be part of the Church of England, has inevitably come to resemble more closely the gathered churches, and that is one of the reasons why Methodism has drawn closer to the rest of what are now called the Free Churches; yet its ethos has features clearly distinguishable from those of a gathered church, even one with a connexional system such as Presbyterianism. Methodism, like every other church, should seek not only to learn from other churches, but to preserve its distinctive contribution, albeit in creative interplay with them, until it can be brought into what we may still call, in an old ecumenical phrase, the coming great church. When we fully make that contribution, I hope that we shall recognize our debt to John Wesley, the organizer.

10

John Wesley: Apostle of Social Holiness

David Guy

On 30 January 1751, having received 'a pressing letter', John Wesley rode to Oxford that he might vote 'in the election for a member of Parliament which was to be next day'. It was not a short or easy journey. Setting out early with a few companions, Wesley rode over icy roads into the teeth of a biting wind. A friend's horse slipped and sustained injury.

> Nevertheless, about seven in the evening God brought us safe to Oxford. A congregation was waiting for me at Mr Evans', whom I immediately addressed in these awful words, What is a man profited if he shall gain the whole world and lose his own soul?[1]

So there we see him, citizen of two worlds, prepared to travel at some hazard of life and limb to participate in the affairs of an earthly kingdom, but exhorting his hearers to set their affections on a heavenly realm.

How are we to assess this gentleman-evangelist with his feet on the earth (or in the stirrups) and his head in the clouds – or so it would appear to our contemporaries – and how judge the social consequences of his life and work? Was his message a direction or a distraction?

Leaving aside the 'this-worldly' emphasis in Wesley's call to salvation (though we shall have cause to note it shortly) we may remark that it is impossible to evaluate Wesley's social influence fairly if we forget that he was a man of the eighteenth century, not the nineteenth or twentieth.

His parents quarrelled over family prayers for a usurper king, and dynastic questions far more than social or economic problems dominated the pulpit whenever the preacher wandered into the political arena. That particular issue was not settled until the collapse of the '45 rebellion, when John Wesley was already into his stride as an itinerant preacher. He was an old man when the French Revolution began to change the agenda, but even then the preoccupation was with political theory rather than economics. To criticize Wesley's approach to social questions because he was pre-Marx, pre-Beveridge and pre-Keynes is to take an attitude hardly worthy of serious consideration. But on the other hand, we shall fail to do justice to Wesley's social impact if we are so much the children of our own age that we judge social progress only in terms of shared material wealth or improved environment.

Human life is a unity and progress which cannot be measured only in moral or spiritual terms, but neither can it be truly assessed if such considerations are disallowed. Wesley's significance emerges when, and only when, the importance of moral transformation in the individual – and his immediate and sometimes widening circle – is given due weight. Then we begin to understand why, in the words of G. M. Trevelyan, 'a new chapter in the religious, social and educational history of the working class'[2] began with the work of the Wesleys and Whitefield.

This has been said so often that it loses its edge unless we bear in mind the state of the labouring classes in the England of Wesley's youth and early manhood. In 1752, the Bishop of Gloucester wrote to his colleague in the See of Cloyne:

> Your lordship calls this the freest country in Europe. There is indeed freedom of one kind in it . . . a most unbounded licentiousness of all sorts . . . a regard to nothing but diversion and vicious pleasures. . . . Our people are now become what they never were before, cruel. These accursed spiritous liquours which, to the shame of the Government, are so easily to be had, and in such quantities drunk, have changed the very nature of our people.[3]

Gin was one undoubted factor: apathy, despair and ignorance also played their part. The aggression of the Epworth villagers to the Wesley family may have expressed not only resistance to unwonted religious zeal but resentment of the régime of squire and parson smouldering in half-remembered hopes of the generations which had hailed false dawns at the time of the Civil War or the Glorious Revolution. Again, we must stress that it is against this background that Wesley's social impact must be seen.

It hardly needs saying that Wesley did not set out to alter the structures of society, nor did he view himself as a social reformer, except in the sense that every evangelist hopes to see a changed society through changed people. But that he expected a practical result cannot be doubted. From his earliest days, and especially after reading Law's *Serious Call*, Wesley's concept of religion was both emotional and practical – the power of God producing inner peace and empowering outward conduct. Hence, 'you have nothing to do but save souls', for the converted would press on towards that holiness which was to be always 'social holiness'. And as they followed after perfection they would serve the present age.

The Revival did change England, though it did not, of course, produce that root and branch transformation of which revivalists dream.

The converted remained a minority that effected change in many areas of national life. In his life of Cromwell, Thomas Carlyle distinguished between a 'valet-population' in which 'knaves and cowards and cunning and greedy persons' can claim 'almost with general consent' that they 'were the orthodox party', and a moral society which does its best to discourage them. If the eighteenth century began with a valet-population gaping in admiration at the ruthless rich and ostentatious oppressor, and gave way to a nineteenth century which – with all its faults and pockets of humbug – did hold sincerely to other ideals, this was itself a social transformation.

It was not all that the godly had hoped for and it was not all the work of the Wesleys; evangelical Anglicans shared the labour and the heat of the conflict and the Enlightenment was not without its effect. But it was Wesley and his preachers who took the light into places where the darkness was deepest and who challenged evil in its heartlands – Wesley preaching against slavery in Bristol which depended on the trade for its prosperity is an example that springs immediately to mind.

Wesley, then – or rather, those who would do him justice 200 years later – must claim a lion's share of credit for national resurgence seen in moral terms and social advance. As has been said, England was changed because men and women were converted. But to Wesley also – and in this he stands alone – belongs the credit for the other great result of the Revival: the emergence of a disciplined minority, able to raise themselves socially and point their contemporaries to similar possibilities. In the words of Professor Plumb:

> Methodism gave far more than emotional release; it brought a sense of purpose and a field for the exercise of both will and power.
>
> To men and women who were just climbing out of utter poverty by the dint of their own thrifty endeavour this concentration of will and purpose was particularly appealing. The oligarchical and rigid nature of local institutions meant that there was little hope for ambitious men and women *with a social conscience.*
>
> All doors were closed to them, including, of course, those of the established Church, but Wesley provided an organization in which they could fulfil their need for power and their sense of duty.[4]

With this background to our thinking we must assess Wesley's influence by scratching the surface of three areas of interest:

1. Wesley's personal response to social problems by preaching, teaching action and attitude.

2. Wesley's influence upon his converts and later generations influenced by his life-style and holiness teaching.

3. Wesley's experiments in social service and the relevance of his teaching to both community care and social protest.

To turn to the first: Wesley's concern for the poor – like his passion for scriptural holiness – preceded his evangelical conversion and can be seen in his student days at Oxford where, in Tyerman's account, he sold the pictures on his study walls to relieve the distress of a servant girl for whose education the Holy Club had already made provision. The man who could never keep money in his pocket was later to challenge his wealthy hearers to heed the cry of the poor.

> Having food and raiment . . . we may, if the love of God is in our hearts, 'be therewith content'. But what shall they do who have none of these? . . . how many are there in this Christian country

that toil, and labour, and sweat, and have it (food) not at the last, but struggle with weariness and hunger together? . . . You that live at ease in the earth, that want nothing but eyes to see, ears to hear, and hearts to understand how well God hath dealt with you, is it not worse to seek bread day by day and find none? Perhaps to find the comfort also of five or six children crying for what he has not to give! Who can tell what this means unless he hath felt it himself? I am astonished that it occasions no more than heaviness even in them that believe.[5]

To Lord Dartmouth, leading evangelical layman and member of the Government, Wesley wrote in 1775 that 'trade in general is exceedingly decayed and thousands of people are quite unemployed. Some I know have perished for want of bread; others I have seen creeping up and down like walking shadows'.[6]

Aware of need but with no political solutions – though he did suggest some economic panaceas which did not carry conviction then and are not highly regarded by modern students – Wesley's recourse was to call for true discipleship or practical religion. And this he proceeded to do, without fear or favour, though he learned by experience how many went away sorrowful because they had great possessions.

In Sermon 23 'Upon Our Lord's Sermon on the Mount: Lay not up for yourselves treasures upon earth', Wesley pleads for purity of intention in ordinary business. By this he means seeking God's glory in the use of wealth rather than personal security or aggrandisement. He calls on preachers to warn the wealthy against seeking to be richer yet: 'It may be one in a thousand will have ears to hear. . . .' Having admitted that a man must provide for his family and invest sensibly in his business, Wesley insists that

whoever he is that, owing no man anything and having food and raiment for himself and his household, together with a sufficiency to carry on his worldly business . . . seeks still a larger portion on earth, he lives in an open, habitual denial of the Lord that bought him.[7]

In this preaching Wesley was swimming against the tide. Asa Briggs has noted the 'change in attitude to the making of wealth' that accompanied the Restoration and was accepted without question by Hanoverian times. 'After 1660 moral or ethical debate on permissibility of interest gave way to practical discussion concerning its level. . . . "Did men content themselves with bare necessaries, we should have a poor world". . . .'

The preacher of today who echoes Wesley may expect a similar reaction from many of his hearers, but the fearless correspondent's challenge to Sir James Lowther, '. . . examine yourself whether you do not love money? If so, you cannot love God',[9] has a strangely New Testament ring to it, more, perhaps, than attaches to the more fashionable strictures of some of today's popular evangelists.

And yet the problems remain; 'matted problems', William Sangster called them, remarking that it is 'hard to believe . . . that a man of Wesley's mental stature really believed that he was commending a complete cure'.[10] But the challenge of his teaching endures.

It formed a necessary foundation for the call he made to his followers to renounce some of the respectable (or locally accepted) ways of increasing their worldly wealth and to seek only for the true riches that endure.

This call included denouncing the taking of bribes when the practice was part of the electoral pattern, and a warning against participating in smuggling at a time when large sections of the population engaged in evasion of hated – and heavy – customs duties.

Wesley's social protest included his pioneering of the attack on the Slave Trade. His pamphlet *Thoughts on Slavery* was published in 1774 when the trade seemed entrenched and unstoppable; his well-known letter to William Wilberforce, one of his last writings, was the word of a veteran who knows how long the walls of Jericho may resist the blowing of the trumpets of the Lord's people.

All this is well known, but it is sometimes forgotten that Wesley offered a challenge to the class divisions of the eighteenth century which was every bit as disturbing to his contemporaries as any attack upon their money-making methods. The challenge was not so much in what he said as in his readiness to say it to duke as well as dustman, and those who became uneasy when they heard ladies and gentlemen included among the lost sinners that Jesus came to save were right to be worried, for this was a levelling Gospel and socially subversive in the true sense. As Arnold Lunn has said:

Wesley was so obsessed by the eternal values that he completely lost all sense of class values . . . (he) told people exactly what he thought of them, but there was no hint of condescension in his 'openness'. He never patronised people. . . . He did not spare people when he thought them wrong, but the preachers who resented Charles' condescending manner accepted without question John Wesley's quiet assumption of autocratic power.[11]

It is to those preachers, and to the class and band leaders and the committed folk in the meeting houses that we must now turn our attention. Had Wesley been only a preacher he would – under God – have made a tremendous impact on the England of his day, but his continuing influence is seen through the ongoing life of the Societies he organized and their offshoots.

It is registered in the lives of his followers and of those they in turn influenced; in the official policies of movements and the day-to-day service of individuals; in the immediate response of contemporaries and the ongoing work of later generations within the Wesley tradition.

Where do we begin? With the vast numbers influenced by the preaching and hymns of the Revival and far outnumbering Wesley's official followers? It is easy enough to find evidence of social change there, though to a more limited degree. In 1772 Wesley referred to some newly-built factories where the work-force had been notorious for swearing and blasphemy but where some of the women employed, influenced by the local Methodist meetings, had so impressed their workmates that 'in three of the factories no more lewdness or profaneness was found for . . . blasphemies were turned into praise'.[12]

Was this social progress? Working conditions remained the same – unless one includes among working conditions the moral tone, the effect of conversation on conduct, relationships and character. (There may even be some of our contemporaries, suffering sexual harassment amid hygenic conditions, who would sigh for a change of the kind Wesley noted in the 'dark, satanic mills'.)

Or should we note the social consequences of the quest for Christian Perfection among those who embraced Wesley's teaching in its entirety? Certainly their patient endurance of persecution, upright honesty and unfailing industry impressed those around them. Typical, perhaps, is the story of Hudson Taylor's forebears in Barnsley who slowly wore down the opposition of their persecutors by patience and principled living. It was the practice of Hudson's father, James Taylor, never to delay the repayment of a debt even by a day because his creditor would lose interest, even though a trifling sum.[13]

But for an all-round summary of the effect of Methodism on Wesley's followers we must borrow the words of David Edwards.

> He (Wesley) insisted on temperance. . . . He was equally emphatic about cleanliness and hygiene generally. And he gave these working men and women a new vision of what life could be. . . . He encouraged them to read the Bible day by day – and much else, ordering his preachers to carry books and pamphlets around with them. For his people's benefit he supplied concise guides to the Bible, history, literature, philosophy, politics, economics, medicine and science. He encouraged them to educate their children . . . to hope for heaven, and meanwhile to work for heaven on earth, transfiguring their daily labours in the spirit of Charles Wesley's hymn, 'Forth in thy name, O Lord, I go'. Those who were not willing to live and to labour in this spirit were told to go forth more rudely.[14]

The last point is important. Assurance must be balanced by conduct: by their fruits ye shall know them. What could have been an orgy of emotionalism was protected, purified and directed by an insistence on godly living that was not under law but did employ rules. Hence the comment of Max Warren:

> There is something wholly one-sided and inaccurate in the popular picture of Evangelical religion as being one of unbridled individualism. The disciplined fellowship of religious societies is the real clue to Evangelical religion.[15]

So it was and, thanks to Wesley's continuing influence, so it continued to be. Compare Wesley's advice to his preachers with William Booth's orders to his soldiers one hundred years later.

John Wesley's rules for preachers, delivered at Conference in 1763 began: 'Be diligent, never unemployed or triflingly employed.' In 1769 he was writing to a preacher in Ireland:

Be active, be diligent; avoid all laziness, sloth, indolence. Fly from every degree, every appearance of it; else you will never be more than half a Christian. . . . Be cleanly . . . use all diligence to be clean. . . . Whatever clothes you wear, let them be whole. . . . Let none ever see a ragged Methodist.[16]

William Booth, who said, 'For me, as a young man, there was one God and John Wesley was his prophet,' found himself the leader of a new religious movement towards the end of the nineteenth century. Like Wesley before him, Booth set out simple lines of guidance for his converts and assistants. *Orders and Regulations for Soldiers of The Salvation Army* (1898) stated:

Industry: No circumstances are an excuse for being idle or unemployed. . . . He (the soldier) should never allow himself to be inactive. If he has nothing to do for himself he should do something for others. If he has nothing for his hands to be engaged upon he should engage his mind . . . he can always engage his soul in prayer. . . . Cleanliness: As far as his trade, calling and employment will allow, the Salvation Soldier should be clean in his hands and clothing.

I am not suggesting that William Booth deliberately modelled his regulations on Wesley's advice to his followers, but it seems clear that the nineteenth-century evangelist retained many of the emphases impressed upon his mind in formative years.

Wesley's teaching on scriptural holiness also finds an echo in Booth's call to regular, weekly self-examination in which the salvationist should ask himself (among other things): 'Am I conscious of any pride or haughtiness in my manner or bearing? Do I conform to the fashions and customs of the world? . . . Am I in danger of being carried away with worldly desire to be rich or admired?'[17] That Wesley's call to Christian Perfection, the 'grand depositum' that was to characterize his followers and be their special care, should leave its mark on the Booths is not strange when one considers that it played its part in leading them to break with the Methodist New Connexion that they might devote themselves entirely to evangelism among the poor. Some months before that departure, Catherine Booth told her parents that she and her husband had given themselves to renewed and more earnest study of Wesley's holiness teaching, and the unexpected result, for Catherine, had been 'a renewal of the evangelistic question'. Previously rebuffed when they had asked Conference to agree to William Booth's setting aside to full-time revivalistic work, the young couple were becoming reconciled to their situation – until the search for holiness revived 'the evangelistic question', first for Catherine and then for William. The wife, who had previously held back, wrote:

> Such an unexpected surrender on my part, of course, revived William's yearnings toward the evangelistic work, though in quite another spirit to that in which he used to long for it.[18]

It is indisputable that John Wesley's call to holiness stands behind evangelism and social service in five continents, beginning as it did in a man's abandonment to seeming obscurity in East London because of a spiritual renewal that drove him back to his essential work but 'in quite another spirit'.

The Salvation Army, whether viewed as an evangelistic movement or an expression of social service, was not, of course, the only outcome of the great revival of the previous century. Dr M. G. Jones wrote of how the 'religious revivals, by stressing the sense of individual responsibility, changed a trickle of private and semi-private benevolence into a spate of organised philanthropy'.[19] The onflowing spate was a varied stream; we may note individuals and associations, organizations and trends; Britain was not the only land affected, and the results were seen in political action as well as philanthropy. Let Wesley himself lead us into our third and final area of interest – practical service to the needy.

John Wesley was a practical man. Describing the beginnings of Methodism to the Rev. Vincent Perronet, he wrote first of evangelism, then of the organization of the converts, then of the relief of want. Under this last heading he described the work of a 'Visitor of the sick. . . . To relieve them if they are in want'. But this opened up another area of need.

> . . . many who were not sick, were not able to provide for themselves . . . chiefly feeble, aged widows. I consulted with the Stewards how they might be relieved. They all agreed if we could keep them in one house it would not only be far less expensive to us, but also more comfortable for them . . . we have nine widows, one blind woman, two poor children, two upper

servants, a man and a maid. I might add, four or five preachers; for I myself, as well as the other preachers who are in town, diet with the poor on the same food and at the same table; and we rejoice therein as a comfortable earnest of our eating bread together in our Father's kingdom.[20]

He went on to mention the founding of a school for widows and orphans and the care of (at that time) sixty children, also a scheme to help those in a small way of business who had, in modern terms, a temporary cash-flow problem. In all these endeavours there is a complete lack of that spirit of patronage or lordly paternalism which was later to disfigure so much of the philanthropy of the succeeding era, and the picture of Wesley enjoying a simple meal with poor widows and some of his preachers and finding it a sacramental experience – a comfortable earnest of our eating bread together in our Father's kingdom – is a delightful one.

Those who followed him into costly and consistent caring were not always among his declared followers, but were often inspired by their example and by the social dimension of that holiness doctrine which Wesley constantly commended. Among those beyond the bounds of official Methodism we may note Hannah More who, in 1785, under the influence of the Wesleyan call to perfection, resolved to dedicate herself to God 'with a more entire surrender than I have ever made'. The consequences included association with Wilberforce in his many reforming endeavours and the setting up, in her own locality, of a school for poor children. This aroused the wrath of local property owners who saw the seeds of revolution in the education of those whom Providence had decreed should be ignorant, but Hannah had made 'a more entire surrender' and did not draw back.

Among those who enjoyed a specifically Wesleyan upbringing was Hudson Taylor, who, at seventeen, wrote that he was longing 'for this perfect holiness'. Out of the joys and agonies of that period came a sense of acceptance for service: 'From that time the conviction never left me that I was called to China.'[21] Wesley's holiness teaching and the eventual emergence of the China Inland Mission are not unrelated.

Social service leads to social protest – as many of Wesley's children were to discover. The revelation of human need set against a vision of the kingdom draws out the implications of a call to Christian perfection and can produce a Christian radicalism described by Theodore Runyon:

> When *Christian perfection* becomes the goal of the individual, a fundamental hope is engendered that the future can surpass the present. Concomitantly, a holy dissatisfaction is aroused with regard to any present state of affairs. . . . Moreover, this holy dissatisfaction is readily transferable from the realms of the individual to that of society.[22]

I have not forgotten that John Wesley's particular doctrine of entire sanctification was a cause of controversy during his lifetime and of some bewilderment to many of his followers. It has its problems. It is not, however, the theory that matters so much as the vision. By placing before his converts the prospect of freedom from all conscious sin, Wesley inspired in many an intolerance of personal imperfections that was to become in time a refusal to settle for the injustices and wrongs perpetrated by society. Compassion for the poor very easily translated into passion for social progress and this involved political action.

To ask if Wesley – a man of the eighteenth century, as I have said – would have approved of the Chartists or the early-day socialists is as sensible as to ask if Nelson would have welcomed steam-driven ironclads. Politically Wesley was a man of his time. But his preaching – and, as we have seen, his insistence on disciplined living – raised up a task force for change.

That this task force did not always enjoy the approval of those who had legally inherited Wesley's mantle, is well-known.

> Even after the 1832 Reform Act the Methodist Conference issued another of its warnings against listening to political debates 'with too warm an interest'. . . . Many individual Methodists, particularly in the splinter groups, continued to defy such discouraging guidance.[23]

By 1844, however, the voice of Methodism was to be heard in other than the 'splinter groups'. When the Home Secretary, Sir James Graham, resisted the demand for a restriction of women's and children's labour to ten hours per day on the grounds of expense to the nation, but was willing to settle for twelve hours, a writer in the *Wesleyan Methodist Magazine* commented:

If the protection for which Lord Ashley contended is right, let it be granted; and in granting it let the legislature do homage to that never-failing Providence which ordereth all things in Heaven and Earth. If it is wrong, let it be shown so, and let not an argument of injustice and humanity on one side be met with an argument of pounds, shillings and pence on the other.[24]

Mention of Lord Ashley – later the Seventh Earl of Shaftesbury – reminds us that the ongoing work of the revival was shared, as the Revival itself had been shared, by Evangelicals outside the Wesleyan tradition, but the influence of John Wesley had been paramount and remained powerful. In the 1880s a woman's voice – Catherine Booth's – denounced the enthronement of market forces in the realms of human need, appealing for 'wholesome houses for the poor at such a rental as they could comfortably pay' and recognizing that such provision would require 'a benevolence willing to lend, hoping for nothing again'.[25] This was almost as impractical as John Wesley's call to despise money – and as scriptural and relevant to human need.

A hundred years after Catherine Booth, Dr Donald Burke writes that,

Wesleyan theology, when linked to the establishment of the Kingdom of God, should not motivate us so much to the provision of social services which are merely ameliorative or cosmetic. The commitment to the Kingdom motivates us to strive for social reform or, perhaps, more appropriately, social recreation.[26]

John Wesley, apostle of social righteousness: by his words, attitudes and example, challenging the social evils of his own day; through his evangelistic ministry and leadership raising up a people motivated to good works and serious living who would follow after that holiness which would be seen as a goal for their own souls and – in many cases – a challenge to the accepted ways of society. Wesley's mission was used to bring about change – often immediate in the personal realm but also long-lasting and developing in the social.

Men and women were liberated for service and advance. 'To you,' wrote Joseph Priestly in his *Address to the Methodists* in 1791, 'is the civilization, the industry and sobriety of great numbers of the labouring part of the community owing.' And that was only the beginning.

11

Wesley and Women

John A. Newton

Gordon Rupp's piquant comment on Frank Salisbury's celebrated portraits of the two founding fathers of American and British Methodism, comes rather close to the truth: 'He (Salisbury) made Francis Asbury look like an old man, and John Wesley look like an old woman.' Yet true or not, Rupp's critique may serve as a reminder that the feminine element in Wesley's complex make-up was certainly highly developed. There are numerous hints in the records of his life that this was so. His careful grooming of his long hair (contrary to eighteenth-century custom, he never wore a wig); the fastidious neatness of his person and dress; his tact, sympathy, and consistent courtesy of manner: these all point to the strength of his feminine side. Many women found Wesley charmingly attractive. Some fell in love with him – Sophy Hopkey, Grace Murray – but found at best an equivocal response from Wesley as would-be husband. In middle life, Molly Vazeille actually married him, but it was a union that proved bitterly disappointing to both parties. A much larger group of women found in him a friend, pastor, spiritual adviser, and a leader prepared to treat them as trusted colleagues in the work of the Methodist Societies.

Wesley's collected letters reveal the astonishing range of his friendships with women. Young and old, married and single, drawn from the nobility, the middle classes, the labouring poor, these women shared certain common characteristics. They were evangelical believers, mostly Methodists. They had energy and commitment. They brought together spiritual idealism and practical good sense. They were not afraid of hard work, and they strove to express their faith in active charity and good works. They were examplars of the Pauline ideal, which was for Wesley the essence of the Christian life, 'Faith, working through love'. Within the bonds of that Christian love, Wesley worked creatively with his many women colleagues. With woman as lover and wife he never came to terms. Perhaps he could not. But with the women he called his 'Sisters', it was a very different story. To them he was an elder brother; or alternatively we may see him as father-in-God to a large and lively brood of daughters.

This familial analogy reminds us that Wesley grew up in a home where he was surrounded by sisters – Hetty and Keziah; Martha, Nancy, Sukey, Emily and Molly. They were spirited and intelligent girls, and Wesley relished their companionship, as he was to relish female company all his life. Later, as religious leader, he treated his Methodist 'Sisters' much as he had treated the girls at home – as his confidantes and friends who were now, in addition, his co-workers. His consistent style of address, in the many letters he wrote to them, was 'My dear Sister' – the title which the late Dr Maldwyn Edwards seized on for his study of 'John Wesley and the women in his life'. These 'Sisters' may be seen as part of Wesley's surrogate family. In terms of spiritual consanguinity, they were his 'Sisters in the Lord' – a usage which reflects the Gospel passage he cited in a letter of 19 June 1773 addressed to Selina, Countess of Huntingdon:

> My dear friend, you seem not to have well learned the meaning of those words, which I desire to have continually written on my heart, 'Whosoever doeth the will of my Father which is in heaven, the same is my brother and sister and mother,'
> I am, my dear Lady, your affectionate,
>
> John Wesley.

Wesley's usage derives not only from the Gospels, reflecting the new family relationships created by the Kingdom of God. It looks back equally to the first Christian communities of the Acts of the Apostles, where 'Brother' and 'Sister' were common form among those who had been brought into the household of faith. At Oxford Wesley had been nicknamed 'Mr Primitive Christianity', and he never lost his profound respect for the life-style of the first Christians. 'My dear Sister . . .' carries that apostolic resonance too.

There were, then, many women in John Wesley's life; but the first and most important was his mother, Susanna. When Elsie Harrison published her biography of Wesley in 1937, she provoked a storm of criticism. *Son to Susanna: The Private Life of John Wesley* was not sufficiently hagiographical for some Methodist reviewers. It was, they claimed, too racy, speculative, psychologizing, in its portrait of the man. It made him human, all too human. Yet when all legitimate criticism of the book has been allowed, it still stands up, fifty years later, as a work which puts the accent where it belongs, on the crucial human relationship of Wesley's life. It is hard to exaggerate the enormous significance of the bond between mother and child, especially when the mother is as gifted and single-minded as Susanna. Some of the women who have written on Wesley – Julia Wedgwood, Elsie Harrison, Mabel Brailsford – have brought a quality of feminine insight to their studies which we need if we are to begin to understand him. They discern both his massive strengths and his human frailties. They have certainly grasped that 'Mothers are the makers of spirit', and that behind every great and good man or woman, there is a mother of distinction.

Wesley's mother is an outstanding case in point. She shaped his development, of course, by the quality of her maternal care and affection, as any good mother inevitably must. Susanna, however, went far beyond this basic, elemental nurturing. She influenced John – and indeed all her children – by being both their school teacher and their spiritual mentor. For six hours a day she turned the Rectory at Epworth into her schoolroom, and gave both boys and girls all their primary education. With a large family – three boys and seven girls – she was driven to devise a basic structure of eight 'bye-laws' for their conduct and discipline. For the early eighteenth-century classroom these ground-rules were remarkably enlightened, as the first one exemplifies:

1. It had been observed that cowardice and fear of punishment often lead children into lying; till they get a custom of it which they cannot leave. To prevent this, a law was made that whoever was charged with a fault, of which they were guilty, if they would ingenuously confess it, and promise to amend, should not be beaten.

Susanna taught and trained her young in reading, writing, manners, morals and religion. She was herself the daughter of a

distinguished Puritan minister, Dr Samuel Annesley, and had
browsed freely in his superb library as a girl. The mother of the
Wesleys was unusually widely-read, well-educated, and an able
theologian. It was surely significant for John Wesley that the first
woman in his life was one who had a trained mind, a liberal culture
and a genius for education. He was thus made aware, from his
most formative years, of the intellectual and organizing, as well as
the domestic, talents of women. He never forgot that lesson, and
throughout his long life as leader of the Methodist people he would
seek to encourage and employ the gifts of women to the full. He
would never restrict the role of women to the chores of the church,
but allow ample scope for their leadership and responsibility. He
could hardly have been his mother's son had he done otherwise.

If Susanna was John's earliest and most formative teacher, she
was also his first pastor. This woman of superlative gifts, confined
to a rough parish in the backwaters of Lincolnshire, made a
conscious decision to devote all her powers to the upbringing and
Christian formation of her children. Had she been the Reverend
Mother of a religious house, she could hardly have been more
utterly consecrated to her calling. She wrote for the children
detailed theological expositions of the Creed, the Lord's Prayer,
and the Ten Commandments. She instilled into them a pattern of
private prayer and family worship, and devised a detailed system
of personal counselling to foster their Christian development. This
latter innovation followed the great fire of 1709, when the Rectory
was burnt down, and the children had to be boarded out among
families around the village. In Susanna's view, this disruption of
home life meant that their manners, morals and religion all took a
turn for the worse. To reverse the decline, she instituted a series of
personal counselling sessions, as a means of family reformation:

> On Monday, I talk with Molly; on Tuesday, with Hetty;
> Wednesday with Nancy; Thursday with Jacky (i.e. John);
> Friday with Patty (i.e. Martha); Saturday with Charles; and
> with Emily and Sukey together, on Sunday.

So the fire, disastrous as it was, had indirectly positive results for
the children.

Nevertheless, the conflagration was a traumatic event in the life
of the young Wesleys. For John, it was overwhelmingly so. He was
the last to be rescued from the blazing house, trapped in his

bedroom, and pulled out through the window just seconds before the roof fell in. No wonder Elsie Harrison, in a startlingly apt metaphor, calls her chapter on the event 'Fire Curtain'. For John, the fire motif – in the Methodist hymns, in his theology, and in those unconscious levels of his mind which are outside time – was to remain always powerfully evocative. Fire symbolized not only the love of God and the power of the Spirit but also destruction, mortal danger and the fierce flames of passion and erotic love. As a missionary in Georgia, in love with his teenage protegée, Sophy Hopkey, John would draw back from betrothal and commitment with the biblical question, 'Can a man take fire into his bosom, and not be burned?' A burnt child dreads the fire; and there was certainly fear in the self-questioning.

After the Rectory fire, and John's providential escape, Susanna confided to her devotional diary a vow to take special care of the six-year-old child who had been snatched from the blaze, and who would ever after regard himself as 'a brand plucked from the burning'. She recorded, in one of her meditations before God:

> I would, if I durst, humbly offer Thee myself and all that Thou hast given me, and I would resolve (Oh give me grace to do it) that the residue of my life shall be all devoted to thy service; and I do intend to be more particularly careful of the soul of this child that Thou hast so mercifully provided for, than ever I have been, that I may do my endeavour to instil into his mind the principles of thy true religion and virtue. Lord, give me grace to do it sincerely, and prudently, and bless my attempts with good success.

Not that Susanna neglected the religious formation of any of her children; but she had a special care for John. Consequently we find evidence of a particularly close bond between mother and son which endured until her death and no doubt beyond. That is not to imply that the umbilical cord was never cut, or that Wesley was held in infantile dependence on his mother. He grew up, as did his brothers and sisters, into spirited independence of character. Yet the bond, even in his maturity, still held. Before they sailed to Georgia as missionaries, John and Charles laid their whole scheme before their mother, to win her approval and consent. John would continue to consult Susanna on matters of moment, whether personal or theological, as long as she lived. After his decisive experience of the grace of God at Aldersgate Street, on 24 May 1738, Wesley compiled a careful account of his spiritual development for the thirty-five years of his life up to that date. Having compiled it, he promptly read it over to his mother for her confirmation of its truth. Charles did no such thing, after his similar spiritual experience. The fact that John felt it imperative to do so surely speaks volumes for the relationship between his mother and himself.

One other great debt Wesley owed his mother, beyond her teaching and pastoral care. Not only was she well-educated herself, but she ensured that all her daughters should be so too. Her conviction shines through one of the rules she devised for her family, namely, her insistence

> . . . that no girl be taught to work till she can read very well; and then that she be kept to her work with the same application, and for the same time, that she was held to in reading. This rule also is much to be observed; for the putting children to learn sewing before they can read perfectly is the very reason why so few women can read fit to be heard, and never to be well understood.

She was not, of course, simply concerned with basic literacy, but with reading skills as giving access to the world of learning. As a result, Wesley was privileged to grow up among sisters who were not only lively and intelligent girls, but also recipients in their home of an education equal to their brothers'. Without acknowledging the striking effect of Wesley's early experience of able women in his own family, we cannot well understand his mature relationships with the women of Methodism, who provided some of his outstanding colleagues and friends. To them we now turn.

The Church has, sadly, often confined the ministry of its women members to domestic chores in the household of faith, or to the dispensing of tea and sympathy. John Wesley would have none of that. He gave to women positions of genuine leadership, trust and responsibility. Grace Murray, in charge of the Orphan House at Newcastle-upon-Tyne; Hannah Ball, organizing pioneer Sunday School work at High Wycombe; Nancy Bolton, exercising pastoral care and leadership in the Society at Witney: these were the prototypes. Wesley encouraged women to use the varied gifts they had been given – in teaching, preaching, nursing, organizing and pastoral oversight. He never belittled them, patronized them or talked down to them. On the contrary, he drew freely on their advice, friendship and encouragement. He went further. He was ready to receive from his closest women colleagues the kind of rebuke which he had earlier accepted from his mother and his sisters.

The fruitfulness of Wesley's partnership with his many women colleagues comes out in the lively exchanges of his pastoral letters. If we take a sample from one of the volumes of John Telford's edition of Wesley's *Letters*, we can see their range and significance. Volume Five covers the years 1766 to 1772, when Wesley was in his sixties. These were years of steady growth among the Methodist Societies, marred chiefly by the fierce attacks on Wesley from his Calvinist opponents during 1770–71. Of the 103 personal correspondents in the volume, 34 are women; and Wesley writes, in general, far more frequently to his women correspondents than he does to the men. He writes to his 'Sisters' not about trivia, but on weighty matters, both pastoral and theological. He is concerned both for their bodily health and their spiritual progress. He takes them seriously, and gives detailed spiritual guidance suited to each one's needs, without either arrogance or condescension. He is concerned that they should make advancement in their Christian living; that they should, indeed, 'press on to perfection'. His tone is familiar and affectionate, yet with a pastor's seriousness of concern. He writes, for example, to Mrs Woodhouse on 17 May 1766:

> Surely His grace is sufficient for you: sufficient to subdue all things to Himself. I want you to be all like Him. Your openness and freedom of behaviour when we were at Epworth endeared you to me much. At any time you should speak to me without reserve just what rises in your heart. The peace that passes all understanding keep your heart and mind in Christ Jesus.
> I am, my dear sister, Your affectionate brother,
>
> John Wesley

He used great frankness, whether he was writing to Selina, Countess of Huntingdon, or to Sarah Ryan, who had begun life as a servant-girl. On 28 June 1766 he wrote to Mrs Ryan, who was then helping to run an orphanage in Leytonstone, in terms which combine plain speaking with his customary courtesy:

> My Dear Sister,
>   For some time I have been convinced it was my duty to tell you what was on my mind. I will do it with all plainness. You may answer or not, as you judge best. Many things I have observed in you which gave me pleasure; some which gave me concern: the former I need not mention; the latter I must, or I should not myself be clear before God. . . .
>   I am afraid you are in danger of enthusiasm. We know there are divine dreams and impressions. But how easily may you be deceived herein! How easily, where something is from God, may we mix something which is from nature! Especially if we have a lively imagination, and are not aware of any danger.

To Lady Maxwell (8 July 1766) he writes with equal directness:

> I rejoice to hear that you have the resolution to sleep and rise early. The uneasiness of it will soon be over, but the advantage will remain for ever. O fear no cross! God is on your side, and will command all to work together for good.
>   I am, my dear Lady, Your most affectionate servant.

He often expresses concern for the physical, as well as spiritual, health of his women friends. To Lady Maxwell (23 February 1767) he urges:

> Exercise, especially as the spring comes on, will be of greater service to your health than an hundred medicines; and I know not whether it will not be restored in a larger measure than for many years when the peace of God fixes in your heart. . . .

On 13 June 1771 he seeks to dispel criticisms which had been levelled at Mary Bosanquet for preaching, and so, allegedly, going directly contrary to St. Paul's injunction that a woman should keep silence in the church. Wesley writes to her:

> My Dear Sister,
>   I think the strength of the cause rests there – on your having an *extraordinary* call. So I am persuaded has every one of our lay preachers; otherwise I could not countenance his preaching at all. It is plain to me that the whole work of God termed

Methodism is an extraordinary dispensation of His providence. Therefore I do not wonder if several things occur therein which do not fall under the ordinary rules of discipline. St. Paul's ordinary rule was, 'I permit not a woman to speak in the congregation.' Yet in extraordinary cases he made a few exceptions; at Corinth in particular. – I am, my dear sister,
Your affectionate brother.

Like his Master, Wesley is prepared to flout public opinion and bend the religious rules in his relations with women. He has two prime aims: to enable them to use their gifts to the full; and to maximize their contribution to the work of the Kingdom.

This sampling of Wesley's voluminous correspondence with his women friends and helpers is entirely typical, and may serve to indicate its range and quality. He valued his women colleagues greatly. He both upheld them in their own work and drew support from them for his own. He needed their understanding sympathy and shrewd judgment. If we ask what were the qualities he most prized in women, he gives us the answer in the pen-portraits he draws of them. Of Grace Murray, he wrote that she was, 'indefatigably patient and inexpressibly tender; quick, clean and skilful; of engaging behaviour and a mild, sprightly, cheerful and yet serious temper; while her gifts for usefulness were such as he had not seen equalled'. In Nancy Bolton, he acknowledged, he had found 'all the qualities which I wanted, meeting together in one person: seriousness, liveliness, sweetness; and all that springing free from the true Fountain, Faith that worketh'.

These descriptions of the women he most admired are strongly redolent of his mother's character and gifts. That can hardly be accidental. Susanna had set the standard of womanhood for him. It was a high standard, so high, perhaps, that no other woman could ever attain to it. John Wesley gave and received much in his wide range of friendships with women: they were to him advisers, co-adjutors, supporters and colleagues. His mother had been to him all these and more. Though he might have many 'Sisters', he had only one mother. He remained, first and last, 'Son to Susanna'.

12

Health and Healing in the Ministry of John Wesley

Morris Maddocks

The manner in which God calls his servants is not only as varied as their personalities, but is also significant for their future ministry. Wesley's conversion was no exception. It was total and holistic in that it affected his whole being. His ministry was also to be total and holistic. The salvation by faith he proclaimed was nothing less than the salvation of the whole human being. The Lord he served was his total Redeemer: there was no part unhealed by lying outside salvation. And he was at one with the writer to the Hebrews, 'How shall we escape if we ignore such a great salvation?' (2.3)

In recording his conversion he obviously chose his words with care and accuracy. He felt his '*heart* strangely warmed', the seat of the emotions, the centre of one's being that brings light and love and compassion to all other activities. It was this large and compassionate heart that would enfold all he sought to touch for Christ in a desire for their total health and healing, their wholeness and salvation. Again, he felt he did '*trust* in Christ, Christ alone for salvation'. He *felt* he did *trust*. It was not merely a cerebral acceptance of intellectual truth. He entirely resonated with the truth that gripped his whole being – a total salvation/healing in Christ. It was a total experience, not merely a clicking of an intellectual truth into place. For he continues to describe the overwhelming experience of forgiveness, again total and immense: 'an assurance was given me that he had taken away *my* sins, even *mine*, and saved (healed) *me* from the law of sin and death.' Here is the holistic experience of inner healing; the consciousness of one's glaring sins and shortcomings in their vivid colours, overwhelmed and cleansed by an experience of the healing touch of Christ, in which he transforms them into something beautiful, into an instrument more useful in his service, manifested in an ability to pray fervently for one's persecutors, which Wesley proceeded to do.

The final testimony to the genuineness of his experience was the 'buffeting with temptations' he had to endure on his return home. In his old life his striving was under the law as well as under grace, and sometimes he was beaten. There was now a changed situation. He was always victor, in the healed state in which he found himself to be, in Christ. Always, from his waking moment each and every day, 'Jesus, Master' was invariably in his heart as well as on his lips. He knew he had to keep his eye firmly fixed on the One he now fully served. Of course there would be setbacks, a soreness in his heart indicating that there were still a few wounds not fully healed, but he knew that even in his life the Kingdom was now breaking in, as it was in the lives of many, for with new powers of listening, he heard of 'the wonderful work which God is beginning to work over all the earth'. How right he was to give God thanks 'for the mightiness of his Kingdom'.[1]

The pattern and totality of his conversion launched Wesley into a ministry that was to change the face of his own country and others. Few men or women in the history of humankind have had such a formative influence over their fellow human beings. Wesley's influence was such because his gospel message, like that of his Master, was total. He not only preached, but he actually ministered healing and salvation. He saw the needs of men and women and met them head on. Like his Master's, Wesley's ministry was to the whole person. Like his Master, Wesley met people at the point of their need. But of all the ways in which he bore the imprint of his Master, the most significant was that he had a great desire for God which issued in a great desire for the salvation/healing of humankind, both of individual souls and of the whole of society. This was the fire that burned within him, the fire that warmed his heart in Aldersgate Street, the fire that burned on until it was extinguished in death, constantly fanned into flame by his single-mindedness in 'keeping my eye fixed upon him and my soul waiting upon him continually'.[2] This was his secret, as on his 'delightful ride to Keswick, having my mind stayed on God'.[3] He had set his heart first on the Kingdom of God and his righteousness (Matt. 6.33; Luke 12.31). That was the priority that inspired his whole life and work.

The Kingdom of God was the dynamic symbol used by Jesus to encapsulate his message that his Father wills to reign in every part of his creation. It is the key concept in the thought and message and activity of Jesus. When taken seriously it is bound to be translated into terms of healing and salvation. Once grasped by the vision, as Wesley undoubtedly was, he could but follow his Master in a ministry of compassion to the poor, in a ministry that would reach the whole person, in short, in a ministry of preaching and healing, a proclamation of the gospel by word and deed.

The health and healing of the people to whom he ministered was always as much the purpose of his ministry as the salvation of their souls. In December 1746 Wesley mentioned to the society 'my design of giving physic to the poor. About thirty came to the next day, and in three weeks about three hundred. This we continued for several years, till, the number of patients still increasing, the expense was greater than we could bear. Meantime, *through the blessing of God*, many who had been ill for months or years were restored to perfect health' (my italics). Physic and prayer for God's blessing of health were the joint prescription of that holy man. And God answered his prayer, for he observed 'the power of the Lord was present to heal them'.[4]

Wesley of course practised what he preached. He would pray equally for God's healing for his own infirmities. Only a month before the above incident, he recorded the following entry in his journal: 'In the evening, at the chapel, my teeth pained me much. In coming home, Mr Spear gave me an account of the rupture he had had for some years, which was perfectly cured in a moment. I prayed with submission to the will of God. My pain ceased, and returned no more.'

An incident in May 1741, also recorded in the *Journal*, illustrates even more forcibly Wesley's belief in the healing power of Christ:

I was obliged to lie down most of the day. In the evening my weakness was suspended while I was calling sinners to repentance. But at our love feast which followed, beside the pain in my back and head, and the fever which still continued upon us, I was seized with such a cough that I could hardly speak. At the same time came strongly into my mind 'These signs shall follow them that believe.' I called on Jesus aloud to 'increase my faith', and to 'confirm the word of his grace'. While I was speaking, my pain vanished away, my bodily strength returned, and for many weeks I felt neither weakness nor pain. 'Unto thee, O Lord, do I give thanks.'

The word of God is indeed not bound. The Kingdom *must* be proclaimed. God honours the faith of his servants.

Sometimes Wesley records a case of inner healing. It is worthy of note how many such healings happen in response to a faithful proclamation of the gospel, either in preaching or writing. The word of God is indeed sharper than any two-edged sword, for 'it penetrates even to dividing soul and spirit, joints and marrow; it judges the thoughts and attitudes of the heart'. (Hebrews 4.12). The entry in his *Journal* (21 January 1739) is worth quoting at length:

> We were greatly surprised in the evening, while I was expounding in the Minories. A well-dressed, middle-aged woman suddenly cried out as in the agonies of death. She continued to do so for some time. When she was a little recovered, I desired her to call upon me the next day. She told me that about three years before she was under strong convictions of sin, and in such terror of mind that she had no comfort in anything, nor any rest day or night: that she sent for the minister of her parish, and told him the distress she was in: upon which he told her husband she was stark mad, and advised him to send for a physician immediately . . . who ordered her to be blooded, blistered and so on. But this did not heal her wounded spirit. So that she continued much as she was before: till the last night, he whose word she at first found to be 'sharper than any two-edged sword' gave her a faint hope that he would undertake her cause, and heal the soul which had sinned against him.

This entry also underlines Wesley's assiduous pastoral care in making the appointment for the following day and listening to the troubled soul with such prayerful attention. His practice of follow-up was one of the constants of his ministry.[5] That his ministry was truly a healing ministry was demonstrable by its fruits.

Such a person as Wesley, large in heart, large in mind and totally committed to God as Creator, Redeemer and Sanctifier, was inevitably a man of the future in the sense of being a man of vision. He would have agreed with the dictum of Sir Edwyn Hoskyns, 'Bury your head in a dictionary and rise in the presence of God.' Life for Wesley was a voyage of discovery, a journey of total adventure to be lived to the full glory of God. He was for instance intensely interested in the latest discovery – electricity. He began to ask such questions as: What use can be made of this for the betterment of humankind, for the good of the sick and the poor? Has this new discovery healing properties? An entry in the *Journal* for 17 February 1753 shows how Wesley's mind was working:

> From Dr Franklin's *Letters* I learned that electrical fire (or ether) is a species of fire, infinitely finer than any other yet known; that it is diffused, and in nearly equal proportions, through almost all substances . . .; that if any quantity of it be collected together, whether by art or nature, it then becomes visible in the form of fire, and inexpressibly powerful. . . . What an amazing scene is here opened for after-ages to improve upon!

Wesley must have pursued his interest in electricity and especially in relation to his healing ministry,[6] because three and a half years later we find the following entry:

> Having procurred an apparatus on purpose, I order several persons to be electrified, who were ill of various disorders; some of whom found an immediate, some a gradual cure.[7]

Wesley also 'prescribed' this treatment with other remedies for his own pains. On his way to the South Coast, his horse shied and fell on his leg. His consequent sickness was relieved 'by a little hartshorn and water'. His soreness was healed by applications of treacle twice a day. His lameness was alleviated and mended slowly by 'being electrified morning and evening'.[8] Wesley was in his sixty-third year and had commented before the fall, in the October of that year: 'It pleases God that I . . . find no disorder, no weakness, no decay, only that I have fewer teeth and more grey hairs.' But when misfortune, illness or suffering came, Wesley was not above prescribing such a remedy as electrification either for himself or for others, which on one occasion included his brother

Charles. 'Let him be electrified, not shocked, but filled with electric fire,' he wrote in a note to the Reverend Samuel Bradburn, shortly before his brother's death in March 1788. Presumably he carried the apparatus with him on his travels and was therefore able to use it regularly. He must also have persuaded some of his colleagues to purchase one.

Wesley's most painstaking work in this field must have been to collect the many remedies handed down from generation to generation, which he published in his small but invaluable volume *Primitive Physic* in 1747. The preface unfolds Wesley's theology of healing. Originally there was no need for physic nor for the art of healing. 'The entire creation was at peace with man, so long as man was at peace with his Creator.' But man's rebellion changed all that: 'the seeds of wickedness and pain, of sickness and death, are now lodged in our inmost substance.' Moreover the rest of creation conspires together to punish the human rebels: 'sun and moon shed unwholesome influences from above; the earth exhales poisonous damps from beneath' (modern discoveries about skin cancer show he was not far off the mark). Can nothing be done?

Yes it can, says Wesley. In the very threat from God, 'In the sweat of thy face shalt thou eat bread', he sees a message of hope. The power of exercise is able both to preserve and restore health. Furthermore, from the beginning physic as well as religion probably came down from father to son, so that the art of healing was handed down to each successive generation. Much was learned from mere accident and was then handed down. But complicated theories involving the introduction of astronomy and astrology, and of natural philosophy, tended to obscure the art of healing and eventually to deter men and women from taking more natural remedies to assist the healing of themselves and of their neighbours.

Wesley sought to remedy this state of affairs in his remarkable work, far ahead of his time, listing sometimes two or three remedies for each condition and advising that if the first has no effect, then try the second. He also added a few 'easy rules' for which he was indebted to a Dr Cheyne. Some are still relevant to our lives today and therefore bear repetition: 'The air we breathe is of great consequence to our health.' Tender people need 'sound, sweet and healthy' beings around them. Health is preserved by maintaining cleanliness in the house, in one's clothes and in the furniture. Food should always sit 'light and easy on the stomach'. Highly-seasoned food is unwholesome. Hard work, abstinence and plain food are recipes for health. Water is the most wholesome of all drinks, quickening the appetite and strengthening the digestion most of all. Alcohol is a certain, yet slow, poison. 'Coffee and tea are extremely hurtful to persons who have weak nerves.' Tender people should eat light suppers two or three hours before going to bed and should be early to bed and early to rise. 'A due degree of exercise is indispensably necessary to health and long life.' Walking is the best exercise. Any weak part of the body can be strengthened by exercise. For instance, 'the lungs may be strengthened by loud speaking, or walking up an easy ascent'. The studious especially need regular exercise 'at least two or three hours a day', should frequently shave, and wash their feet. Those who read and write much should learn to do it standing. Other admonitions deal with the wearing of fewer clothes by night or day as an aid to hardiness of health; cold bathing as an advantage to health when approached with due caution; the passions which greatly influence health, violent and sudden passions disastrously.

Most of all however, the love of God is the panacea for our diseases and illnesses: 'It effectually prevents all the bodily disorders the passions introduce; by keeping the passions themselves within due bounds; and by the unspeakable joy and perfect calm serenity and tranquility it gives the mind, it becomes the most powerful of all the means of health and long life.'

The book ran to three impressions in the first four years and was regularly revised. Wesley's purpose throughout was 'to set down cheap, safe, and easy medicines; easy to be known, easy to be procured, and easy to be applied by plain unlettered men'. It was indeed a book that aimed to help the poor and for the most part employed natural means and common household substances. In the revision of 1760, however, he strongly advised the use of electricity: 'I cannot but entreat those who are well-wishers to mankind to make full proof of this. Certainly it comes the nearest to a universal medicine of any yet known in the world.' He also repeated a word of advice in two other prefaces to revisions: 'In complicated cases or where life is in immediate danger, let every one apply without delay to a physician that fears God.' Anyone practising the Christian healing ministry today would want to offer the same counsel.

As to the whole, it was a work far in advance of its time, and though some of the remedies may now occasion a smile, it is full of common sense and a deep concern for the well-being of God's poor. He himself practised a majority of its remedies, as is shown by the comment 'tried' by many of them, and also by entries in his *Journal* such as the following on 27 April 1755: 'As I walked by, I saw a good old man bleeding almost to death. I desired him immediately to snuff vinegar up his nose, and apply it to his neck, face and temples. It was done, and the blood entirely stopped in less than two minutes.' It recalls to mind the Good Samaritan pouring in oil and wine to the bleeding wounds. He also advised the kiss of life for three children who had fallen down a well, and as a result two out of the three lives were saved.[9]

The little volume was an offering from a man of God who not only had a very great devotion and commitment to the Lord he knew himself privileged to serve, but who also had a very great desire for the salvation and healing of the bodies, minds and spirits of those among whom he travelled and ministered.

When he was seventy-two, he looked back on his life and saw as one of the reasons for his health his never travelling less, by sea or land, than four thousand and five hundred miles in a year. On his eighty-fourth birthday he gave two major reasons for the alertness of his faculties and general good health; the first was 'doubtless to the power of God, fitting me to the work to which I am called, as long as he pleases to continue me therein'. The second reason he ascribed 'subordinately to this, to the prayers of his children'. He then gave five 'inferior means', more of which later.[10]

The first two reasons – the power of God and the prayers of the faithful – are of extreme interest. There is little doubt that health and wholeness are promoted by being in tune with the will of God. Health has been described as a resonance with the music of heaven. An acknowledgement of the power of God in one's life and an ordering of that life to ensure it is attuned to the will of God and to the strong call he has laid upon us to fulfil our destiny according to his will is a recipe to be within the healing process that leads to wholeness and ultimate health. Wesley saw the power of God fitting him to the work to which God had called him, enabling him to be within the will of his heavenly Father, and so ordering his destiny ordained by God. This, as he saw it, was the primary reason for his health and longevity – a healed and wholesome relationship with God.

Linked with this, but subordinate to it, he cited the prayers of his (spiritual) children. I recall one of our church leaders in this country telling me on the day he took office what a wonderful experience it had become for him to be carried on the prayers of others. I also know from my own small experience how essential it is when engaged in the preaching, teaching and healing work of Christ to be undergirded by the prayers of the faithful. They seem to open one's being more fully to the grace of God which alone enables such a ministry. How Wesley must have experienced this 'amazing grace', made even more vivid to him through the faithful intercession of devoted souls to whom he had ministered. Here was health indeed, a healing for him as he endured the many hardships of his ceaseless travels and constant demands for his ministry. Indeed, how dare any of us engaged in the preaching and healing ministry venture forth in the Lord's name to do his work unless equipped with such a wholesome benefit as the unremitting prayer of the faithful?

It was only after stating these as the two primary reasons for his health which tell us so much about the firm foundations of his great ministry, that Wesley went on to list the 'inferior means'. The first of these was his 'constant exercise and change of air', which received regular mention when Wesley suggested recipes for health. Dr Fothergill had prescribed this in November 1753. Urging him not to stay in London a day longer, he added: 'If anything does thee good, it must be the country air, with rest, asses' milk, and riding daily.' Wesley would also prescribe exercise for others: 'I found Mr Fletcher a little better, and proposed his taking a journey with me to Cornwall, nothing being so likely to restore his health as a journey of four or five hundred miles.' Unfortunately in this case the physician refused to agree to such a course of action![11] It was in fact not always the panacea Wesley believed it to be. He tried to save John Cowmeadow, 'another martyr to loud and long preaching', but it was apparently too late: 'To save his life, if possible, when he was half dead, I took him to travel with me. But it was too late.'[12]

Throughout his life, Wesley believed in fresh air and exercise as the elixir for many of life's ills and encouraged others to hold the same view. He was also blessed by being a good sleeper, doubtless helped by his regular hours. He always rose at 4 a.m. and preached at 5 a.m. On his eighty-fourth birthday he gave all these reasons for his longevity and continued active life and ministry. Retirement at seventy, let alone sixty-five, would have been unthinkable. The people to whom he ministered must have been greatly encouraged by Wesley's vigour in old age.

The sick and poor among whom he travelled were Wesley's first concern. It was they who first had to hear the good news of the Kingdom. The Gospel must first be preached to them. But poor and unlettered people, sick and seriously ill men and women are not in a position to accept a faith that is only cerebral. They need to be touched by the compassion of Christ at every level of their being. They need a whole Gospel that will minister to their needs holistically, to the healing of both mind and body, of soul and spirit. It was these people, in this way, Wesley sought to touch for Christ.[13]

The 'poor' included children, and Wesley was keen to lay the foundations of health and wholeness of body, mind and spirit in the young. Learning much about Christian education from the Moravians he founded Kingswood School in Bristol (now in Bath). At the opening of the school on Midsummer Day, 24 June 1748, he preached on the text 'Train up a child in the way he should go; and when he is old he will not depart from it.'[14] And as if to lay emphasis on the focal point of the education at Kingswood, he and his brother Charles on the same day 'administered the Lord's Supper to many who came from afar'.

The ethos of the school was well set out in an appeal of 1763 'to make Methodists sensible of the excellency of Kingswood School' which contains the following passage:

> It is well known that the children want nothing; that they scarce know what sickness means; that they are well instructed in whatever they are capable of learning; that they are carefully and tenderly governed; and that the behaviour of all in the house, elder and younger, is as becometh the Gospel of Christ.[15]

One of the main reasons for this achievement was because Wesley had laid solid foundations, being most careful about the choice of staff: 'I saw none would answer my intention, but men who were truly devoted to God; who sought nothing on earth, neither pleasure, nor ease, nor profit, nor the praise of men; but simply to glorify God, with their bodies and spirits, in the best manner they were capable of.'[16] With such a staff it is not surprising that health of body and soul was well catered for and that sickness was a rare occurence, when all was ordered 'as becometh the Gospel of Christ'.

There would be many happenings in today's world and church of which Wesley would disapprove; some developments he might even consider to be disastrous. But there is at least one fact that would rejoice his heart, the proclamation of the healing Christ and the practice of his healing ministry in all the churches. He would rejoice as one who sought to bring to his generation a great desire for God, a massive zeal for prayer and a consuming compassion for the sick and suffering, God's poor. Little would surprise him of modern methods where Church and medicine work together: prayer and physic were for Wesley a vital partnership for the wholeness of people and society and for the furtherance of the Gospel of Christ. He would have rejoiced at seeing, as I do from my home in Dorothy Kerin's Foundation, Burrswood, the day-to-day working out of this partnership in the context of worship and Christian community life. Neither would he be surprised at the sudden outpourings and manifestations of the Holy Spirit in today's Church. Describing the symptoms of people affected by the Spirit during the preaching, in this case of Mr Whitefield, though it frequently happened during his own sermons, Wesley commented: 'From this time, I trust, we shall all suffer God to carry on his own work in the way that pleaseth him.'[17] Twenty years later he observed that the same symptoms were caused 'not from sorrow or fear, but love and joy',[18] but also that these happenings usually occurred at 'the beginning of a general work of God'.[19]

In many ways, John Wesley was a man who was a century or more ahead of his time. He would have spoken a telling word to our contemporary generation, two hundred and fifty years after his birth. It would have been a word direct from the Lord he loved and served and obeyed so faithfully, for his was no second-hand Gospel. It would have communicated truth to a generation that is learning afresh the meaning of wholeness and integration as it learns more of the miracle of the human species. Wesley would have welcomed the rediscovery in both Church and medicine of the art of healing, aware as he was of the constant potency of

Christ's healing power. He would have seen this discovery in the Church as a vital ingredient of the proclamation of the Kingdom of God. Of all preachers he was a herald of the full salvation/healing Gospel of Jesus Christ. His God wanted men whole. As for medicine, it was unthinkable that it should be practised other than for the glory of God. He also believed this about his 'electrification' treatment, that it was to God's glory. Medicine has only followed this up for patients with mental distress (ECT), though an 'electric' heat is frequently transmitted during the Christian ministry of the laying on of hands, with beneficial results. For this, as for all John Wesley's ministry of healing, glory should be given to God.

13

John Wesley and Death

Wesley A. Chambers

The eighteenth century was brutal. Illegitimate children were abandoned in the streets. At the height of the gin era (1740–1742) burials in London were twice as many as the baptisms.[1] The pillory often proved a fatal punishment for minor offences while the number of offences punished by death soared to two hundred.[2] Public hangings were popular spectacles: the public burning of women, dead or alive, was still practised in English law.[3]

The Wesley family was part of this society. Of the nineteen children born to Samuel and Susanna Wesley only nine reached maturity. The same cloud of death hung over Charles Wesley's family. Of his eight children five died in infancy. In John's lifetime prior to his sailing for Georgia, a brother had died in 1705, an unknown sibling in 1709, sister Mary in 1734, and his father in 1735.

John Wesley's theology of death

From early childhood John Wesley had been carefully instructed in the teaching of the Church of England. According to the baptismal liturgy all men are conceived and born in sin,[4] and partake of original sin which inclines to evil. Therefore every person born into the world deserves God's wrath and damnation.[5] By baptism a child is regenerate[6] and spared condemnation, yet the infection remains.

In preparing for ordination Wesley was obliged to give such issues closer consideration. His correspondence with his brother Samuel shows he grappled with the fate of those condemned to hell, i.e. with whether there is a second death or eternal punishment. To avoid such a fate there was need for great holiness, for without it none could with confidence appear before God.

Wesley's *Notes* on the Old and New Testaments reveal his mature thinking. Commenting on Romans 6.23 he classified death under three headings – temporal, spiritual and eternal. Temporal death was brought about by Adam's sin. In it the body is forsaken by the soul, and becomes dust. Wesley's exposition of Genesis 3.21 makes the point that the skins of animals were not only for our primal parents' clothing but also to teach them precisely what death is. Adam's tilling the ground was to keep him humble and to remind him of his latter end. Yet while our primal parents were excluded from the privileges of the state of innocency, they were not abandoned to despair 'God's thoughts of love designing them for a second state of probation upon new terms'.[7]

Spiritual death is the result of sin in the second state of probation. Sin, which is the sting of death, is full of hellish poison, and works death in a person.[8] Without sin death could have no power.[9] Yet a person physically alive can be spiritually dead, i.e. 'absolutely devoid of all spiritual life and as incapable of quickening yourselves as a person literally dead'.[10]

Eternal death is the second death which takes place in the 'lake of fire' and is the portion of those who have not overcome the fear of death in times of persecution.[11] At the general resurrection of the dead, death gives up the bodies and Hades the souls of the departed, so that each person is reunited in body and soul. In the following judgement the saints have everlasting joy[12] but the fearful, unbelieving, idolaters, etc. suffer the second death. This judgement is eternal because the sentence pronounced is irreversible and its effects remain for ever.[13]

Yet victory has been made possible through Christ's conquest of death, sin and Hades.[14] Indeed death is totally conquered.[15] In the meantime death is 'King of a vast domain',[16] terrible to natural man and particularly terrible when death is violent.[17] Everyone who knows not Christ fears death to some extent.[18] Such a person is 'subject to bondage and in a slavish, uncomfortable state'. True believers are delivered from this bondage.[19]

Wesley's emphases are exposed in his selection of hymns for his hymnals. In the Charles-Town Hymnal, published in 1737, there are hymns on 'Triumph over Death'[20] which is inherent in

'Faith in Christ'.[21] Further, there is the possibility of 'Heaven Begun on Earth',[22] yet the haunting question remains:

> When rising from the bed of death
>   O'erwhelmed by guilt and fear,
> I view my Maker face to face,
>   O how shall I appear?[23]

What strikes the reader is Wesley's head-knowledge that was to become the heart-experienced reality of later years. Such themes as 'triumph over death' and 'heaven begun on earth' were to become the joyous experience of the Methodist people. In the 1779 hymnal there were fourteen hymns on death, thirteen on judgement, thirteen on heaven, and one on hell which reflects Wesley's early observation that repentance induced by fear is transitory unless it is accompanied by a real love of goodness.[24] Though Wesley believed in and had clear views on the reality of hell and the second death, his mature emphasis lay upon the possibilities of the soul being restored in the divine image and the joy of heaven being experienced on earth and consummated in heaven. This stands in marked contrast with the popular image of him as a hell-fire preacher and marks him off from many evangelicals who were not so sparing in their threats of hell to induce repentance.[25]

John Wesley's experience of death

While Wesley was sorting out his theological understanding of death it is apparent that he had personal problems in relation to it. The death of 'Robin' Griffiths (1727) in particular made him acutely aware of the shortness of life which imperilled the process of sanctification and therefore of readiness to appear before God in judgement. It was a stressful time for all concerned, not least for Wesley, who had been in close touch with the deceased. To relieve the grieving father Wesley preached on the Sunday after the funeral and commented in a letter to his mother:

> I never gave more reason to suspect my doctrine did not agree with my practice for a sickness and a pain in the stomach, attended by violent loosness, which seized me the day he was buried, altered me so much in three days, and made me look so pale and thin, that those who saw me could not but observe it.[26]

We know that up to this time Wesley's own skirmish with death in the Epworth rectory fire still exercised a continuing 'strong impression' on his mind. In this letter Wesley clearly states that his body language did not harmonize with his intellectual belief. One can legitimately infer that in all probability Wesley had not come to terms with death in his own experience. Between what he knew and what he felt there was an incongruity which may well be taken to indicate an unresolved trauma.

This view is supported by his reaction to the violent storms experienced in the Atlantic crossing of 1735. Wesley honestly recorded his reactions: afraid to die – unwilling to die.[27] The same is true of his reactions to storms on land.[28] In theory death meant being with Christ; but the dreadful thought of appearing before the judgement seat of God made him realize that he did not have the kind of faith that could overcome the fear of death. As he realized at 'Robin' Griffith's funeral, so he realized in the death-threatening storms of the Atlantic. His head told him his faith should overcome his fear of death; his emotional reactions revealed the poverty of his faith and his unreadiness to die. How to overcome this fear of death – and the ensuing experiences of the soul – was Wesley's major problem.

Back in the security of London he reflected upon his spiritual plight:

> . . . I have a fair summer religion. I can talk well: and believe myself when no danger is near. But let death look me in the face, and my spirit is troubled. Nor can I say 'To die is gain!'
>
> > I have a sin of fear, that when I've spun
> > My last thread, I shall perish on the shore.
>
> . . . Oh, who will deliver me from this fear of death? What shall I do? Where shall I fly? . . .[29]

Searching for an answer to the fear of death

In his search for an answer, Wesley had sought help from a friend who advised him to look upon this fear as his cross to quicken his good resolutions. When the fear was dormant he should forget about it and get on with his ministry.[30] Who this friend was we do not know. However well meant, this advice did not solve Wesley's problem nor resolve the disparity between his belief and his involuntary reactions.

More help came from his introduction to the writings of Bishop Jeremy Taylor and of Thomas à Kempis. Fundamental to Taylor's work is the omnipresence and omniscience of God, who is 'the great eye of the world aways watching over our actions, and an ever open ear to hear all our words'. He is especially present in the consciences of all people, good and bad, by way of testimony and judgment. 'He is the remembrancer to call our actions to mind; a witness to bring them to judgment, and a judge to acquit or condemn.'[31] In short, Wesley learned ultimate accountability. As one who must give an account, he began to keep a diary in order to be able to reflect upon how his time, i.e. his life, was spent.

In Taylor Wesley also discovered a way to overcome his 'sin of fear'. If saints cannot sin because they always behold the face of God, then if men practised the presence of God, they too would not sin.[32] In effect holiness was the key to overcoming his problem. Wesley wanted assurance in this matter but found Taylor unsatisfactory, although his teaching about pardon for sin encouraged him to believe that change was possible.[33]

If Taylor taught Wesley the practice of the presence of God as the means of achieving holiness, à Kempis gave him understanding of inward holiness. Wesley's initial criticisms were overcome by his mother, who gave him a clearer perception of à Kempis's concept of Christian perfection as necessary not only for happiness in time but also in eternity.[34] This clearer perception launched Wesley into a decade (1725–35) of intensive following of à Kempis, whose work he translated and published in English as *The Christian Pattern*.

Wesley's introduction to *The Christian Pattern* is a window into his religious understanding prior to his leaving for Georgia. The essence of Christian perfection is love which unites the soul to God. Perfect love implies entire humility, absolute self-renunciation and the union of the will with God. This perfection is only achieved by passing through several stages viz, the purging of all wilful and habitual sin; the practising of all the virtues of Christ; the union with God by love. The chief instruments of Christian perfection are the grace of God and, subservient to this, prayer, self-examination and the holy communion.

Wesley acknowledged the priority of grace as the chief means of perfection, but the emphasis of his practice was upon imitating

Christ in both attitude and behaviour. He clearly defined the form of godliness in terms of love: the power was derived from emulation and the holy communion.

In 1729 this personal quest for Christian perfection was enriched by the formation of the Holy Club.[35] The members had supper together, reviewed the events of the day, read the Greek New Testament, attended the sacrament weekly and did what good they could. Doing good was the form of godliness; communicating was the power to do it.[36] Different members added specific activities which fleshed out the general concept of doing good. William Morgan began visiting the local prison and a prisoner under sentence of death; Wesley initiated instruction for poor children and took an interest in the freshmen at the university; John Clayton began visiting poor families and the workhouse. In the course of time these activities were allocated to different members of the group who followed up the people involved in a caring manner.[37]

The power for this work lay in communicating weekly, for the sacraments were effective vehicles of divine grace, as were scripture reading, prayer and mutual correction.[38]

John Clayton of Brazen-Nose College also introduced the fasts and festivals of the Church into the practice of the first Oxford Methodists. On the principle that the nearer the source the purer was the fountain, the earliest commentators were regarded as the truest interpreters of scripture, and the primitive church was thought to provide the truest practice of the church. Wesley was strongly influenced by this non-juror influence and became an avid reader of the writings of the early fathers. This was not historical nostalgia; it was an attempt to recover the form and power inherent in the faith which for him at least was the answer to his urgent personal problem. What power enabled the martyrs and confessors of the church to overcome the fear of death and to die triumphantly? Wesley was seeking to locate the source of the power inherent in the Gospel: power which he believed to be available to him and to his generation if only he could find it.

It was the Georgia experience which brought him into contact with a group of Christians who had the kind of faith that overcame the fear of death. He caught a glimpse of it on 25 January 1736, when he recorded in his *Journal*:

> . . . at seven I went to the Germans . . . In the midst of the psalm wherewith their services began (wherein we were

mentioning the power of God) the sea broke over, split the mainsail in pieces, and poured in between the decks, as if the great deep had already swallowed us up. A terrible screaming began among the English. The Germans (looked up and without intermission) calmly sang on. I asked one of them afterwards, 'Was you not afraid?' He answered, 'I thank God, no.' I asked, 'But were not your women and children afraid?' He replied mildly 'No; our women and children are not afraid to die' . . . This was the most glorious day which I have hitherto seen.

Here was the power to overcome the fear of death. Wesley wanted it. He eagerly sought opportunities to talk with the Moravian settlers in Georgia, and later with Peter Böhler.

Wesley and Böhler had much in common: a university background, a missionary zeal, a concern for the disadvantaged, an experience of death which deeply shocked each.[39] But Böhler also represented a group of Christians who had overcome the fear of death and whose ecclesiastical simplicity, akin to the primitive church, was much admired by Wesley. In the first of thirteen contacts, Böhler pointed out that Wesley must allow the scriptures to speak for themselves, then introduced him to the nature of saving faith and encouraged him to preach it though he did not then possess it. Doing so, Wesley observed the difference in people's behaviour when he spoke to them about turning to God.[40] This led to a conversation about the fruits of saving faith, viz. holiness and happiness. Amazed, Wesley found verification of it in the scriptures. Preaching to Clifford (a condemned prisoner) from Hebrews 9.27, Wesley saw him change from fear of death to a sense of pardon, and die with composed cheerfulness, enjoying 'perfect peace in the confidence that he was accepted in the Beloved'.[41]

But Clifford's death posed real problems for Wesley. He disbelieved in death-bed repentance, because much time was needed to cultivate the virtues of Christ essential to appearing before God with any confidence. Yet Clifford died in peace with God and in composed cheerfulness . . . the fruit of saving faith. Böhler's assertion that faith could be given in a moment was beyond Wesley's comprehension. Turning to the Scriptures he found it to be the norm. Böhler then spoke about the object of saving faith and several people testified that for them it was 'the blood of Christ' which effected their passing from 'sin and fear to holiness and happiness'. Bohler had not finished yet. Faith in 'the blood of Christ' must be seen in the context of the grace of God.[42] On 3 May he spoke to both John and Charles about the nature of the one, true, living faith whereby through grace alone we are saved. This was exciting. After preaching from Romans 8.32 Wesley recorded in his *Journal*: 'My heart was now so enlarged as to declare the love of God to all that were oppressed by the devil, that I did not wonder in the least when I was afterwards told "Sir, you must preach here no more." '[43]

Wesley's preaching had turned one hundred and eighty degrees. Instead of preaching the necessity of our love to God in terms of I Corinthians 13.3, he now preached God's love to us from Romans 8.32. He was excited about it. It was God's love that, in a moment, issued in the change from sin and fear to holiness and happiness. It was the experience of the first Christians. It was the experience of newly found friends and strangers. It was good news to proclaim, not a duty to be enforced. It was hope for solving his problem, the fear of death.

Bohler's final contact was by letter on the eve of his departure for America. In it he emphasized 'how great, how inexpressible, how unexhausted' is 'God's love in Christ and urged Wesley to put Christ in mind of his promises assuring him that He could not refrain from doing for him what He had done for so many others.[44]

On 24 May Wesley went unwillingly to a Society meeting in Aldersgate Street, where Luther's preface to the Epistle to the Romans was being read. Wesley records:

> About a quarter before nine, while he was describing the change which God works in the heart through faith in Christ, I felt my heart strangely warmed. I felt I did trust in Christ, Christ alone for salvation; and an assurance was given me that He had taken away my sins, even mine, and saved me from the law of sin and death.[45]

Faith in Christ had overcome the terrors of the law and its consequence, death.

In the fortnight that followed he was buffetted by many temptations, but he was sure of two things – he had peace with

God and victory over sin. But joy was fickle. Most disturbing was a letter from Oxford which asserted that whoever had any degree of doubt or fear was not weak in faith, but had no faith at all.[46] This really questioned the validity of his experience. From the scriptures he concluded that he was a 'babe in Christ' and felt so 'sawn asunder' by such doubtful disputations that he determined to visit Herrnhut in the hope that mature Christians there would establish him in the faith and enable him to go from strength to strength. Almost a year later he was to assess again his spiritual progress and conclude that he was not a Christian. He never questioned God's love to him, but he questioned his love for God. He had no feeling for God, little to show of the fruits of the Spirit, and the love of the world still possessed him. He saw himself as having the faith of a servant rather than the faith of a son. One suspects that his sense of assurance was fulfilled only when he discovered his role as an evangelist which his *Journal* records as the opening of a 'new period' of his life.[47] Prior to Aldersgate he had a vocation but no good news to proclaim and no assurance of salvation – only a great fear of death. Through Bohler he discovered the message and at Aldersgate Street experienced the grace of God and some of the fruits of saving faith. At Hanham Mount there was a fusion of his newly discovered theology of saving faith, his vocation as a servant of God's mission to the poor and neglected, and his experience of the divine love. There he opened his mission with the same words as his Master in the synagogue at Nazareth. It was to proclaim liberty from sin and the fear of hell.[48] From this fusion of vocation, message and personal experience flowed an amazing era of evangelistic activity which even the Wednesbury riots of October 1743 could not stop. Some say he was a figure larger than life: others that he suffered from a martyr complex. Whatever he had, the fear of death no longer terrified him. Rather he was prepared to accept death when, where and however required. 'Hereafter no man can take anything from me, no life, no honour, no estate; since I am ready to lay them down, as soon as I perceive that Thou requirest them at my hands . . .'[49]

The fear of death had been conquered.

How then did this conquest of the fear of death effect Wesley's post-Aldersgate ministry?

Death in Wesley's preaching, pastoral care and polity

Attention has already been drawn to the difference in texts from which he preached before and after Aldersgate. Instead of pressing the duty of love to God, he proclaimed the love of God to all mankind. This does not mean that the theological significance of death was neglected. He took that seriously, warning his hearers that death was the consequence of unrepented sin. But any man who preaches for a verdict has the solemn responsibility of continuing spiritual oversight of those who respond. In Wesley's subsequent counselling death was also an important component. 'Do you deserve to die?' the penitent was asked. Acquiescence in the divine judgement upon his sin was taken as evidence of genuine repentance. To such the promises of Christ were spoken. When the divine grace was accepted, the penitent was asked 'Are you willing to die?' Willingness to die was seen as readiness to appear before God trusting in Christ alone for pardon and acceptance. In this way death was used to awaken the careless and to test the genuineness of the penitent and the reality of the experience of the pardoned.[50]

Wesley classified his hearers as 'natural man', 'awakened', 'babes in Christ' and 'fathers in Christ' and directed his preaching and fashioned his counselling and polity accordingly. The following table broadly illustrates Wesley's integration of these factors.

Spiritual condition of the hearer	Aim of the Preacher	Theme	Polity
natural man	to awaken to spiritual peril	judgement, death	field preaching
awakened	to bring to a sense of pardon and peace with God	the promises of Christ, atonement, love of God	Society meeting
babes in Christ	to encourage growth in love to God and man	sanctification of the whole of life	Class meeting
fathers in Christ	to encourage to press on to perfection in love	entire sanctification as a present possibility	Band Meeting

While delegating much of his pastoral responsibility to preachers and class leaders in connexion with him, Wesley gave much time to personal counselling in interviews and letter writing. Special concern was given to those skirmishing with death.

Soldiers

In the course of duty soldiers were subject to the real possibility of violent death. It is not surprising that Wesley showed them special concern. Letters from some of them appear in his *Journal.* John Haime records the overcoming of his fear of death by an overwhelming sense of God's love to him; Sampson Stanisforth not only knew the indwelling peace of God driving out his fear of death, but while advancing into battle told his comrades of the happiness of the man who has God's peace in his heart; John Evans, with both legs taken off by a chain-shot, lay across the barrel of the cannon 'praising God and exhorting all that were round about him, which he did till his spirit returned to God'.[51]

Condemned prisoners

Early Methodists also gave special attention to condemned prisoners. Conspicuous in this work were John and Charles Wesley, Silas Told and Sarah Peters. After visiting ten condemned men for over a week, Charles Wesley and Mr Bray spent the night before the execution with them in their cell. The time was spent in prayer and concluded with the sacrament. Charles Wesley accompanied the men to the gallows in the death cart and witnessed the execution. 'None showed any natural terror of death: not one showed any struggle for life.' He had never seen 'such calm triumph' and noted in his *Journal* 'that hour spent under the gallows was the most blessed hour' of his life.[52] He had witnessed the power of the Gospel to overcome the fear of death, enabling men to die with dignity, peace and joy.

The sick and dying

Assiduous visitation of the sick had always been part of Wesley's pastoral practice, but after 1738 this had not only the previous force of facing death squarely but also provided a specific opportunity to counsel the sick to an assurance of salvation so that they could die in peace with God and in the hope of sharing in a blessed immortality. This ministry was often enriched by the local

Society meeting around the sick-bed and sharing in the eucharist. Such meetings had a double importance. Being legal in canon law they enabled members of Society to receive sacramental nourishment when they were excluded from the parish communion: they also gave the sick and the dying a sense of continuing fellowship with the people of God here and hereafter. One has only to read the obituaries in the Methodist Magazines for the record of scores of ordinary Methodist people who 'died triumphantly' in 'full assurance of faith'[53] and the Minutes of Conference from 1778 for many of Wesley's preachers who died 'fully delivered from the fear of death', finishing 'their course with joy', 'in full triumph of faith'.

This strong sense of the unity of the church militant and triumphant found voice in Charles Wesley's eucharist and love feast hymns, and even in the tea meeting grace. Realized eschatology was part of their lives in Society, Class and Band meetings. These were a sip of the cup of joy which lay beyond death. On this basis what need was there to fear? They died believing, in hope, in peace, with joy, with dignity and in anticipation of the fulfilment of their lives in heaven. In short, they died triumphantly.

This they owed to John Wesley who sought, found and shared his theological answer to his deeply felt psychological problem – the fear of death.

14

Wesleyan Theology

Melvin E. Dieter

In this essay I hope to provide some sense of how the Aldersgate event of two hundred and fifty years ago shaped a theology in which persons today still are finding windows to a renewed vision for a Church that is groping for direction within a welter of confusing change. Some degree of oversimplification and presumption is inescapable in so brief an attempt to describe John Wesley's theology, but, appropriately for this occasion, his account of his Aldersgate experience provides us with as useful a paradigm in as manageable a form as any we have available to us for sampling the essence of his thought. His terse words of testimony will be quoted again and again as we commemorate the significance of the events of 24 May 1738:

> About a quarter before nine, while he [Luther, through a reader of his preface to the Epistle to the Romans in the Aldersgate assembly] was describing the change which God works in the heart through faith in Christ, I felt my heart strangely warmed. I felt I did trust in Christ, Christ alone for salvation: And an assurance was given me, that he had taken away *my* sins, even *mine*, and saved *me* from the law of sin and death.[1]

What is there in these words that intimates the distinctive emphases in his *via media* of Christian thought, a way which Wesley always defended as fully confirmed in the grand themes of scripture and yet was one that was also not wholly consonant with the great theological systems which had risen out of the Protestant Reformation or out of medieval Catholicism before it? Wesley's witness to his Aldersgate experience here and in other commentary of his upon it brings into focus three elements which characterized his thought. In each of these elements Wesley expanded, or even altered, the theological perspectives on the nature and ends of the divine plan of salvation and the Christian life which shaped the prevailing Christianity of the eighteenth-century England of his day. These three elements are: 1. An enlarged perspective of the nature of justification and the new birth. 2. An altered understanding of the work of the Holy Spirit in bringing persons to salvation and establishing the life of God in the heart of the believer. 3. An expanded expectation of the work of God in his people and of his people in the world.

Before we can consider that story more fully, however, we must respond to several questions which some may raise concerning the propriety of such a project itself. The first of these is, 'Why?' The obvious answer may be an adequate one: 'To commemorate and celebrate one of the great moments within Christian history.' A much more relevant inquiry may be whether or not a theology shaped by an event two hundred and fifty years ago can have meaning today for the people of God as they regroup for ministry under the onslaught of unprecedented change. In the light of the increasing interest in Wesley studies in religious circles our answer is that whenever movements find themselves in the middle, or more accurately, the 'muddle', of radical dislocation, they often turn to the past for guidance. They search for new paradigms for leaving the past behind and moving into the future. Old normative categories of thought and action often begin to lose their power to give focus and meaning to traditions in transition. At such times, movements attach new importance to the views of persons who are still regarded as faithful to a fundamental mission, but whose perspectives have in the past been overshadowed by those views which dominated the shaping of failing cultural norms. This is one of the dynamics which is producing the new burst of interest in Wesley studies. Growing numbers of individuals are looking to his work in an effort to identify authentic alternatives of Christian thought and action to replace those whose usefulness seems to be waning.

Another contemporary issue which always presses to the fore is whether writing about Wesleyan theology or that of any other particular Christian group is appropriate in an age in which persons all across the Christian spectrum are sensing the deep need for greater commonality and unity in the faith. Wesleyans respond to this concern with an unhestitating affirmation of their commitment to as full a participation as possible in the universal body of Christ. They believe in a holy and catholic church and want to promote its unity and mission. Nevertheless, it is just as true today as it was in Wesley's time that one cannot be a 'catholic Christian' unless one first finds a home among a group of Christians who are functioning as a part of the inclusive family of Christians. However, particularity of experience and understanding of the Gospel is authentic only as it contributes to, or serves, the creation of the richer and broader community of Christian faith. The readiness of the whole to recognize and accept the grace which it can receive only by due recognition of God's gifts to each member is equally important. Wesleyans, therefore, seek to bring whatever strengths of Christian experience and spiritual understanding that God's grace may have worked in them to the service of all the people of God. They also need the enrichment of their own thought and life which comes from all others in the body of Christ.

Another preliminary question is whether theology is really important to the Wesleyan movement. Writers commonly have praised Wesley for his ardent evangelism and for his promotion of experiential and practical religion. However, not until our own times have they begun to value him as a theologian. The Wesleyan movement has usually been viewed as an essentially experiential tradition. The initial impetus to this non-theological bent of Methodism was born out of the nature of the Aldersgate event itself. The overbearing experiential import of that moment of personal spiritual enlightenment tends to overshadow the abiding significance of basic Christian doctrines to John Wesley and his Methodists. Does one readily conceive of a Lutheran theology? Yes. A Reformed theology? Yes! But a Wesleyan theology? Historically, a positive answer to that question has always come grudgingly, if at all.

We may even raise the question whether Wesley himself allowed that doctrines and theological opinions played any significant role in true religion. He cautioned his followers against getting too deeply involved in controversial writings. He admonished them not to be caught up in anything but the living and the preaching of the Gospel. Winning souls, calling them to holiness, caring for the poor, becoming representatives of God at work in the world were to be Methodism's priorities. To those critics who charged that his own answers to the doctrinal questions with which they challenged him were always too brief, he made the rather abrupt retort that the time he was already giving to such writing would have to suffice. But those who have used such references, and others like them, to determine the whole of Wesley's judgment on the importance of doctrine and theological definition fall into the trap of proof-texting. The simple fact is that like Luther and others thrust into the limelight of leadership in abrasive and even revolutionary movements he spent much more time in defending and explicating his doctrinal commitments than the forenamed aversions and cautions would suggest.

His sermon on the 'Catholic Spirit' demonstrates, as well as any of his writings, his attempt to maintain a proper balance between the experimental-practical and the doctrinal-theoretical polarities of the Christian faith. Wesley's deft use in that sermon of his text, 'Is thine heart right, as my heart is with thy heart? . . . If it be, give me thine hand' [2 Kings 10.15],[2] enables him to rise above the obstacles which so commonly have prevented genuine Christian love for those with different opinions and Christian practices, means of worship, etc., from our own. He concludes that genuine religion is the knowledge of God in the heart and may be present there in spite of faulty doctrine or religious opinion.

However, many of those who quote this sermon of Wesley's to deny the importance of a good doctrine to true Christianity abuse his meaning here as much as at any other point in his writings. They fail to stay with him and hear him out to the end. He concluded his sermon by observing that the greatest danger in making such broad statements as he had made was that some would use the ideal of the catholic spirit as an excuse for their own lack of personal conviction in belief or practice. The absence of decisiveness in fundamental Christian beliefs is 'an irreconcilable enemy . . . to true catholicism'. Persons of truly catholic spirit are always ready to hear and consider the opinions of others but, at the same time, they are 'fixed as the sun' in their judgements concerning 'the main branches of Christian doctrine', or 'the elements of the Gospel of Christ'. The 'royal way of universal love' which he had described was to be no hiding place for people 'of a muddy understanding' and 'unsettledness of thought'. Any such wavering concerning the faith was 'the spawn of hell . . .'[3] Wesley *did* think beliefs were important and *was* concerned about basic doctrinal definition!

We can now turn to a brief look at Wesley's way of thinking about theological matters and then go on to an analysis of his own understanding of 'the elements of the Gospel of Christ', and the 'main branches of Christianity'. Finally, we must consider whether any of Wesley's theological insights are at all helpful to the church today.

First, a word about his method. *Wesley's theology is dialogical and incarnational.* It is a theology of the life of God in the souls of men and women; true religion is a constant dialogue between God's Word and promise and the faithful response of men and women as God brings them to salvation and lives in them through Christ in the Holy Spirit. Humankind's holiness and happiness in God are the ultimate goal of the work of salvation in this life.[4] Its most basic tenets lie grounded in the maxim that God will not save us because of ourselves, nor will he save us without ourselves. The merit of our salvation, Wesley came to realize at Aldersgate, lies in God and Christ alone, and is ministered to all persons at all times, in every place as the Holy Spirit seeks to bring them to accept the saving revelation of himself. The ability of men and women to believe and to accept the 'Good News', however, is also the free gift of God; persons must receive grace as freely as God has given it before salvation can come to them.

Aldersgate radically reformed and reordered all his prior theological understanding, especially that of justification and sanctification. But the new experiential relationship with God which the event initiated and the passion to witness which it inspired in him did not make his concern for the importance of proper doctrines irrelevant to his future life or ministry. Rather, it allowed him to bring biblical convictions and doctrinal beliefs into the service of his mission of saving his own soul and the soul of every other person he could touch. After his evangelical conversion he never again could approach questions of beliefs and doctrines as he and many of the theologians in the church before him had been accustomed to doing. His theology became a working theology, not averse to the usefulness of the historically accepted objective, logical or systematic discussion of truth, but never satisfied to stop there. From that time on, all purported knowledge of God, Christ, the Holy Spirit, the Christian life, the church or its mission would have to take into account what such knowledge meant to the everyday life of the Christian and the church in the world. It had always to address such questions as these. How does it encourage the development of the life of God in the souls of men and women? How does it compel and empower those who experience the wholeness of entire sanctification to love other Christians, to reach out, in the name of Christ, to the poor and oppressed and to promote righteousness and justice wherever and whenever they have opportunity? Christian doctrine which did not speak to questions like these was deficient and possibly even destructive of true Christianity. Without doubt his Aldersgate experience set the pattern for an understanding of biblical truths which gave more prominence to the subjective elements of the faith than the largely objectively-orientated theologies of the Protestant Reformers before him.[5]

Nevertheless, Wesley lived, ministered and reasoned with the assumption that he shared an underlying common core of agreement with all believers on what he called 'the elements of the Gospel', or 'the main branches of Christian doctrine.'[6] In all else, he demonstrated such an unusual openness that he was accused of borrowing from everyone and of being a party to every tradition from which he learned.[7] But Wesley was no eclectic, picking and choosing indiscriminately to suit his own purposes at any given moment. Rather, he drew upon sound spiritual and doctrinal teaching wherever he discovered it, so long as it measured up to the Gospel of Jesus Christ as revealed in the Word of God. As a result, his theology is more like a recipe of God's plan of salvation and the Christian life than it is like the ordered propositions of logic which characterize the usual efforts to describe beliefs. Consequently, we cannot explain the Christian life by scriptural descriptions alone (although Scripture alone was the final arbiter for all his 'opinions'). We also must take into proper account the best reasoning which can be brought to the service of understanding faith; reason, too, is God's gracious gift. We must engage in sober reflection on the nature of the work of God in us and in the life of the whole Christian community, both present and past, particularly in the more pristine life of the early church. Guarded and guided by biblical revelation, all of these ingredients became part of his recipe for scriptural Christianity. The result was a carefully proportioned blend of biblical, practical religion which concerned itself chiefly with understanding and experiencing Gods plan of salvation. It was a way of looking at the Christian faith which placed the principle of divine love at the heart of it all. It had a flavour and texture about it sufficiently distinct from the doctrinal systems generated in the Protestant tradition before him, to create new options for understanding, practising, and promoting Christianity.[8]

We can turn now to those elements in Wesley's Aldersgate testimony which illustrate for us the most significant of these distinctive features, at least in their seminal form.

1. There was an enlarged understanding of justification and the new birth: 'I felt I did trust in Christ, Christ alone for salvation . . .'

First and foremost the conviction came to him that God was the sole source of his salvation. Wesley came to Aldersgate with a heavy heart and a heavy load of the conventional theological baggage of his time. The one element in his spiritual quest which was most real to him even then and always thereafter was a vision of the holiness and happiness which he believed to be the grand end of all of God's redemptive work in men and women in this life. This vision first came to him in 1725 at Oxford as he reasoned out the faint outlines of true religion. Five years before Aldersgate he carefully described the vision in his sermon on 'The Circumcision of the Heart',[9] a major pre-Aldersgate sermon which Wesley allowed to stand as part of his later collections of major sermons.[10] By that time he had immersed himself in the study of the Bible. Everything he found there confirmed his vision. From that moment on he was never willing to give it up, in spite of the extreme difficulties he experienced as he defended its validity both within and without his movement.

But before Aldersgate, he had come up dreadfully short in his progress toward his goal of whole-hearted love for God and others and the happiness it promised. In company with so many other individuals in his day, and in spite of the much more evangelical theology which he voiced daily as he followed the Anglican ritual, he was following the path of personal moralistic striving. He and other sincere seekers for understanding of God's work in the world were little different from their contemporaries, the deists, whose philosophies permeated the popular mind. God was a far-off God for both parties; he had established the rules for the game of life in the world and the church, but the ordering of society and the working out of one's salvation were chiefly the concern of men and women. Reason, discipline and dedication would win the prize and bring the vision of a better world and happiness and holiness to reality. But it didn't, either for the deist or for this heaven-bent Anglican priest.

Long before Aldersgate, Wesley had already joined the 'fellowship of the frustrated'. The path from his present state of spirituality to the bright light of the vision which had been beckoning him on to holiness and happiness seemed to stretch out farther than it had when he caught the first glimpses of it at Oxford more than ten years before. A new sense of his own inability and of God as his only hope of salvation were the first steps toward the 'new theology', shaped by Aldersgate. Wesley became aware of the radical measure of his own depravity, forsook his efforts to commend himself to God and joined the company of Luther, Calvin and all the other less-renowned souls of the Reformation of the sixteenth century who came to know for themselves that salvation is from God alone and by his grace through faith alone. Analyzing his own condition before and after the event, he noted that previously he had been 'fighting' with all his might, grounding his hope of justification on his '*own* works and righteousness'. Now he was 'always conqueror' as he trusted in Christ as his 'sole justification, sanctification and redemption'.[11] After Aldersgate, Wesley never wavered: it was Christ alone for justification, Christ alone for forgiveness, and Christ alone for the regeneration and sanctification, for himself and for all humankind. His encounter with a God who offered him pardon and forgiveness without condition so upset all his previous ideas of how one comes to holiness and happiness that we may still say that Wesleyan theology, along with most everything else Wesleyan, began at that point.

There is nothing distinctively Wesleyan, however, in his discovery of salvation in Christ alone and by faith alone; Wesley was just catching up on one of the most fundamental truths of scriptural salvation – justification by faith alone. Luther and the Moravians had shown him the way home to God. It is with reference to the content of the word, *salvation*, that nuances and emphases appear in Wesley's teaching which pushed his thought beyond the parameters of prevailing evangelical Protestant understanding of the new birth. When he began to lay the expectations of those theologies alongside the biblical vision of holiness and happiness as the ends of God's work in men's and women's lives he believed that they came up short. Prompted by that vision he gave new attention to the regeneration of the believer and the restoration of new life 'in Christ', which were part of the Aldersgate experience. Wesley affirmed that the righteousness which comes to believers when they trust in Christ consists not only in God's imputation of Christ's righteousness to their account for the justification of their sins, but is at the same time the impartation of the life of righteousness to the believer in whom Christ now dwells through the indwelling Holy Spirit. He would never allow that God called someone righteous as a mere legal or objective gesture. The scriptural promise was much broader than that. Through the indwelling power of the Holy Spirit, God would enable believers to overcome sin and to do works pleasing to him; God's promise was the assurance of his provision. He freely justified believers in Christ. The end, however, is not merely a question of righteous standing, but rather that they may become 'partakers of the divine nature'. But more of that later when we discuss Wesley's doctrine of sanctification, which he always regarded as a process distinct from justification but begun in the regeneration of life which came with the new birth. Wesley realized that by God's grace he not only was saved in Christ but that by the Holy Spirit Christ was living in him. Which leads us to our next consideration.

2. There was an altered understanding of the work of the Holy Spirit: 'And an assurance was given me that he had taken away *my* sins, even *mine* . . .'

The personal relationship which God confirmed to Wesley through the witness of God's Holy Spirit to his own spirit brought to him a new inner sense of acceptance and peace. As he sought to understand and explain what had occurred, he turned for instruction, as he often did, to the theology and testimony of early Christians. In this instance he imbibed deeply at the springs of Eastern Orthodox teaching concerning the work of the Holy Spirit.[12] What he learned there reinforced his conviction that true Christianity did not rest upon verbal formulations or propositions of faith alone but had to have the dialogical dimension by which the life of God – life in the Spirit – is realized in the lives of believers; that experiential realization in turn becomes valid data for fuller reflection upon the revelation of God from whom it sprang. A personal assurance of personal acceptance by God had confirmed the reality of salvation which he had experienced. In later sermons on this witness of the Spirit with that of our own spirit, he defined his understanding of the inner word of assurance which had warmed his heart at Aldersgate.[13] God's Word affirmed that all of the Christian's life is in the Spirit. The Holy Spirit communicates the grace and life of God to us by his prevenient presence (the grace of God which always comes before any action or knowledge of our own) which brings us to salvation and sustains life in believers by his continuing presence. Christian life, then, becomes an inspiration, an 'inbreathing of the Holy Spirit' into the new-born soul. God establishes a conscious, developing relationship with the believer in which the Spirit 'is continually received by faith' and then 'is continued back [to God] – by love, by prayer, by praise, and thanksgiving . . .' It constitutes a 'new kind of *spiritual respiration*' which becomes the life- giving source of spiritual knowledge and growth in the love and service of God and others.[14] A Christ-centred trinitarian pneumatology became the heart-beat of Wesley's understanding of a believer's relationshp with God. At every point it is life in and from the Holy Spirit, whether it be the first intimations of the gracious presence of God in granting persons the grace of conscience or the grace to see his wisdom in creation, or the revelation of himself in his daily providence, wooing and nudging them on to faith in Christ for their salvation, or calling them on to the whole-hearted love of God and neighbour. Although in later reflections on his doctrines of 'assurance' Wesley did not insist that such an initial sense of assurance as he had enjoyed and had once insisted upon was always prerequisite to authenticate one's relationship with God, nevertheless it remained a keystone of his understanding of evangelical salvation because it was the common experience of those who believed they had fully trusted in Christ and were living obediently in the Spirit.

It is Wesley's understanding of the fundamental importance of the work of the Holy Spirit to the whole continuum of salvation that again moves his perceptions of the nature of the Christian life into arenas of thought which were not common to the prevailing theologies of his time. The Spirit is always present and working with individuals before and after salvation, seeking to bring them to the salvation which God in Christ had already provided for all who will believe. This prevenient grace which always precedes all our inclinations to seek God and all our faithful responses to grace was Wesley's answer to the doctrines of particular predestination to salvation or damnation by divine decree which dominated the theologies of the Reformation. It is this new daily, living relationship with God and Christ in the presence and power of the Holy Spirit – the Holy Spirit giving assurance, wisdom, discipline and holiness to individual believers and the church – which has led revival movements in subsequent Wesleyan history to understand themselves in Pentecostal categories. Wesleyans believe that Christmas, Good Friday and Easter all find their fulfillment in Pentecost, the people of God living daily 'in Christ' and witnessing to his righteous kingdom in the presence and power of the Holy Spirit.

This brings us to the final point of our brief survey of the theology intimated at Aldersgate.

3. There was an expanded conception of the work of God in his people and of his people in the world: '. . . and *saved* me from the law of sin and death'.

As we have already noted, Wesley was a person who immersed himself in Scripture. Its imagery and cadences flowed into his descriptive and analytical language naturally and habitually. His Aldersgate witness echoed the words of St Paul: 'The law of the Spirit of life in Christ Jesus has made me free from the law of sin and death' (Romans 8.2). The end of salvation was the happiness of people who represented the holiness of God's love and the love of God's holiness in their lives in the world. It is no easier today to talk of Wesley's understanding of 'being saved from the law of sin and death' than he himself found it to be in his time. It was at this juncture in his teaching that his views clashed most directly with those Reformation traditions which from the time of Luther and Calvin had emphasized the imperfectibility of believers in this life. Wesley not only believed that the whole tenor of Scripture denied that position but ardently urged upon his followers and all Christians the necessity of going on to the entire sanctification of their hearts and lives – to both *inner* and *outer* holiness. A key question for his people was: 'Do you expect to be perfected in love in this life?'[15] He used a number of terms to describe the essence of this climactic experience of grace through faith and the relationships in divine love which it made possible both with God and neighbours. 'Christian perfection', 'perfect love', 'scriptural holiness', 'entire sanctification' or simply 'sanctification' turn up interchangeably in his writings. The same Holy Spirit who had led him into faithful response to God's saving work in Christ would by the same grace and faith make him a 'partaker of the divine nature'. This freedom from the old 'law of sin and death' and the freedom to 'be' under the 'royal law of love' is the ultimate gift of the indwelling Spirit. It is nothing less than the restoration through the 'second Adam' of the quality of love for God which the 'first Adam had enjoyed'.[16] The fall of humankind was not the result of illicit desire which broke a relationship of love, but rather the breaking of the relationship of love which led to illicit desire. The ultimate end of salvation then was a restoration of love. If love failed, all failed. If love prevailed, God's 'royal law' was ruling. It is the moment by moment possibility of victory over faithlessness. This wilful failure to exercise faith (Wesley's essential definition of sin) is the ultimate ever-present problem at every point in the Christian's progress – even at the heights of a relationship with God. Even those perfected in love can fail, as Adam himself would affirm. By faith we have the power to love God, but it never abrogates the freedom to forsake love; it is not, therefore, sinless perfection. It brings calm assurance of perseverance and final salvation, but not its infallibility.

But the end of the Gospel of salvation is not complete in the establishment of his people in true holiness. Christian holiness sacralizes not only the whole of the person, but all of life. From its first intimations long before Aldersgate, his vision of holiness and happiness was a social vision; Christians were entirely or wholly sanctified to minister the love of God to men and women everywhere, but especially wherever injustice and unrighteousness violated God's royal law of love. By his own precept and example Wesley taught that Christianity's special obligation was to the poor and the weak. It is always 'faith working by love',[17] fulfilling the great commandment. Love rules the heart and love works in a fallen world: both polarities must be present in any doctrine of Christian holiness if it is to represent the biblical promise and possibility. Wesley put the essence of this complex balance of theological elements into the tightest of summaries when he wrote:

> . . . 'the end of' every 'commandment is love, out of a pure heart', with 'faith unfeigned': the loving of the Lord their God with all their heart and their neighour as themselves: and the being purified from pride, anger, and evil desire, by a 'faith of the operation of God'.[18]

God had implanted and nourished within him God's own life, a life always on the move from grace to grace, stamped with the Spirit's seal of divine integrity at every point, yet always reaching out toward a richer and deeper experience of God, a *scala sancta* of grace, which finally led to the ultimate perfection: an eternity of love, an unbounded enlargement upon enlargement of fellowship with the triune God, Father, Son and Holy Spirit in heaven itself. Wesley identified this understanding of the biblical pattern of the life of the people of God in the world as a special 'depositum' of truth and evangelistic responsibility which God had entrusted to Methodists to preach and live.

Does all of this have any significance for us today, other than its commemorative value? The responses of contemporary Methodists would vary greatly at that point, as all who have participated in ecumenical Methodist theological institutes well know. But one observation always seems to come to the fore. It is that after all the qualifications have been made for contemporary political and cultural contexts, after all of the current theologies have raised the many legitimate questions which they do, it is difficult to leave John and Charles Wesley and Aldersgate behind. To be biblical and useful, theology must still speak to men and women who have to live the life of God in sinful and unjust societies. Wesley's doctrinal and practical affirmation of the scriptural word that God in Christ is always present in the Holy Spirit, working with men and women, wherever they are and within whatever context, calling them to love him with all their hearts, does just that. Such relevance assures that he will rise out of history to participate in future discussions of doctrinal formulation and missional strategy not only in Methodism but in broader councils of the whole of the Christian Church. He will be there, not as an authoritarian patriarch, nor as a mystical guru, but as a *peer* whose authentic life and thought have earned him the right to be heard.

15

The Relevance of John Wesley's Message for Today

William R. Davies

Are there people who think John Wesley's message irrelevant today? The very title of this article may imply that the case for relevance needs to be proved. Certainly there are few who would agree that his message as we find it in his sermons can stand exactly as it is. Apart from anything else, the language is archaic and some of his vocabulary would not be understood by modern readers. Others, and these would comprise a considerable number, would say that his message is relevant but needs re-interpreting, that the heart of it is true, but how we express and apply it needs a face-lift. Others, none Methodist, one hopes, would say his message is no longer relevant either because they do not believe in God anyway or because they would argue that God does not reveal himself in so personal a way as Wesley claimed to have experienced.

It is impossible to review the whole of his message, but certain major strands of it may be discussed in order to affirm the proposition that Wesley's message is not only relevant, but was never needed so much as it is today, even though there may be the need for reinterpretation. The doctrines to be looked at are those of salvation, assurance, scriptural holiness and social righteousness.

Salvation

Whether one reads Wesley's sermon on 'Salvation by Faith' or that on 'The Marks of the New Birth', there is no doubt that he believed it possible for a person, on hearing the good news of God's love and forgiveness, to exercise faith in Jesus and thereby experience a radical change. He describes such a change in a variety of ways: salvation by faith, justification by faith, being reconciled to God, being born again – born of God, etc. [1]

By faith in Jesus there could be a change of mind, heart and will which resulted in a changed life-style. It is expressed very much in black and white terms and something he apparently regarded as instantaneous. Today, whilst there is recognition of the significance of crisis moments, there would be a healthy scepticism of anything to suggest that so complete a change happened as instantaneously as the one Wesley described in his sermon on 'The Marks of the New Birth'. What committed Christian would claim to have complete power over sin, constant peace and hope and be so filled with God's love as to love one's neighbour as oneself?'[2] Even Wesley's Aldersgate experience, crisis though it was and significant though it proved, was not a complete and instant change, for Wesley himself expressed doubt about its validity later on. We find him writing on 4 January 1739, some seven months after Aldersgate Street, 'My friends affirm I am mad because I said I was not a Christian a year ago. I affirm I am not a Christian now. . . .'[3] Despite what Wesley said about his state of grace before Aldersgate Street there is no doubt that he had faith, even though it had not yet touched the whole of his personality. He gave mental assent to the saving truths of the Gospel and led a righteous life. In fact, what we see in his search before Aldersgate Street and his questioning afterwards is a man in the state of spiritual growth within which there was a most important crisis-experience.

St Paul's dramatic experience on the Damascus Road, crisis though it may have been, was the culmination of an inner conflict which had been going on for some considerable time since he witnessed the stoning of Stephen, whose faith in life and forgiveness of his murderers at the point of death, left a lasting impression. That does not rule out the significance of the crisis.

William James's often quoted book *Varieties of Religious Experience* has much to say about the once-born and the twice-born, but in the end it matters little whether a person's saving faith in Jesus grows gradually, whether it comes in a dramatic, momentary fashion, or whether there is crisis within growth. What matters is its reality.

There is still the need to preach about a saving faith as long as it is clearly understood and made explicit that both growth and crisis are equally valid and that, indeed, for some types of personality, the crisis of the moment will not be their experience.

Recently, in a Sheffield church, an older man responded to the invitation for public commitment to Christ. Afterwards he said that he had known faith in Jesus for many years. He could point to no crisis experience but he knew that his faith was real. His response to the appeal was simply to register the reality of what had been a gradual growth in faith.

Assurance

In Wesley's own description of what happened at Aldersgate Street on 24 May 1738 he writes: 'an assurance was given me that He had taken away my sins, even mine, and saved me from the law of sin and death'.[4] Wesley's sermon on the 'The Witness of the Spirit' seems to reflect such assurance, for in it he describes the testimony of the Spirit as 'an inward impression on the soul, whereby the Spirit of God directly witnesses to my spirit, that I am a child of God; that Jesus Christ hath loved me, and given himself for me; and that all my sins are blotted out, and I, even I, am reconciled to God'.[5] Though this may appear to be subjective, Wesley applied objective tests: in essence, the fruit of the Spirit would be outward evidence of the inward reality. Wesley was most concerned that the witness of the Spirit should not be confused with the voice of a person's own imagination, and both his sermons on this topic illustrate that concern.

Indeed, Wesley questioned his own assurance. On 4 January 1739, he is writing that he does not have the fruit of the Spirit, yet in the entry immediately preceding, for 1 January 1739, he writes of a love-feast in Fetter Lane when 'the power of God came mightily upon us, insomuch that many cried out for exceeding joy, and many fell to the ground'.[6]

Such questioning is surely a healthy sign and not unlike the experience of Jesus himself. At his baptism, having experienced the Holy Spirit descending upon him and having heard God's voice from heaven saying 'Thou art my beloved Son', he is led into the wilderness where the devil's first words are 'If you are the Son of God. . . .' It could be argued that the first temptation was not 'stones into bread' but that of self-doubt.

In Christian experience, the fact that one's assurance is sometimes assailed by questioning and doubt is a healthy sign. It demonstrates that what a person has is assurance and not presumption, and in such circumstances doubt may be the reflex action of faith.

How relevant is such assurance for Christians today? In view of the well-nigh universal craving for inner peace, a sense of well-being, of the desire to be accepted and of knowing one is accepted and loved, it is very relevant indeed.

Paul Tillich wrote of a certainty which no argument of reason could give but which 'dwells in those who have the Spirit . . .' their 'eternity is present to them'.[8] Elsewhere he writes that when grace strikes, 'at that moment a wave of light breaks into our darkness, and it is as though a voice were saying: You are accepted . . . by that which is greater than you. . . .'[9] Both statements are really concerned with this question of assurance.

In the modern charismatic movement this concept has much relevance. Michael Harper, writing of himself and other Christians who have had the charismatic experience of being filled with the Spirit, says: 'We may hear no voice from heaven, but we do receive a deeper assurance of God's love for us and of our status as His children.'[10]

Here are two writers expressing in different ways the possibility and reality of assurance. Even if there are times when such assurance is assailed by questioning, there can be no doubt of its value. For the sake of health and well-being, if for no other reason, this message of knowing that we are loved and accepted by God is important and relevant. In a world of stress, pressures and self-doubt, to know this is a blessing indeed.

'Scriptural Holiness'

The Deed of Union says that 'in the Providence of God Methodism was raised up to spread Scriptural Holiness through the land'.[11] Scriptural Holiness is variously described as Christian Perfection, Entire Sanctification and Perfect Love.

In his sermon on Christian Perfection John Wesley describes in what sense Christians are not perfect (not free from ignorance, mistake, infirmities or temptations) and in what sense they are perfect (they do not commit sin, do not continue in sin, are made free from outward sin, are freed from evil thoughts and tempers and are delivered from all other inward sin such as pride, anger and self-will).[12]

Wesley used the term 'second blessing' for this experience,[13] thus implying an instantaneous experience subsequent to new birth. Elsewhere he qualified this by writing: 'there is a gradual work, both before and after that moment, so that one may affirm the work is gradual, another it is instantaneous, without any manner of contradiction'.[14]

R. N. Flew was critical of Wesley's teaching and argued that sin could not be expelled or rooted out like a cancer or a rotten tooth, but was more like a poison which was in every part of a man's system. He went on to say: 'Whilst it is therefore possible, and even likely, that a complete emancipation from certain lower and easily recognizable kinds of sin will be gained by anyone who has entered into a new and transforming experience of God, it is not so likely that the subtler sins of Pharisaism will be once and for ever uprooted in that same spiritual crisis.'[15] A number of Christians today, with the exception of certain holiness sects, would probably agree with that viewpoint. They would want to go along with the idea of the work of sanctification being a life-long process with crisis experiences within it in which a person became aware of definite spiritual advance, perhaps in the overcoming of known and obvious sins. This is more a doctrine of relative Christian Perfection: that is, whatever perfection there may be is related to an awareness of conquering known wrong; there will be much wrong to be dealt with of which one is unaware.

One clue about our understanding of Wesley's doctrine of Scriptural Holiness today is to accept W. E. Sangster's description of it as 'the vision of a goal'.[16] Whatever one's present personal condition, that is the end in view.

Another clue is to follow Wesley's understanding of it as perfect love, 'that love of God and our neighbour which implies deliverance from all sin' and 'loving God with all our heart, soul, mind and strength' which implies 'no wrong temper' and by which all thoughts, words and actions are governed by pure love.[17] Here, the emphasis will be not on the implied deliverance from all sin but on loving God and our neighbour with heart, soul, mind and strength. In other words, the positive attitude of love, no matter that we slip and make mistakes, is of prime importance.

Life is about relationships, and any doctrine which encourages us to build bridges, be sensitive to others' needs, to relate well to people of all backgrounds and origins must be good news. The encouragement to reach out to others in love is far healthier spiritually than to become wholly preoccupied with one's own spiritual condition, which is a form of self-centredness.

Christian perfection may not be attainable in this life except perhaps in a relative sense, but it is the goal to which all Christians look, it can inspire within us a positive attitude of love towards God and neighbour, and remains a main plank of our faith.

Social righteousness

Much modern criticism of traditional Methodism has been that it is too personal and individualistic. In the past there used to be fairly general agreement that to change society, there was the prior need to change people. Today there is a strongly held view amongst some that if political and economic structures were more just and equitable, people would have a healthier and better environment to grow in every way, for what hinders people in personal growth is oppressive political structures and a lack of basic rights. Thus change the structures and you will have better people.

It is a highly debatable question. The truth of the matter is that both individuals and the structures of society need to be changed and these things should be happening in parallel. Wesley was concerned with both personal change (as we have already seen) and social change.

His interest in education is seen in his support of founding schools, to which there are several references in his writings. For example, his *Journal* contains a short account of the founding of Kingswood School 'to teach chiefly the poorer children to read, write and cast accounts'.[18]

Wesley's concern for general physical health and well-being is seen in the publication of his *Primitive Physick* in 1747[19] even though some of his suggested cures may have been quaint and very primitive!

Six references in his *Journal* refer to his abhorrence of smuggling, referring to it as 'robbing the king . . . which I could no more suffer than robbing on the highway'.[20] Today he would probably have felt the same about income tax and other forms of taxation.

Supremely, his social awareness and concern are expressed in his opposition to slavery. In October 1787 he wrote to Granville Sharp protesting his 'perfect detestation of the horrid slave-trade',[21] and the last letter Wesley wrote on 24 February 1791 was a final protest against 'that execrable villany, which is the scandal of religion, of England and of human nature'. This letter to William Wilberforce encouraged Wilberforce in the fight against slavery and included this exhortation: 'Go on, in the name of God and the power of His might, till even American slavery (the vilest that ever saw the sun) shall vanish away before it.'[22]

There can be no doubt that for John Wesley his personal religion had to find expression in a social context. For him, social righteousness was the outworking of personal holiness.

Today, there is no problem in reminding Methodism about the relevance of traditional teaching on social righteousness. Perhaps what we need to rediscover with renewed enthusiasm is that the other areas of Wesley's teaching are as much needed today as ever they were.

16

Wesley the Outdoor Preacher

Donald Soper

If it is true to say that Methodism was born in song, it was certainly bred in the open air. Methodism took its place alongside the great movements of Christian revival in as much as it expressed and renewed the one great and eternal gospel (the faith once declared to the saints), but like all evangelical revivals it possessed elements and characteristics which gave it a special and recognizable voice.

One of the early and unique sounds of Methodism was the singing of Charles Wesley's hymns. There is, however, another and equally unique sound – the sound of John Wesley's field preaching.

Methodism was nurtured in the open air. Moreover, just as the Methodist singing is preserved for us in Charles Wesley's hymns, so the story of the Methodist open-air evangelism is recorded in John Wesley's *Journal*. Here are some typical passages from the *Journal* which indicate the conditions under which this Anglican clergyman resorted to the open air, and equally exemplify the nature and environment of this open-air preaching to which he committed himself.

Wesley began his life-long commitment to field preaching largely from the prompting of that other great eighteenth-century evangelist, Whitefield, and with considerable 'perturbation', as he wrote in his *Journal* on 31 March 1739:

In the evening I reached Bristol, and met Mr Whitefield there. I could scarce reconcile myself at first to this strange way of preaching in the fields, of which he set me an example on Sunday; having been all my life (till very lately) so tenacious of every point relating to decency and order, that I should have thought the saving of souls almost a sin, if it had not been done in a church.

On 2 April 1739 Wesley wrote:

At four in the afternoon, I submitted to be more vile, and proclaimed in the highways the glad tidings of salvation, speaking from a little eminence in a ground adjoining to the city, to about three thousand people.

So it began, and the *Journal* records example after example of this field preaching. As he wrote in Dublin fifty years later: 'In a course of years, necessity was laid upon me to preach in the open air.'

Here are a number of quotations which give something of the scenario and flavour of this remarkable ministry. John Nelson has this to say after hearing Wesley make his first address at Moorfields:

Oh! that was a blessed morning for my soul! As soon as he got up upon the stand, he stroked back his hair and turned his face towards where I stood, and I thought he fixed his eyes on me. His countenance struck such an awful dread upon me before I heard him speak, that it made my heart beat like the pendulum of a clock, and when he did speak, I thought his whole discourse was aimed at me. When he had done, I said, 'This man can tell the secrets of my heart.'

Wesley's deliberate, unemotional magnetism produced, much more than Whitefield's emotive appeals, violent reactions in the field preaching of those early years. At Wapping, for instance:

Many of those that heard began to call upon God with strong cries and tears. Some sank down, and there remained no strength in them; others exceedingly trembled and quaked; some were torn with a kind of convulsive motion. . . . I have seen many hysterical and many epileptic fits; but none of them were like these.

Once in Bristol 'the street was filled with people, shouting and cursing and swearing', who were not dispersed till the Mayor's officers took the ringleaders into custody. In Cardiff's Shire Hall he found an attentive audience with 'many gentry', but at his next stop in Newport met 'the most insensible ill-behaved people', including one 'ancient man' who spent Wesley's sermon time in non-stop swearing and cursing, and in repeated attempts to throw a 'great stone', which fortunately proved too heavy for him. At Upton, near Bristol, 'the devil knew his kingdom shook, and therefore stirred up his servants to ring bells and make all the noise they could. But my voice prevailed.'

From the foregoing excerpts there emerges a picture of this field preaching (or rather it is possible to discern the outline of that picture), the subject matter, the arrangement of the constituent elements that go to make it up and the various colours that distinguished it. What can only be suggested is the impact of this ministry, for like the great impressionist paintings, this ministry was much more than the sum of its parts. Ultimately, John Wesley in the open air was a phenomenon. He *appeared*, and his appearance was invested with psychological (or as I would want to put it, spiritual) dynamism, an impression that defies analysis, yet is not totally unknown to such a disciple as myself.

The main characteristics that accompanied this field preaching are doubly valuable. They indicate certain requirements for success which are basic and unchanging. At the same time they would warn Wesley's disciples of the vast changes that have taken place since his day, many of which make some of his methods unrepeatable, and have altered what may be called the 'receptivity' of his hearers.

In as much as Wesley took to field preaching largely because many church doors were shut against him, he took his sermons into the open air. There must have been modifications in the manner of their delivery, and the interruptions which made the flow of his speaking often spasmodic rather than continuous. The evidence such as it is, and it is tantalizingly little, is that he offered Christ to the crowd and set that offer within the framework of a conversion experience open to all who would repent of their sins, and yield themselves to the everlasting mercy of God. The emphasis was moral; what evidence he advanced was the word of God as infallibly expressed in the Bible. He called for immediate decision and couched that call in the language of his brother's hymns. The effects of such preaching were indeed immediate. Over and over again the response was dramatic. The records tell, as I have quoted, of convulsions which convinced those who experienced them that the devil was being thrust out of the penitent sinner's life. Whether they fell in swoons or acclaimed their salvation by shouts of deliverance, there can be no doubt that a genuine revival experience took hold of many as they listened and as they responded. There were other immediate effects. Wesley was often met with hostility, he was threatened physically, he was occasionally molested and was protected and ushered into safety on more than one occasion. The *Journal* is laconic about meetings which must have been riotous, but the results of this field preaching are beyond doubt. A religious revival happened in eighteenth-century England, and it was largely due to the taking of the Gospel out of doors by this neat little evangelical Anglican priest.

Now if all scripture is written for our learning, so is history; and in the present age with its declining churchmanship, its ever-increasing agnosticism and its apocalyptic dangers, then a religious revival must be the hope of organized Christianity.

What can be profitably learned from the history of John Wesley's field preaching? The beginning of the answer must lie in the personal, social and intellectual circumstances that character-ized that eighteenth-century evangelism compared with the circumstances which belong to such open-air preaching today. The differences are as obvious as they are critical. The crowds to whom Wesley preached (and in terms of numbers asserted in the *Journal* it is prudent to divide by three at least to get anywhere near the size of his audiences) were largely uneducated by modern standards. Whatever their lack of theology in general, it is clear that they were susceptible to the threat of hell. They were equally aware of the prospect of heaven for those who received the gift of salvation from sins which were a constant cause of anxiety because they seemed beyond the power of the sinner to refrain from them. Moreover their acquaintance with the world around them was in many cases non-existent, or inevitably fragmentary.

At the same time the emergence of the proletariat of the Industrial Revolution alongside the rural population which had changed relatively little for centuries was already heralding the 'economic' man, although the economic theory to explain him was still in the future. Such a generalization, however, should be accepted in the light of Professor E. P. Thompson's epic work on

The Making of the English Working Class. Yet, whatever exceptions there were to the foregoing description of those who listened to John Wesley out of doors, the format of his meetings was relatively unchanging whether he was preaching to tin miners in Cornwall, or coal miners in Durham, or country folk up and down the land. It was an evangelical sermon taken outside the church doors, hymns now and then, no collection of course, but a proclamation culminating in an appeal and resulting in a response. As he records in his *Journal*, he was frequently heckled, occasionally shouted down, but not argued with or questioned, as is the pattern of open-air meetings in Hyde Park today. In one sense the campaigns of modern evangelists like Dr Billy Graham represent the contemporary equivalent of Wesley's field preaching. The range of his voice determined the size of his crowd (which included those who were ready to mingle in any crowd whatever the occasion). The range of the mechanical loudspeaker makes for much larger crowds today but entirely inhibits the 'to and fro' and the intimacy of comment and argument. The hearer is invited to respond; he is not invited to participate. Whether or not this form of field preaching will provide the seeds of revival, which the church indoors is failing to achieve, is speculative. I would only venture the feeling that its appeal, particularly in these islands, lacks universality and, on the available evidence, tends to shuffle and reshuffle an already existing pack rather than doing what Wesley did – reaching out to those untouched by any other evangelical method of propaganda. Nonetheless, it would be impudent to appear to write it off, though its effects and prospects lead me to claim the need of another form of field preaching which responds more closely to elements in the contemporary scene. I am satisfied that the kind of outdoor preaching which John Wesley undertook, and in which he was so successful, is insufficient to meet that contemporary situation. There is urgent need for the advocacy of the Christian case which begins in a 'fellowship of controversy' shared by speaker and audience. The reason for such a claim lies in the fact that whereas Wesley could count on an over-all sense of guilt among his hearers, the preacher today can only, initially at least, count on a sense of doubt.

Moreover, there is another all-important difference between the condition of those who were attracted to Wesley's preaching and those who tend to listen to open-air evangelism today. The modern crowd is 'informed', however superficially. The press and especially radio and television have opened up areas of awareness about the world around them, and communicate the prevailing social and political ideas, of which in their day John Wesley's hearers were totally ignorant. We know that ignorance breeds superstition, but a little knowledge, however thinly spread, is dangerous in quite a different way. It breeds scepticism.

John Wesley's call to salvation could and did produce an immediate response time after time, because there were few inhibiting doubts in the hearers' minds to interfere in that straightforward process. Despite the sudden conversions that accompany the open-air witness today, the overall response, if any, is conditioned by speculation which inevitably slows down the impetus of the challenge.

Conversion is rarely instantaneous. At best it is a series of choices rather than one all-embracing response. Nevertheless, an increasing number of preachers today, myself included, have come to believe from the experience of taking the Gospel out of doors, and especially out of the church doors, that this is where a return to the faith in the Gospel could happen, and with comparable results with those which were reached by John Wesley's field preaching 200 years ago.

Why? Surely because the root problem is fundamentally a moral one and repentance is now, as ever it has been, the gateway to forgiveness and the coming of the Kingdom of God. The threat of a nuclear calamity gives an unprecedented immediacy to this problem. We need to repent at once, to be forgiven at once, and to seek that Kingdom at once, and all for one supreme reason. Hitherto the end of the world was exclusively in the hands of God. We could speculate on its timing but we could neither facilitate nor delay this awful occasion. It is no flippancy to say that in relation to this apocalyptic prospect we human beings now have a 'do-it-yourself kit'. We have the nuclear bomb, and if it explodes life on this planet could end suddenly and irrevocably. Therefore the moral response to such a final calamity is urgent as it has never been in the great disasters of the past like plague, drought, climatic shifts and of course all the wars of the centuries.

To mobilize the moral case in this global emergency demands the imperative use of every form of the media, the pulpit, the press, radio and television, and every means of exhortation and argument, while yet there is time. The medium of the open air is essential in this 'ministry of all the talents'. It might be extravagant to claim that it is the leaven within the lump of advocacy. On the other hand the Methodist Revival could not have happened without the ingredient of field preaching as a vital constituent. The moral and spiritual revival which is the hope, indeed the requirement, of man's future on this planet requires a similar evangelical excursion into the open air today.

17

Wesley as a Writer

A. Skevington Wood

Although his literary output was considerable, John Wesley did not set out to make his name as a writer. What he published was in the interests of the nationwide mission which engrossed his attention. He was concerned with the communication of the Christian message and regarded his writings as an extension of that ministry. He was no mere dilettante who fancied himself as an author and so dabbled in the art to satisfy his own inclinations. Although, as we shall see, he was not lacking in facility, he directed his talent towards a specific goal. As George Lawton points out, almost everything Wesley wrote 'was intended to communicate or to vindicate, to convince, to persuade, and to move'.[1] However, as Lawton insists, it is unjustifiable to assume that because a work has a functional origin it is disqualified from securing recognition for its literary merit. Wesley did not aim to be a man of letters, but the calibre of what he wrote has nevertheless ensured that he deserves honourable mention in any comprehensive survey of eighteenth-century English literature.

Wesley's reputation as a writer has been enhanced of late as critics have increasingly recognized his gifts. Not long before the two hundredth anniversary of Wesley's evangelical conversion Henry Bett, in his Fernley-Hartley lecture on *The Spirit of Methodism*, felt compelled to complain that the contribution of John Wesley, along with that of his brother Charles, had been unjustifiably underestimated, if not entirely overlooked, by literary reviewers.[2] There were, in fact, notable exceptions even then as, for example, in favourable assessments from such distinguished connoisseurs as Oliver Elton and Louis Cazamian.[3] The space devoted to Wesley in *The Cambridge History of English*

Literature may not have been as extensive as some might have wished, but Archdeacon W. H. Hutton's comments were sufficiently laudatory when he saluted the founder of Methodism as 'a master of direct English and simple strength'.[4]

In recent years, however, several surveys have contained appreciative references, including the relevant volume in *The Oxford History of English Literature*.[5] An up-to-date sample is to be found in James Sambrook's evaluation in the Longman Literature in English series.[6] On the other hand, Wesley is dismissed with no more than a brief, incidental comment in some modern accounts – as, for instance, those by David Daiches and Maximillian Novak.[7] But overall it would be true to say that any adverse balance has now been largely redressed and that Wesley's stature in the realm of literature stands as high today as it ever has done. There are competent judges who claim that, at its best, his prose may bear comparison with anything produced in the eighteenth century and that for clarity and effectiveness he is indeed superior to some of his more fashionable contemporaries.

Conditions of writing

Considering that he wrote so much so regularly, and invariably with little leisure to polish or prune his style, it is remarkable that Wesley maintained such a consistent standard. For it must be remembered that the bulk of his writing was done while, like the apostle Paul, he was 'in journeyings often' as well as preoccupied with the care of the Methodist societies. It was only on comparatively rare occasions that he was able to spend a few consecutive days in some undisturbed retreat. More frequently he seized an opportunity to put pen to paper in a short interval between preaching and riding on to the next stopping place in his relentless itinerary. His only library consisted of the few books he could carry with him on horseback or latterly in his chaise. In these circumstances, it is surprising that he was able to write at all, let alone leave behind him such a large legacy of printed works.

An entry in his *Journal* for 6 January 1754 gives us some idea of the pressures which normally made it difficult for Wesley to squeeze out enough time even for minor and occasional projects, and why he needed a longer span if a more substantial production was envisaged. 'I began writing *Notes on the New Testament* – a work which I should scarce ever have attempted had I not been so ill as not to be able to travel or preach, and yet so well as to be able to read and write.'[8] Towards the end of 1753 he had been compelled to suspend his mission in order to recuperate from a consumption which brought him so near to death that he actually composed his own epitaph. Even while under doctor's orders not to write he nevertheless transcribed a section of his *Journal* for the press; then, soon after arriving at Hotwells near Bristol to take the waters there, he set about the task of preparing the *Explanatory Notes upon the New Testament* for the benefit of his preachers. 'I went on now in a regular method, rising at my hour, and writing from five to nine at night; except the time of riding, half an hour for each meal, and the hour between five and six in the evening.'[9] We can only wonder at Wesley's stamina if as a convalescent he could adhere to such a demanding schedule. As if this was not enough, he soon added a brief exhortation to his conduct of family prayers each evening when a number of neighbours asked if they might attend.

At the end of February 1754 Charles Wesley travelled down from London and the brothers spent several days together examining the Greek text of the New Testament and consulting Philip Doddridge's *Family Expositor* and John Heylin's *Theological Lectures*.[10] In ten weeks the rough draft was completed and John Wesley began transcribing the comments on the four Gospels. It was not, however, until the autumn of the following year that he was able to finalize his work and despatch it to the printers. On 25 August 1755 Wesley embarked on a tiring tour of Cornwall, eventually returning to Bristol at the end of September. 'I was weary enough when we came to Bristol,' he admitted, 'but I preached till all my complaints were gone, and I had now a little leisure to sit still, and finish the *Notes on the New Testament*.'[11] The *Notes*, of course, were officially recognized, along with the Standard Sermons, as indicative of Methodist doctrine. Not all who value them as such are perhaps aware of the personal sacrifice involved in their compilation, even though in the main they represent a compacted translation from the Latin of Bengel's *Gnomon* rather than a wholly original composition.

Extent and range

The sheer magnitude of Wesley's literary achievement is impressive in itself. Richard Green's *Wesley Bibliography* lists no less than 233 works – many quite short – directly from his pen, together with

100 more which he edited and abridged or from which he selected extracts, 8 for which he supplied a preface or annotations and 30 in which he assisted or was assisted by his brother Charles. This makes a total of 371 titles altogether – a substantial contribution indeed in quantitative terms to eighteenth-century literature. The sermons alone constitute a formidable body when compared with those of other prominent preachers of the period which have survived in print. As arranged in the latest edition of Wesley's works they number 151. Only 78 of George Whitefield's sermons are extant and no more than a handful from such celebrated figures as George Berkeley, Joseph Butler and Jonathan Swift.[12] It was in 1771 that Wesley initiated the republication of all his prose writings to date with certain specified exceptions. In 1808 the Conference directed Joseph Benson to supervise the preparation of a new edition which appeared in 17 volumes from 1809 to 1813. A more authentic text was aimed at by Thomas Jackson in his 14 volume set published between 1829 and 1831 and since reprinted. The critical edition currently in progress from Abingdon Press is planned to comprise 34 volumes when complete.

The range of Wesley's writings is as unusual as their extent. 'Few English literateurs played so many parts as Wesley did', declares Lawton.[13] Both Lawton and Elton have attempted to classify the material.[14] Wesley is no doubt best known as a journalist, in the strict sense of that term, for he kept and published part by part a daily record of events in his life as a missioner to the nation. His collected letters and Standard Sermons are reasonably familiar, especially to Methodist readers. But Wesley was also a controversialist, an educator, a translator and an editor. He chronicled the rise of Methodism and produced a series of popular tracts. He even ventured into the realm of biography with his life of Fletcher which Elton described as 'a plain and graceful record'.[15] We must therefore look a little more closely at some of Wesley's variegated compositions before briefly assessing the quality of his English style.

Journal

John Wesley's *Journal* has for long been regarded as a classic of its kind. According to George Sampson, it 'has something of the charm of Pepys'.[16] In its passages of spiritual autobiography it can be placed alongside John Bunyan's *Grace Abounding* and George

Fox's *Journal*.[17] As a record of revival it is of the same genre as
Jonathan Edwards's *Narrative of Surprising Conversions* in the
American awakening – an account which aroused Wesley's
interest in the possibility of a similar movement of the Spirit in
Britain. As reflecting the personality and outlook of a prominent
eighteenth-century figure, it matches the diaries of less widely
influential churchmen like James Woodforde and William Cole.
And viewed simply as a travelogue it provides a fascinating
picture of the contemporary scene which complements such
acclaimed reports as William Cobbett's *Rural Rides*, Arthur
Young's *Journeys* and John Byng's *Torrington Diaries*. Wesley's
descriptive powers have called forth the admiration of literary
critics in the past and still do so today. Elton went so far as to
affirm that in this respect Wesley is the equal of Horace Walpole or
James Boswell and that his fertility of thought rivals that of Daniel
Defoe.[18]

It was through reading Jeremy Taylor's *Rule and Exercises of Holy
Living and Holy Dying* that, while studying at Oxford, Wesley was
first persuaded to check his stewardship of time by keeping a
shorthand diary. During his visit to Georgia he began to expand
his private jottings into what developed into a published *Journal*. It
was to run to twenty-one parts, covering the years from 1735 to
1790. 'I had no design or desire to trouble the world with any of my
little affairs,' Wesley explains in the Preface to the first extract.[19]
He did not intend to reproduce what he had written only for his
own use but 'which would answer no valuable end to others'.[20] He
was concerned with information and edification rather than
merely with self-expression or even self-justification.

The poet Edward Fitzgerald, who translated the *Rubaiyat* of
Omar Khayyam, had occasion to compare three of his favourite
books – Walpole's *Letters*, Boswell's *Life of Johnson* and Wesley's
Journal. After he had first discovered the *Journal*, he shared his
excitement with his friend Edward Cowell, from 1867 Professor of
Sanskrit at the University of Cambridge. 'Another book I have
had is Wesley's *Journal* . . . If you don't know it, do know it; it is
curious to think of this Diary of his running almost coevally with
Walpole's Letter-Diary; the two men born and dying too within a
few years of one another, and with such different lives to record.
And it is remarkable to read pure, unaffected, and undying
English, while Addison and Johnson are tainted with a style which

all the world imitated.'[21] Fitzgerald later learned that Thomas Carlyle knew Wesley's *Journal* and shared his high opinion of it.[22]

Letters

Wesley's contemporary, Samuel Johnson, believed that 'the cool of leisure, the stillness of solitude' were essential for the production of a good letter.[23] As we have seen, such ideal conditions were rarely available to Wesley and, more perhaps than the rest of his writings, his letters were composed in odd moments sandwiched between other assignments. 'Considering that I am usually obliged to write in haste,' Wesley told Mary Cooke (later to be Adam Clarke's wife), 'I often doubt whether my correspondence is worth having.'[24] He was, moreover, diffident about his accomplishments in this area. 'I have often wondered that you were not weary of so useless a correspondent', he candidly confessed to Lady Maxwell, 'for I am very sensible the writing of letters is my brother's talent rather than mine.'[25] Despite his modest estimate of his own effectiveness and the fact that he invariably wrote hurriedly with little time to remove any infelicities of expression, John Wesley's letters are still well worth reading. The collection in the most recent edition of his works will total 3,500 but that, according to Frank Baker, represents only a fraction of what he originally penned.[26]

The earliest letter which has survived was written from Oxford in 1721 and addressed to Ambrose Eyre, Treasurer of Charterhouse School, where Wesley had been a gown-boy. As Telford points out, his style is as clear and direct as in his maturity.[27] His last extant letter, almost seventy years later, urged William Wilberforce to press on with his campaign for the abolition of slavery. Between these dates Wesley wrote to a host of recipients, from the great in the land to the poor and disadvantaged, and even on occasion to criminals. He covered a remarkable variety of subjects but his letters of pastoral counsel are of particular value. He acted as a spiritual director to scores of his followers – more especially women, it must be acknowledged – and if to the modern mind his tone seems at times to be unduly inquisitorial and demanding, his advice is usually sound and scriptural. Throughout his prolific correspondence Wesley wrote as he spoke. As his Irish friend Alexander Knox testified, he in effect talked on paper.[28] That no doubt is why he proved to be such a helpful postal counsellor. Those who received his letters felt that somehow he was actually speaking to them. As a result, present-day readers tend to agree that they are introduced to the real Mr Wesley through this medium more than through anything else he wrote, even including the *Journal*.

Sermons

It is difficult for us to understand the enormous popularity and influence of published sermons in the eighteenth century. A major proportion of printed material during the period of the evangelical revival consisted of such discourses. They proved to be best-sellers, and publishers vied with each other to obtain copy from the foremost preachers. Some clergymen saw here an opportunity to supplement their income. Laurence Sterne, for example, expected to be paid more for a set of sermons than for his novel *Tristram Shandy*, even though that turned out to be by no means unprofitable.[29] When John Wesley entered the field it was certainly not for financial gain, since the proceeds from the sale of all his works were devoted to charitable causes. His aim was to spread the message of universal salvation and scriptural holiness, while at the same time providing his preachers with a standard of doctrine and homiletical method.

Wesley was second only to Whitefield as the voice of the revival. But whereas Whitefield's dramatic and impassioned sermons must have made more impression when they were delivered than perhaps they do when read, that is not the case with Wesley. What Wesley proclaimed was more readily transferred to print, and still retains something of its original impact by reason of its lucidity and logic. Scholars are not altogether of one mind as to whether the printed sermons were preached more or less as they stand or had been studiously edited and altered for the press. James H. Rigg and W. Lamplough Doughty thought that the substance was much the same but that the language was adapted to appeal to readers rather than hearers.[30] John Lawson disagrees and insists that what we are left with is 'not a collection of dummy sermons'.[31] Both George Lawton and James Downey come down on Lawson's side.[32] In the Preface to the first selection of sermons, made in 1747, Wesley announces that he designed 'plain truth for plain people'.[33] He had endeavoured to adapt his presentation to the capacities of the rank and file who constituted the majority of his congregations, especially in the open air. 'I now write', he declares, 'as I generally speak, *ad populum* – to the bulk of mankind.'[34] His statement would seem to justify the assumption that there was little or no difference in language between his preached and printed sermons.

This conclusion appears to be confirmed by the single instance where we can compare a report of one of Wesley's oral sermons with its written counterpart. It is No 91 in the revised list, 'On Charity', with I Corinthians 13.1–3 as the text. It was written in London in 1784 – a year in which it had been preached a dozen times. A manuscript now housed in Drew University Library in Georgia contains an eye-witness account of a service in St John's, Clerkenwell, on 16 December 1787, when Wesley used the identical message. The précis suggests that the sermon as delivered was virtually the same both in content and expression as the printed version.[35] Moreover, William Gurley recalled that in May 1785, during one of his brief visits to Ireland, Wesley had preached from I Corinthians 13 as he stood on a table at the end of the Mall in Waterford. 'It was a most able discourse,' Gurley commented, and then added significantly, 'just the same as printed.'[36]

Although Wesley's sermons are usually couched in language that he hoped was intelligible to the uneducated masses of the people, he could modify it to suit a special occasion. On 23 November 1777 he preached on 'The Reward of the Righteous' (Matt.25.34) before the Humane Society in Lewisham Parish Church. In it, so Albert Outler demonstrates, he raised his rhetoric and expanded the scope of his classical and literary allusions.[37] Wesley had made a similar adjustment when he prepared what was to be his only published sermon addressed to a civil court, at the opening of the Assizes in St Paul's Church, Bedford, in 1758. But even in his regular messages to congregations composed largely of very ordinary hearers, the scholar in him kept breaking through, however hard he tried to simplify his utterance. The range of his vocabulary and references and the depth of his theological insights combined to constitute a brand of eloquence which Dante characterized as 'the illustrious vulgar' – vernacular speech which nevertheless conveys an air of distinction and authority.[38] Although some modern readers apparently find them rather hard to absorb – hence recent attempts to bring their language up to date – set alongside the ornate oratory which flowed from many eighteenth-century pulpits, Wesley's sermons emerge as models of clarity and cogency.

It is as such that they retain their status today. In terms of their content, they embody the heart of the evangelical faith. These are the messages which helped to inspire and sustain a revival. In terms of their form, despite some lapses, they represent a notable contribution to homiletical literature. Indeed, Downey can go so far as to contend that 'no other English sermons, not even those of Donne, Tillotson, or Butler, have enjoyed such widespread attention and influence'.[39]

Controversial writings

The eighteenth century has been dubbed the age of controversy. A spate of pamphlets and lengthier treatises poured from the printing presses, in which the contestants advanced their arguments and counter-arguments, often in the language of bitter and biting invective. Most of such polemic was political or between academics, but the Church was not spared the spectacle of internecine conflict of this kind. John Wesley was himself a reluctant controversialist. He frankly admitted that theological debate was uncongenial to him and was content where possible to leave it to others to take up the cudgels to defend the Christian faith or the Methodist interpretation and practice of it when these were under attack. He described defensive apologetic as 'heavy work, such as I should never choose; but sometimes it must be done'.[40] As Gerald R. Cragg explains, some misconceptions might be ignored but fundamental errors in the understanding of the Gospel had to be corrected. Silence on Wesley's part could have implied consent. 'By giving free course to falsehood, he might have diminished the impact of truth'.[41]

'I have no time to write largely in controversy,' Wesley confessed.[42] He felt that there were more profitable ways of employing his gifts and promoting God's glory. As a consequence, he dealt with his critics briskly and even peremptorily. 'If short answers to opponents will not suffice, I cannot help it; I will not, I cannot, I dare not spend any more time in that kind of writing than I do.'[43] Yet, despite his reticence, Wesley proved to be a formidable debater. His training in logic at Oxford stood him in good stead. He quickly identified the vulnerable areas in his antagonists' arguments and with razor-sharp incisiveness exposed their fallacies. He steered clear of abuse and slander and always tried not to misrepresent those with whom he disagreed, although it must be conceded that he did not always reproduce extracts from their writings with absolute accuracy.

Notable among his replies are those to Edmund Gibson, then Bishop of London, containing what Gordon Rupp regarded as some of the most moving paragraphs Wesley ever penned; to George Lavington, Bishop of Exeter, rebutting his ill-informed charges of 'enthusiasm'; to William Warburton, Bishop of Gloucester, who sought to vilify Wesley as a fraudulent mountebank; to the pseudonymous 'John Smith' in what Rupp described as 'not so much a confrontation as a continuing conversation'; and to George Horne, Fellow of Magdalen College, Oxford, held in high esteem by Wesley and with reference to whom he declared, 'Oh that I might dispute with no man! But if I must dispute, let it be with men of sense.'[44] Wesley's longest theological work, *A Treatise on the Doctrine of Original Sin*, was a response to what he regarded as the insidious reductionism of Dr John Taylor. He refuted Taylor's contentions point by point in an exhaustive and indeed exhausting scrutiny. In his *Appeals* Wesley aimed to meet the charges brought against the Methodist societies during a campaign of pamphlet abuse in a way which he hoped would satisfy 'men of reason and religion'.[45] With these and other controversies in mind, Elton said of Wesley: 'It was well that he could write, with so many good writers ranged against him.'[46]

Educational purpose

We can do no more than glance at other aspects of Wesley's literary activity. He was a determined educator. In an age when the majority were deprived of adequate schooling, Wesley was concerned that his preachers in particular and his followers in general should be given an opportunity to learn. He was convinced that the influence of the revival would decline in one generation if the Methodists were not a reading people. The *Explanatory Notes upon the New Testament* were compiled 'chiefly for plain, unlettered men' and were supplemented by an exposition of the Old Testament, drawn mainly from the commentaries of Matthew Poole and Matthew Henry.[47] Wesley edited the fifty volumes of his *Christian Library* in order to make available such a collection of divinity as 'is all true; all agreeable to the oracles of God; as is all practical, unmixed with controversy of any kind, and all intelligible to plain men'.[48] To achieve this end, he sometimes tampered with the text in such a drastic fashion as to shock the purists, although his motives were commendable.

But Wesley's educational concern extended beyond the spiritual sphere. He issued an English grammar for the use of pupils at Kingswood School, and followed it with similar textbooks to cover the Hebrew, Greek, Latin and French languages. His English dictionary, if something of a curiosity today, no doubt met a need when it was released. Works on philosophy, logic, history, natural science and medicine must be added to the list – most of them supplying a 'reader's digest' version of books by various authors. Wesley also displayed an unusual gift as a translator of hymns in the German Pietist tradition as well as composing some of his own.

Literary style

Wesley insisted that obscurity is an inexcusable fault in any writer on practical religion.[49] As an instrument employed in the service of Christian communication, his prose is marked by clear thought and direct expression. 'I dare no more write in a "fine style" than wear a fine coat', he declared.[50] He aimed to 'use the most common words, and that in the most obvious sense'.[51] Hence, according to John H. Whiteley, 'his prose has the muscular form and incomparable vigour with which the bulk of the English people then spoke.'[52] Downey emphasizes the same feature: 'Wesley's prose is best described as athletic.'[53] As an evangelist travelling up and down the land, constantly meeting a representative cross-section of society and especially the lower strata, Wesley was more familiar than were most writers with the everyday speech of the masses.

This contact with the vernacular was reinforced by the fact that Wesley's mind was saturated with the strong cadences of the English Bible. He told John Newton that the Bible was his standard of language as well as of sentiment.[54] He strove 'to express Scripture sense in Scripture phrase' for he believed that 'the Bible language is like Goliath's sword, that "there is none like it"'.[55] According to Frank Baker, the sources of Wesley's style are to be traced to his classical education, his familiarity with the

Authorized Version and the Book of Common Prayer, and his call to communicate the Gospel to the poor.[56] These determinative factors combined to produce distinctive prose which, however its literary merits may be assessed today, undoubtedly served the purpose for which it was intended in the circumstances of writing at the time.

But Wesley the writer cannot be summarily dismissed as a figure of merely antiquarian significance. He must surely not only be accorded a place among the more noteworthy authors of religious literature but also recognized as a craftsman whose style is still to be admired and indeed emulated. If good prose is that which 'allows the writer's meaning to come through with the least possible loss of significance and nuance, as a landscape is seen through a clear window', then John Wesley deserves to be included in the roll of those who have succeeded in producing it.[57]

Bibliography

Frederick C. Gill, *The Romantic Movement in Methodism*, Epworth Press 1937.

Richard Green, *The Works of John and Charles Wesley: A Bibliography*, Methodist Publishing House ²1906.

Thomas W. Herbert, *John Wesley as Editor and Author*, Princeton University Press 1940.

George Lawton, *John Wesley's English: A Study of His Literary Style*, Allen and Unwin 1962.

Thomas B. Shepherd, *Methodism and the Literature of the Eighteenth Century*, Epworth Press 1940.

George H. Vallins, *The Wesleys and the English Language*, Epworth Press 1957.

18

Wesley the Communicator

Pauline M. Webb

Dear Mr Wesley,

This letter is to invite you to broadcast a series of 'Reflections' on the BBC World Service. These daily talks reach a world-wide radio audience and are intended to set current issues in the context of religious faith. They need to be simple, direct and concise, lasting not more than four minutes and pitched at a popular level. Would you please let me know as soon as possible whether you are willing and able to accept such an assignment?

I would have had no hesitation in sending such an invitation to the Rev John Wesley, if only our lot had been cast in the same age and place. There is little doubt either what his reply would have been. Yes, he would have been willing and certainly he would have been able to speak through a medium which would have given him the opportunity of addressing in one four-minute span an audience a thousand times greater than those he addressed in a lifetime of travel or through volumes of published sermons. For he was pre-eminently a mass-media man, in all the best meaning of that phrase. He enjoyed speaking to the masses, he saw the value of a variety of media and he cherished the gift of plain, direct speech which could truly communicate, that is, share with all the people information or experience which everyone has a right to know and which can bind us together in one (the root meaning of the word 'communicate').

Unfortunately, without a time machine, which not even John Wesley could invent, we cannot bring him to the microphone. But we can through his journals and letters and published works, and above all through other people's recorded memories, recall what an excellent communicator he must have been. Even his very presence, slight and slender of stature though he was, seems to have radiated a charisma that charmed his friends and disarmed his enemies. A fellow man of letters and biographer of Wesley, Robert Southey, wrote of him, 'His presence excited a stir among strangers and made a festival among his friends.'

So I can imagine what a delight it would have been to have him coming into a radio studio, his script already penned in that scrawling handwriting of his, with many crossings out as he had laboured to find exactly the right word to express what he wanted to say. He would have had no difficulty in obeying the advice to keep it simple. He was himself a lover of plain and direct speech, despite his great learning, and once said,

> I dare no more write in a fine style than wear a fine coat. Even had I time to spare I should still write just as I do. I should purposely decline what many admire – an highly ornamental style. Let who will admire French frippery: I am still for plain, sound English.

This was no mere precept. Wesley's own writings afford abundant examples of his ability to translate complex ideas into simple language. Take, for example, his definition of the very word religion. It comes in that sixty-page pamphlet entitled *An Earnest Appeal to Men of Reason and Religion*, which spoke so directly to the heart of the distinguished layman, Nathaniel Gilbert, Speaker of the House of Assembly in Antigua. While searching for peace of mind himself, he picked it up almost by chance and was so impressed that he was prompted to travel especially to Britain to hear this man preach and there, together with two of his accompanying slaves, he was converted. So that pamphlet became as it were one of the founding documents of the Methodist Church in the Caribbean. In it, Wesley had written so simply, using no word of more than two syllables,

> Religion is no other than love, the love of God and of all mankind; the loving God with all our heart and soul and strength, as having first loved us, as the fountain of all the good we have received, and of all we ever hope to enjoy; and the

loving every soul which God has made, every man on earth as our own soul.

Such directness of speech was also used on occasion with devastating effect, for Wesley could pack into one brief sentence a world of meaning. Take his oft-reiterated claim that he had no intention of separating from the Church of England. Sometimes he wrote long, closely argued documents on the theme, but in one brief sentence he conveys all that this had cost him in terms of his own inner struggle. In a letter to his brother Charles near the end of his life, he wrote, 'I submit still, though sometimes with a doubting conscience, to mitred infidels.' You can almost hear him wickedly relishing that choice of phrase, possibly written with tongue in cheek as a polite way of putting his tongue out at the bishops who had treated him badly. Or there was the occasion when he was fiercely criticised by Augustus Toplady, but refused to enter into controversy and simply commented in a letter to George Merryweather dated 24 June 1770, 'Mr Augustus Toplady I know well but I do not fight with chimney sweepers. . . . I read his title page and trouble myself no further.'

Despite the length of many of his own pamphlets and his prolific letter writing, I would have no fear that our broadcasting Mr Wesley would find it difficult to keep within the time limits prescribed for him. He frequently advised his preachers not to go in for long sermons and warned against what he called 'the lust of finishing'. In other words, he wanted people both in their studying and in their preaching to keep to the times allotted to them without drawing things out beyond the limit.

Wesley even specifically advised one of his women helpers, whom he felt unable to recognise as preachers as such, 'Keep as far from what is called preaching as you can; therefore never take a text; never speak in a continued discourse without some break over four or five minutes.' Yet he became persuaded that certain of these women speakers did clearly have 'an extraordinary call' and comments in a letter to Mrs Crosby:

I do not wonder if several things occur which do not fall under ordinary rules of discipline. St Paul's ordinary rule was, 'I permit not a woman to speak in the congregation'. Yet, in extraordinary cases he made a few exceptions, at Corinth in particular.

So no doubt we would have had a lively discussion in the studio on the current Anglican debate on women's ordination!

Nor would I have any fear that Wesley the broadcaster would not take well to production. He frequently sought the advice of others, particularly on matters of communication. One of the most striking occasions was when he had been invited to preach the University Sermon at Oxford and worked for some days in the Library of Lincoln College on a manuscript in which he set out to denounce the many vices he found in the city and the decline in values he felt there since his own days as a student. So he prepared a scathing attack on the theme 'How is the faithful city become a harlot!' But the sermon was never preached. Its mutilated manuscript, dated 24 June 1741, was found among Wesley's papers after his death, and he began another sermon, one which was to become one of his most popular, on Acts 26, 28, 'Almost thou persuadest me to become a Christian'. This change from a negative to a positive approach would seem to have come about on the advice of the Countess of Huntingdon, to whom, Wesley recalls in his journal for 28 June of that year, he read a sermon (presumably the harlot one), and she persuaded him not to preach it.

Wesley was well aware of one of the perils of all public communicators, that of being misrepresented or misunderstood. So, even after preaching a sermon, he would still edit it to ensure that any permanent record would represent exactly what he wanted to say. In that he was like many modern preachers who still want to amend transcripts of their own recorded words before allowing them to be published. There is an interesting footnote at the beginning of the pamphlet publishing the famous sermon on 'Scriptural Christianity', again one of Wesley's university sermons which had been very hard-hitting at the prevalent vice in Britain. It was a sermon that was heavily criticized, not least by Bishop Gibson, whose handwritten notes on the subject can still be seen in the Library at Lambeth Palace, where he complains that Wesley is saying that there is no such thing as Christianity in Britain. The sermon was subsequently included in a collection of twelve, among them three others also preached at St Mary's before the University of Oxford, in Wesley's first volume of *Sermons* published in 1746. In this volume too the footnote is kept, where Wesley answers his critics saying,

It was not my design, when I wrote, ever to print the latter part of the following sermon; but the false and scurrilous accounts of it which have been published, almost in every corner of the nation, constrain me to publish the whole, just as it was preached: that men of reason may judge for themselves.

So Wesley clearly knew what it meant to be the victim of the media as well as a participator in them. However, none of that deterred him from his prophetic role as a public communicator. He often himself entered the lists of debate in what was then and still is the powerful mass medium of the newspaper world. *Lloyd's Evening Post* over the years carried many letters to the Editor penned by John Wesley on contemporary social issues, one of the most lengthy and remarkable of which was published in the *Leeds Mercury* and several other leading papers. It was written on 21 December 1772 and addressed the then, as now, urgent question of unemployment and rising prices. Wesley goes into a lengthy analysis of the economic state of the nation, particularly as it affects the rural areas. He adopts a frequent technique of his, that of asking and answering a series of questions, in very frank terms. Thus he writes:

> Why are pork and poultry and eggs so dear? Because of the monopolizing of farms, as mischievous a monopoly as was ever introduced into these kingdoms. The land which was formerly divided among ten or twenty little farmers enabled them comfortably to provide for their families but is now generally engrossed by one great farm. . . .
>
> Where is the remedy? Perhaps it exceeds all the wisdom of men to tell. . . .
>
> How can the price of wheat be reduced? By prohibiting for ever that bane of health, that destroyer of strength, of life, and of virtue, *distilling*. Perhaps this done will answer the whole design.[1]

Reading that, I only wish we could have heard Wesley on a phone-in following the same theme!

Another theme on which Wesley frequently wrote to the press was when he wished to appeal for support of various charitable works. During the wars against the French in 1759 he published a powerful appeal in *Lloyd's Evening Post* on behalf of French prisoners of war, and later wrote regarding the services celebrating the victories at Minden and Quebec, 'The prayer for our enemies in particular was extremely striking; perhaps it is the first instance of the kind in Europe.' Eight years later he appears again in *Lloyds Evening Post* raising funds for people in Britain suffering as a result of an exceptionally severe winter.

Wesley clearly believed in the value of the medium of print. He has been called 'the best gatherer and scatterer of useful knowledge that Georgian England knew'. He became the precursor of all publishers of paper-backs, as he introduced his popular Christian Library, making available to the general public not only cheap versions of religious classics, but also his own publications on innumerable topics. Writing to Thomas Blackwell of Lewisham, on 14 August 1748, he describes the plan for the Library:

> I have had some thoughts of printing on a finer paper with a larger letter not only all that we have published already but, it maybe, all that is most valuable in the English tongue, in threescore or fourscore volumes in order to provide a complete library for those that fear God . . . whenever I can procure a printing press, types and some quantity of paper I can begin immediately.

He took very seriously the task of editing and marketing his books and made an extensive list of authors and subjects he thought worthy of inclusion. His biographer Southey remarks somewhat laconically, 'Many a folio was brought down to the limits of Wesley's favourite duodecimi'. This publishing venture eventually proved a great success; it has been estimated that Wesley could have made some £30,000 from the sale of books, but typically gave it all away to charitable causes. Certainly, eighteen years after his publishing enterprise began he was summing up his accounts and recording that rather than having made any profit he now had a debt of over £1000. He ran into several publisher's difficulties, such as arguments over copyrights and other people trying to get in on the act. Some of his preachers, emulating his example, eagerly began publishing their own sermons, but were severely reprimanded for doing so, lest they lowered the high standard Wesley set for all published work. So in the Minutes of the Conference of 1749 appears the question: 'Shall we require every Helper to answer that question, "Will you print nothing until we have revised it?" The answer is "By all means".' Thomas Butts and William Briggs were appointed as the first Book Stewards, and all printed literature thenceforward bore the imprint, 'Printed and Sold at the Foundery near Upper Moorfields'.

Wesley's own publications proliferated, ranging from *Addresses on the Rights and Wrongs* (mainly the wrongs in his view!) *of the American Revolution*, through *Letters to a Smuggler, Letters to a Freeholder, Letters to a Swearer*, right on to his own four volumes of sermons and his comprehensive *Study Notes on the New Testament*. In his Preface to this latter work, he gives a profile of the kind of readership he intends to cater for, 'I write for plain, unlettered men who understand only their mother tongue and desire to save their souls.' He himself knew at least eight other languages – French, German, Spanish, Italian, Arabic, New Testament Greek, Hebrew and Latin – the sure sign of an eager communicator, and he encouraged even the least educated of his lay preachers to study Greek so that they might read the New Testament in its original tongue. He felt very keenly the need for linguistic skills. On one of his visits to Wales in 1748, he records in his *Journal*:

O what a heavy curse was the Confusion of Tongues! And how grevious are the effects of it! All the birds of the air, all the beasts of the field, understand the language of their own species. Man only is a barbarian to man, unintelligible to his own brethren.

As that *Journal* extract well illustrates, literature is also indebted to Wesley's skills as a communicator in his unpublished work as well as in his books. His own *Journal* ranks alongside those on Pepys and Evelyn in its lively portraits of the contemporary scene, when he delights in recording not only the great preaching events, but even tiny and amusing incidents that occur along his journeys. As a very old man, in 1790, he tells an anecdote about a man who had a large Newfoundland dog and an old raven who had fallen in love with each other. He records in his *Journal*:

The bird has learned the bark of the dog so that few can distinguish them. She is inconsolable when he goes out, and if he

stays out a day or two, she will get up all the bones and scraps
she can and hoard them up for him till he comes back.

Though obviously an excellent raconteur himself, and fond of a
tall story, Wesley warns his preachers never to give in to 'that
hateful custom of painting things beyond the life. . . . Let us rather
speak under than above the truth. We of all men should be
punctual in all we say, that none of our words may fall to the
ground.' Understatement rather than overstatement seems to
have characterized his own style of preaching and utterance. His
style was extempore, as evidenced in an interesting account in one
of the early *Methodist Magazines*:

> On the last Sunday in the year (1788) he had an exceedingly
> large congregation in All Hallows Church, Lombard Street . . .
> 'Sir' said Wesley to his attendant while putting on his gown, 'It
> is above fifty years since I preached in this church. I remember
> it from a particular circumstance. I came without a sermon; and
> going up the pulpit steps I hesitated and returned into the vestry
> under much mental confusion and agitation. A woman who
> stood by noticed my concern and said, "Pray, Sir what is the
> matter?" I replied, "I have not brought a sermon with me".
> Putting her hand on my shoulder, she said "Is that all? Cannot
> you trust God for a sermon?" This question had such an effect
> upon me that I ascended the pulpit, preached extempore, with
> great freedom to myself and acceptance to the people; and have
> never since taken a written sermon into the pulpit.[2]

To this fluent style there is no doubt that as a communicator
Wesley added histrionic skills. His contemporary, Horace
Walpole, describes him as a preacher who is 'wondrously clever
but as evidently an actor as Garrick. He spoke his sermons fast and
with so little accent that I was sure it had been often uttered. Still,
there was elegance in it.'[3] Certainly, Wesley must have been
aware of the importance of gesture and facial expression, of 'body
language' as we call it these days. This is why he took such detailed
interest in the way his followers dressed and appeared to others.
Among the reams of advice he gave to his helpers is one passage
which surely ought to be hung up in the office of every Social
Security Office or on the threshold of every charitable foundation,
as a reminder that gesture and tone convey as much as words:

If you cannot relieve, do not grieve the poor. Give them soft words if nothing else. Abstain from either sour looks or harsh words. Let them be glad to come, even if they go empty away. Put yourself in the place of every poor man and deal with him as you would God should deal with you.

And on the subject of dress, it is delightful to find John Wesley as a very old man refusing to rebuke a young lady whose father had reprimanded her for her finery in dress, which he feared would offend the taste of the ascetic Mr Wesley. But to the father's surprise John Wesley commented, 'For my part I do not wish to see young people dress like their grandmothers' – a comment which no doubt eased the process of communication across the generation gap!

For Wesley was at his best as a communicator in a person-to-person relationship. He seems to have been able to bridge all the usual gaps, of class or age or sex, and was an excellent conversationalist with people in all walks of life. Even the famous Dr Samuel Johnson enjoyed his company, though he complained that Wesley never stayed in one place long enough for a really leisurely conversation! But Wesley himself refuted the idea that he rushed about too much. 'Though I am always in haste,' he once wrote, 'I am never in a hurry; because I never undertake any more work than I can go through with perfect calmness of spirit.' This balanced way of life gave him time to attend to the needs of hosts of individual friends with whom he communicated regularly by correspondence, which for many people became a real source of blessing. When John Haime, a dragoon in the Queen's Regiment, became converted under Wesley's preaching, he joined the company who often travelled with Wesley, and commented:

Mr Wesley took me to travel with him. . . . And when I was absent he comforted me by his letters which were a means, under God, of saving me from utter despair.

And the kind of good advice Wesley gave in such pastoral letters can be seen in a phrase from one of them: 'Through every threatening cloud look up, and wait for happy days.'

This great care for individuals and their many various needs found its focus in the life of the Society for which Wesley cared in the Foundery Chapel. It is recorded that on founding the Society there, he spent two whole days writing out a list of the names of every individual member and learning them by heart, so that he might pray for them personally and attend to their separate needs. And it is reported that when he preached, however great the crowd, he had that knack of so fixing his eyes upon his hearers that each one thought he or she was being addressed individually, rather as in one of those portraits so skilfully painted that the eyes seem to follow the beholder from wherever one stands.

Such individual care understandably strengthened the bonds which attached the people called Methodists to their founding father. Robert Southey says of him:

> No founder of a monastic order ever more entirely possessed the respect as well as the love and admiration of his disciples or better understood their individual characters and how to deal with each according to the measure of his capacity.[4]

Such individual care is the secret of good communication, whether it be on a person-to-person basis or through mass media. Wesley would surely never have thought that the one could replace the other. Even if his words could have been recorded on tape, or his lively countenance have been captured on film, what finally counts is the way in which he personally embodied the love of God and the grace of Christ for all with whom he came into contact. Alexander Knox, who met Wesley when he was a child, wrote of him in later years, 'His countenance as well as his conversation expressed an habitual gaiety of heart. . . . He was, in truth, the most perfect specimen of moral happiness which I ever saw.'

So there seems little fear that Wesley would have been a delightful guest to have in a radio studio or on a television chat show or holding a phone-in and I have a feeling he would have enjoyed it all immensely. So, I present to you John Wesley, communicator par excellence. The green light comes on. Can we guess his opening words? 'I look upon all this media world as my parish . . .' and his out-cue? 'The best of all is, God is with us.'

19

Wesley the Evangelist

Joe Hale

It was the emptiness of John Wesley's experience in America – not the confidence of his Oxford scholarship – which thrust him upon the world as an evangelist. Four months after he returned to England he asked Peter Böhler, 'How can you preach to others, who have not faith yourself?' Böhler told him, 'Preach faith *till* you have it; and then, *because* you have it, you will preach faith'.[1] He had been a missionary in Georgia without having personally experienced God's freeing and reconciling grace, so Böhler's prescription was radical and exceedingly important. Wesley seized the moment two days later and first offered salvation by faith alone to a 'prisoner under sentence of death' named Clifford.[2] He then began in the London churches to preach boldly 'salvation by faith alone'. At St John the Evangelist's 'I preached on those strong words, "If any man be in Christ, he is a new creature"'. The people were offended and he was told to 'preach there no more'. Other churches in the city, St Lawrence's, Great St Helen's, St Ann's, Aldersgate and the Savoy Chapel, followed suit and refused him a hearing. Through God's gracious initiative, the very thing he was preaching to others, 'free salvation by faith in the blood of Christ', was moving toward realization in his life, and in the life of his brother Charles!

'My brother had a long and particular conversation with Peter Böhler', John wrote on 3 May 1738. 'And it now pleased God to open his eyes; so that he also saw clearly what was the nature of that one true living faith, whereby alone, "through grace, we are saved".'[3]

On Pentecost Sunday, 21 May, Charles was ill and recuperating in the Little Britain Street house of John Bray, 'a poor ignorant mechanic who knows nothing but Christ'. He entered into his conversion experience reading Psalm 39, 'And now, Lord, what wait I for? My hope is in thee.' Charles wrote, 'I then moved my eyes and met, "He hath put a new song in my mouth, even praise unto our God . . .' (Psalm 40.3,4). Two days later he wrote: 'I awakened under the protection of Christ and gave myself up, soul and body, to Him. At nine, I began a hymn about my conversion but was persuaded to break off for fear of pride.' Bray encouraged Charles to continue and Charles prayed Christ to stand by him and finished the hymn:

> Where shall my wondering soul begin?
>   How shall I all to heaven aspire?
> A slave redeemed from death and sin,
>   A brand plucked from eternal fire,
> How shall I equal triumphs raise,
> Or sing my great Deliverer's praise?[4]

It was the next evening John Wesley reluctantly went to the society in Aldersgate Street and there 'felt he did trust in Christ and Christ alone for salvation. . . .' He received the assurance that Christ had saved him from the 'law of sin and death'. The scene was glorious when John met Charles at the Bray house a hundred yards away; 'Toward ten, my brother was brought in triumph by a troop of our friends, and declared, "I believe!" We sang the hymn with great joy, then parted with prayer.'[5]

The Methodist shorthand 'Aldersgate', must include a series of important spiritual experiences extending before and after 24 May 1738. Dr Albert Outler writes of the 'ample evidence that fixes the year 1738 as the decisive period in Wesley's change from a faith in faith to faith itself, from aspiration to assurance. At Aldersgate he had passed from virtual to real faith, from hoping to having.'[6] Dr Gordon Rupp says if we bypass the debate between those who would 'play up' or 'play down' the significance of 24 May, 'it was certainly no flash in the pan'. The following Sunday John stood up in a Religious Society at the house of the Rev. John Hutton in Westminster and 'told the people that five days before he was not a Christian . . . and the way for them all to be Christians was to believe and own that they were not now Christians', which brought the famous response from Hutton, 'If you was not a Christian ever since I knew you, you was a great hypocrite, for you made us all believe you was one.' Mrs Hutton was so distressed that she wrote to Samuel, John's father, which does seem to confirm what 24 May meant to Wesley himself.[7] What John Wesley was convinced in his mind lay at the heart of Christianity he *experienced* in his heart at Aldersgate.

On 11 June, at St Mary's, Oxford, John preached before the University on the text 'By grace ye are saved through faith'.[8] This was the first sermon published following the eventful day. It became the manifesto of his herculean ministry and set him apart as a mighty evangelist.

For the balance of his life Wesley preached on average 800 times a year. He exclaimed, 'I do indeed live by preaching!'[9] He travelled up to 5,000 miles year after year for half a century on horse or in chaise, and near the end, in 1789, wrote to the *Dublin Chronicle*: 'It is not for pleasure at this time of life I travel three or four thousand miles a year.' Bishop F. Gerald Ensley adds:

> No, it was not pleasure, but the passion to mediate the divine grace which had so blessed his own life. It lured him from the classrooms, from the lawns and 'sculptured loveliness which is Oxford', to serve the brutal masses. It nerved him for his encounters with hostile mobs. It held him steady when his own followers seemed hopelessly divided. No, it was not for pleasure, but the urge to share the deepest possession of his own life that kept him to his task.[10]

To this end he wrote and edited 400 books, wrote hundreds of tracts in defence of the faith, and published a fifty-volume Christian Library which he personally edited and expected every Methodist preacher to read. His 'eminence is secure – as evangelist, reformer, practical genius', writes Dr Outler in his *Library of Protestant Thought* volume on Wesley. 'Few men in the eighteenth century have left a mark so clear and ineffaceable.'[11]

First, foremost and always, John Wesley was an evangelist. His labour provided fuel for the Evangelical revival. The movement known as Methodism was inspired by his visionary leadership and was moulded by the unusual ability he possessed to attract and mobilize people.

If the word 'evangelist' is suspect today, tarnished by sensational and well publicized abuses, perhaps we can look to the model John and Charles Wesley left of 'some to be evangelists' and find in their exercise of this New Testament gift both effective ministry and honour.

Following Aldersgate and his visit to the Moravians at Herrnhut in Germany, Wesley, back in England on Sunday, 27 September 1738, 'began again to declare in my own country the glad tidings of salvation. . . .' This announcement stretches across his life like a canopy and illuminates Wesley the evangelist: how he understood 'the glad tidings of salvation'; how he sought to deliver this burning message; and what changes occurred as a result, or, as Wesley exclaimed, 'What hath God wrought!'

(i) The glad tidings of salvation

John Wesley sought to bring the offer of free salvation to all persons. He declared:

> If any doctrines within the whole compass of Christianity may be properly termed fundamental they are doubtless these two – the doctrine of justification, and that of the new birth: the former relating to that great work which God does *for us*, in forgiving our sins; the latter to the great work which God does *in us*, in renewing our fallen nature.[12]

A stirring of the Spirit in the London religious societies he knew, and an Awakening across the Atlantic in New England of which he had read in the writings of Jonathan Edwards, moved him 'more narrowly to inquire what the doctrine of the Church of England is concerning the much controverted point of justification by faith'. He concluded, 'Now all I teach respects either the nature and condition of *justification*, the nature and condition of *salvation*, the nature of justifying and saving *faith*, or the *Author* of faith and salvation.'[13] These three words, *all I teach*, accurately describe the heart of Wesley's sermons, appeals, and letters.

The change God brings in the human heart and what flows from that change became the focus of his search and the basis for his vocation. He wrote

> By those words, 'we are saved by faith', we mean that the moment (one) receives that faith which is above described he is saved from doubt and fear, and sorrow of heart, by a peace that passes all understanding; from the heaviness of a wounded spirit, by joy unspeakable; and from his sins, of whatsoever kind

they were, from his vicious desires, as well as words and actions, by the love of God and of all mankind then shed abroad in his heart.[14]

His evangelical premises are beautifully and powerfully expressed in this highly personal plea.

> The faith I want is 'a sure trust and confidence in God, that, through the merits of Christ, my sins are forgiven and I reconciled to the favour of God'. I want that faith which St Paul recommends to all the world, especially in his Epistle to the Romans, that faith which enables every one that hath it to cry out: 'I live not; but Christ liveth in me; and the life which I now live, I live by faith in the Son of God, who loved me and gave himself for me' (Gal. 2.20). I want that faith which none can have without knowing that he hath it (though many *imagine* they have it, who have it not), for whosoever hath it, is 'freed from sin, the whole body of sin is destroyed' (Rom. 6.6,7) in him; he is freed from fear, 'having peace with God through Christ and rejoicing in hope of the glory of God' (Rom. 5.1, 2). And he is freed from doubt, 'having the love of God shed abroad in his heart through the Holy Ghost which is given unto him' (Rom. 5.5), which 'Spirit itself beareth witness with his spirit that he is a child of God' (Rom. 8.16).[15]

Wesley the evangelist was seeking nothing less than the establishment of 'real religion' in the church: 'a restoration of man, by him that bruises the serpent's head . . . a restoration not only to the favour, but likewise to the image of God; implying not barely deliverance from sin but the being filled with the fullness of God'.[16]

He confidently believed this restoration would result in 'a religion of love and joy and peace, having its seat in the heart, in the inmost soul, but ever showing itself by its fruits, continually springing forth not only in all innocence – for "love worketh no ill to his neighbour" – but likewise in every kind of beneficence, in spreading virtue and happiness all around it'.[17] The Gospel was both a powerful vortex drawing persons toward God and a centrifugal, impelling force thrusting redeemed people into the world about them. It was religion *seated in the individual heart* with *its benefits ever flowing to all around it.*

Only God, as Creator, could bring about that kind of *new* creation for the new creation was the gift of God. 'It is a work of omnipotence. It requires no less power thus to quicken a dead soul than to raise a body that lies in the grave. None can create a soul anew but he who at first created the heavens and the earth.' Wesley believed these words in his bones. On the basis of his intellectual grasp of the Scripture and his own experience that God 'had taken away *my* sins, even *mine*, and saved *me* from the law of sin and death', he convinced others it could happen to them, too.[18] Thus the end of life for which we are all created was 'to know God, to love him, to do his will, to enjoy him for ever and ever!'[19] He was sure of the way to begin, 'We preach *inward salvation, now attainable by faith.*'[20] It was for preaching this direct, personal and immediate offer of grace 'that we were forbid to preach any more in any of those churches where, till then, we were gladly received!' These are telling words – *inward, salvation, now, attainable by faith*. They reveal the cutting edge of the Gospel Wesley announced, the 'Glad tidings of salvation' he preached to all who would listen.

(ii) Delivering the glad tidings

In eighteenth century England one was born and baptized into a specific parish of the Church of England. Shifts in population, however, caused the system to break down. The mining areas of Cornwall were among the most populous areas of England, with St Just nearly as large as Manchester and St Ives larger than Liverpool. New industries, like magnets, had drawn into their field of force new concentrations of people. In Cornwall many of those drawn to the west had no ties to a parish and no relationship to a church. Families in need of the Christian Gospel were lost to the faith because they were not found where the established church had determined they should be. Never before had the Cornish people so needed material and spiritual help, but never before had the clergy had so little to offer.[21]

Some new impetus was needed and this was provided by George Whitefield, a young contemporary of Wesley.

George Whitefield was a member of the 'Holy Club' at Oxford, having been introduced to the group by Charles Wesley. He later followed John and Charles Wesley across the Atlantic to Georgia.

He was ordained in Gloucester at the early age of twenty-one, having been converted three years before John and Charles Wesley. Though in London he was derided as a 'boy parson', his early preaching attracted wide notice in England. The trumpet was sounded in crowded London parks and in the fields of Bristol by George Whitefield and the troops began to gather. John and Charles were across the Atlantic at the time many people in London and Bristol, England's premier cities, were beginning to hang on to the Gospel preaching of young Whitefield and to think of him as the original methodist! According to Gordon Rupp, Whitefield was the morning star of the Evangelical revival. 'He was the one great evangelist to share in the Revival as it embraced America, Wales, Scotland, and England.'[22]

This history has been eclipsed in part because Whitefield was eleven years younger than Wesley and died at the early age of fifty-five. John Wesley, active virtually to the end of his eighty-eight years, outlived him by twenty-one years.

When the Wesleys returned to London and found the churches closed to them, John was pragmatic and believed that when one door was closed, God would open another. Whitefield was instrumental in nudging him through a new door, a door that led him to the irregular and strange practice of preaching in the out of doors, first in Bristol. He also accompanied Whitefield to join the action in London.

> Thursday, 14, 1739 – I went with Mr Whitefield to Blackheath, where were, I believe, twelve or fourteen thousand people. He a little surprised me by desiring me to preach in his stead, which I did (though nature recoiled), on my favourite subject, 'Jesus Christ, who of God is made unto us wisdom, righteousness, sanctification, and redemption.' I was greatly moved with compassion for the rich that were there, to whom I made a particular application. Some of them seemed to attend, while others drove away their coaches from so uncouth a preacher.[23]

As Whitefield recorded it:

> June 14, Thursday – Spent the whole day in my pleasant and profitable retreat at Blendon; and in the evening had the pleasure of introducing my honoured and reverend friend, Mr John Wesley, to preach at Blackheath. The Lord gave him ten

thousand times more success than He has given me! After sermon, we spent the evening most agreeably together with many Christian friends at the Green Man. About ten we admitted all to come in that would; the room was soon filled – God gave me utterance. I exhorted and prayed for nearly an hour, and then went to bed, rejoicing that another fresh inroad was made into Satan's territories by Mr. Wesley's following me in field-preaching as well in London as in Bristol.[24]

Kennington Common and Moorfields in London were the great outdoor theatres where Whitefield and the Wesleys fearlessly proclaimed the message God had given them to crude and hostile audiences.

John wrote:

Sunday, 9 – I declared to about ten thousand in Moorfields, what they must do to be saved. My mother went with us, about five, to Kennington, where were supposed to be twenty thousand people. I again insisted on that foundation of all our hope, 'Believe in the Lord Jesus, and thou shalt be saved.' From Kennington I went to a society at Lambeth. The house being filled, the rest stood in the garden. The deep attention they showed gave me a good hope that they will not all be forgetful hearers.[25]

Sunday, 16 – I preached at Moorfields to about ten thousand, and at Kennington Common to, I believe, nearly twenty thousand, on those words of the calmer Jews to St. Paul, 'We desire to hear of thee what thou thinkest; for as concerning this sect, we know that everywhere it is spoken against'. At both places I described (in very plain terms) the real difference between what is generally called Christianity, and the true old Christianity, which, under the new name of Methodism, is now also everywhere spoken against.[26]

Sunday, 23 – I declared to about ten thousand, in Moorfields, with great enlargement of spirit, 'The Kingdom of God is not meat and drink; but righteousness, and peace, and joy in the Holy Ghost' (Rom. 14.17]. At Kennington I enforced to about twenty thousand that great truth, 'One thing is needful.' Thence I went to Lambeth and showed (to the amazement, it seemed, of many who were present) how 'he that is born of God doth not commit sin' [I John 3.9].[27]

Rounds of field preaching like these were the heart and soul of the Methodist awakening.

Dr George Hunter suggests the first objective in Wesley's field preaching was the starting of small classes in which those attending experienced saving grace and disciplined growth. Wesley's practice in open-air preaching was: 1. to awaken people; 2. to enrol awakened people in a class; 3. to teach those awakened to experience their justification; and 4. to teach justified people to expect an experience of sanctification in this life.[28] While Wesley was convinced new believers must be formed into disciplined societies so that the gains would not be lost, I believe his open-air preaching was also meant to call people to experience salvation 'by grace through faith' *then and there*.

Wesley's *Journal* entries include texts of his sermons and describe the call Wesley gave for people to respond to the saving message. In his manner of appeal Wesley resembled at times a retired minister I used to hear at the Presbyterian church in the place where I attended college. Unlike the stereotypical present-day evangelist, this popular and provocative preacher rarely asked persons to 'come forward' at the end of the service, but he *always* gave an invitation! You *knew* you were being challenged to respond! Wesley's urgent preaching touched human need and opened people to see their need for support in fellowship with other believers. Without the preaching of a message that in itself *called for response*, however, the classes would never have got off the ground.

The spoken word driven home by the Holy Spirit unlocked human hearts.

> An hundred gathered themselves together, who I earnestly called 'to repent and believe. . . .' I cried out, with all the authority of love, 'Why will ye die, O house of Israel?' My heart was filled with love, my eyes with tears, and my mouth with arguments. They were amazed, they were ashamed, they were melted down, they devoured every word. . . . I cried aloud, 'All things are ready; come unto the marriage.' I preached 'God hath given us eternal life; and this life is in his Son.' I believe God applied it to many hearts.

Wesley aimed to offer Christ, to announce salvation through Christ as good news for every person and to invite persons to respond to a loving God with their whole beings. Because Wesley and his preachers left no grounds for neutrality, the sheer force of the Gospel message they brought, in contrast to much of that being then offered in the churches, led to opposition and meant life for the early Methodists was anything but easy.

Dr Frank Baker paints a stark picture that present-day Methodists may have trouble grasping. 'In 1740 William Seward was first blinded, and then killed, by a Welsh mob, the first, but not the last, Methodist martyr. Many of the preachers were pelted, beaten, stamped on, kicked, stripped, thrown into ponds, dragged along the ground by the hair, drenched with water from fire hoses, gored by bulls, tarred and feathered.'[29] John's advice was 'Always look a mob in the face,' and he did! 'He cut the cloth of his meeting to cover the situation which confronted him; the length and order were adapted to the mood he found when he arrived.'[30]

On 5 June 1739 in Bath, Wesley met the notorious Beau Nash in a famous encounter. Nash was pretentious, usually travelling from Bath to Tunbridge in a post chariot drawn by six grey horses, with outriggers, footmen, French horns and every other appendage of expensive parade. He always wore a white hat. He was the king of Bath and Bath was the most fashionable watering-place in England. Everyone sought to make a grand appearance in the Pump Room where Beau Nash held forth. One poetically described the atmosphere: 'Anointed with oil, crowned with rose-buds, and decked with purple and fine linen, they sport away their days, chanting to the sound of the viol, drinking wine in bowls, and stretching themselves on couches of ivory!' Nash was the king of revels.

There was great expectation at Bath of what a noted man was to do to me there; and I was much entreated not to preach, because no one knew what might happen. By this report I also gained a much larger audience, among whom were many of the rich and the great. I told them plainly, the Scripture had concluded them all under sin – high and low, rich and poor, one with another. Many of them seemed to be a little surprised, and were sinking apace into seriousness, when their champion appeared, and, coming close to me, asked by what authority I did these things. I replied, 'By authority of Jesus Christ, conveyed to me by the (now) Archbishop of Canterbury, when he laid hands upon me, and said, "Take thou authority to preach the Gospel."' He said, 'This is contrary to Act of Parliament: this is a coventicle.' I answered, 'Sir, the coventicles mentioned in that Act . . . are seditious meetings; but this is not such; here is no shadow of sedition; therefore it is not contrary to that Act.' He replied, 'I say it is; and, beside, your preaching frightens people out of their wits.'

'Sir, did you ever hear me preach?' 'No.' 'How then can you judge of what you never heard?' 'Sir, by common report.' 'Common report is not enough. Give me leave, Sir, to ask, Is not your name Nash?' 'My name is Nash.' 'Sir, I dare not judge of you by common report: I think it is not enough to judge by.' Here he paused awhile, and, having recovered himself, said, 'I desire to know what this people comes here for': on which one replied, 'Sir, leave him to me; let an old woman answer him. You, Mr Nash, take care of your body; we take care of our souls: and for the food of our souls we come here.' He replied not a word, but walked away.[31]

At times religious leaders hurled ludicrous charges. One incident reported in *The Methodist Magazine* occurred in Redruth when Methodists were summoned before a magistrate and events took a humorous turn.

Soon after the Methodist society was formed in Redruth the minister of the parish, who was also a magistrate, desired to root out the sect. He sent his agents to their meetings to take down names. He then appointed a day on which the offenders were to appear before him, that he might take out a Mittimus and send them all to jail. His court was a club-room over the public-house kitchen at the church-town. The Methodists, on appearing, were accompanied by a mixed multitude – some sympathizers, and others rejoicing that now the 'Canorums', as they called them (the Methodists), would be put down. The reverend magistrate took the chair, with pen and ink before him. The room was filled, and all things ready for entering on business, when the floor suddenly gave way and sunk down into the kitchen beneath them. No lives were lost, no bones broken, but much noise and dust ensued. As the gentleman was descending he cried out to one of his friends, 'Joe, where are we going?' 'I don't know,' says Joe. 'Nor I neither,' says his Worship. But though his journey was short, it proved a little disastrous, for he lost his hat and wig by the way, and the contents of the inkbottle, happening to fall on his head, ran down over his face. After a while he got up, and, having recovered his hat and wig, and cleaned his face as well as he could, the Methodists collected around him to know his further pleasure, when he prudently replied, 'Go home, go home; sufficient unto the day is the evil thereof.'[32]

Wesley is not simply an eighteenth-century personality who belonged to a distant religious scene. The movement he led continues right down to the present and has an important place in recent Christian history. The evidence of what happened *then* is seen in what exists *now*.

What hath God wrought!

Toward the end of his life, in the summer of 1787, Wesley preached a sermon, 'The Signs of the Times', from Jesus' words in Matthew 16.3: 'Ye can discern the face of the sky; but can ye not discern the sign of the times?' He was astonished by indifference among the leaders of the Church of England to the Methodist revival and its renewing, refreshing influence. He quoted from a pastoral letter from the Bishop of London, written some years before: 'I cannot imagine what persons mean by talking of "a great work of God" at this time. I do not see any work of God now, more than has been at any other time.'[33]

Wesley rejoined:

At this day the gospel leaven – faith working by love, inward and outward holiness, or (to use the terms of St Paul) 'righteousness, and peace, and joy in the Holy Ghost' – hath so spread in various parts of Europe, particularly in England, Scotland, Ireland, in the islands, in the north and south, from Georgia to New England and Newfoundland, that sinners have been truly converted to God, thoroughly changed both in heart and in life; not by tens, or by hundreds only, but by thousands, yea, by myriads! The fact cannot be denied: we can point out the persons, with their names and places of abode.[34]

Continuing his assessment:

After a candid inquiry into matter of fact, consider deeply, 'What hath God wrought?' Who hath seen such a thing? Who hath heard such a thing? Hath not a nation, as it were, been 'born in a day?' How swift, as well as how deep, and how extensive a work has been wrought in the present age! And certainly 'not by might, neither by power, but by the Spirit of the Lord'. For how utterly inadequate were the means! How insufficient were the instruments to work any such effect![35]

John Wesley knew the West Country well, having visited Cornwall on thirty different occasions. He had seen miners and their families changed by the power of Christ. George Borlase wrote in 1753 of great atrocities being committed along Cornwall's rugged coasts that were shocking even for that day. 'The people who make it their business to attend these (ship) wrecks are generally tynners, and, as soon as they observe a ship on the coast, they first arm themselves with sharp axes and hatchetts, and leave the tynn works to follow those ships . . . They'll cut a large trading vessell to pieces in one tide, and cut down everybody that offers to oppose them.' The story of one shipwreck in which nearly two thousand men died is legendary. The commander, Sir Cloudesley Shovel, was cast up alive on Porth Hellick beach, only to be murdered by a woman for the sake of an emerald ring![36]

Wesley asked on one of his later visits if 'that scandal of Cornwall, the plundering of wrecked vessels, still subsisted' and was told by the old vicar of Cubert, 'As much as ever; only the Methodists will have nothing to do with it.'[37] The sheer increase in the *number* of Methodists in the region had become a powerful leavening influence.

Redruth, once considered to be one of the roughest, became one of the most civilized towns in all of England. The nearby plain at Gwennap, covered from end to end with nearly ten thousand miners when it was so dark they could hardly see one another, was an awesome sight, Wesley wrote. 'There was on all sides the deepest attention; none speaking, stirring, or scarce looking aside. Surely here, though in a temple not made with hands, was God worshipped in 'the beauty of holiness'.' The next morning he was 'waked between three and four, by a large company of "tinners", who fearing they should be too late, had gathered round the house, and were singing and praising God. At five I preached once more on "Believe on the Lord Jesus Christ, and thou shalt be saved." They all devoured the word.'[38] This was one of the seventeen times he preached at the famous Gwennap Pit. The Methodist chapels scattered throughout the then populous mining region are his footprints.

Wesley left two of the most important Methodist societies in England at St Ives and Redruth in Cornwall and 'an organization and apostles who were to spread his simple docine of fearing God and working righteousness throughout the country. He had brought hope to hopeless thousands, and thanks largely to him the Cornwall of 1790 was a far less barbarous place than it had been in 1740. Drunkenness had declined and, though smuggling had never been so prosperous, the inhumanities of wrecking had been checked.'[39]

In the north Midlands, potteries developed in Burslem, and new towns prospered, drawing in people from every side. Wesley wrote in 1781 of the Methodist witness: 'The word of God has had free course among them. Sinners are daily awakened and converted to God, and believers grow in the knowledge of Christ.' When the Prime Minister of England, William Gladstone, laid the foundation stone of the Wedgwood Institute at Burslem a little less than a century later he quoted from Wesley's *Journal* to illustrate how harsh conditions had been softened because of the Wesleyan revival.[40] Artisans and potters came into the Christian faith in large numbers. Many used their skills to create commemorative figures, plates with picture transfers, and pottery busts of John Wesley, which found their way into Methodist homes and chapels across Britain, and indeed are scattered today throughout the world. These popular folk-art pieces attest to the impact of Wesley as spiritual father of the awakening. Such veneration was usually reserved for members of the royal family, prime ministers, or heroes of battle. Enoch Wood, a gifted potter, sculpted the most correct pottery portrait of John Wesley at age eighty. The first edition Enoch Wood bust is extremely rare and valuable. Lesser quality commemorative pieces were cast by the tens of thousands.

For half a century John Wesley single-mindedly pressed on, determined to keep to the course. The sermons he prepared were not to be once preached, once heard, and then forgotten! He refused the advice of the minister who said, 'Once in seven years I burn all my sermons; for it is a shame if I cannot write better sermons now than I could seven years ago.' The urgency underlying Wesley's preaching was that people should experience saving grace, then live to bring glory to God, had little to do with the artful use of words, the turning of a phrase, or polite literature.

> Whatever others can do, I really cannot. I cannot write a better sermon on the Good Steward than I did seven years ago; I cannot write a better on the Great Assize, than I did twenty years ago; I cannot write a better on the Use of Money than I did thirty years ago; nay, I know not that I can write a better on the Circumcision of the Heart than I did five-and-forty years ago. Perhaps, indeed, I may have read five or six hundred books more than I had then, and may know a little more history, or natural philosophy, than I did; but I am not sensible that this has made any essential addition to my knowledge in divinity. Forty years ago I knew and preached every Christian doctrine which I preach now.[41]

His preaching was a consistent hammering home of four 'alls' (*all* need to be saved; *all* can be saved; *all* can know they are saved; and *all* can be saved to the uttermost). Even so, he was ever an avid learner, intensely observing and faithfully recording what he saw. He was *not* enamoured by novelty nor a devotee of the notion that because something is new, it is true.

In all that transpired between John Wesley's reluctant visit to the society in Aldersgate Street where he felt his heart 'strangely warmed' and the time of his death in his City Road house fifty-three years later, he was an evangelist. No other objective he pursued came close to his passion to see a rebirth of vital religion. He was convinced the message of unmerited grace offered a different life to people and that new Christians drawn together in small disciplined classes could bring change in the nation.

There was one clear and undeniable fact for Wesley:

A few years ago Great Britain and Ireland were covered with

vice from sea to sea. Very little of even the form of religion was left; and still less of the power of it . . . God commanded light to shine. In a short space he called thousands of sinners to repentance. They were not only reformed from their outward vices, but likewise changed in their dispositions and tempers; filled with 'A serious, sober sense of true religion', with love to God and all mankind, with an holy faith producing good works of every kind, works both of piety and mercy.[42]

Dr Rupp writes,

That the whole manner of existence of individuals and the character of local communities were changed is beyond dispute. Without exaggeration of the number of converted boozers, men and women were turned from disordered characters into sober, decent people into whose homes there came new stabilities and joys.[43]

In less than two and a half centuries, a movement developed into a dynamic and vital church now found in ninety nations, with a worldwide membership exceeding twenty-five million people.[44]

The relationship between John Wesley and Methodist people is without parallel in any other Christian world communion. Lutherans and Calvinists do not think of leaders, Martin Luther and John Calvin, in the same way. John Wesley provided the Methodists with spiritual direction, theological guidance and a discipline and order for their churches. But more, he gave Methodist people a vision of what God was doing in human history. What he sought in the renewal and restoration of vital religion in England he earnestly longed to see realized in the wider Church and in the whole family of God.

He was utterly convinced all persons were spiritually dead until they received the gospel of salvation; that salvation was for all people and for all the world; and that all might experience the unfathomable love and reconciling power of God. Only the Spirit of God could raise the dead to life. Those embued with new life could collectively be used of God to unleash a mighty moral transformation. Though Methodists dare not take credit for the whole impact of the Evangelical revival, they did their part, scattering evangelists everywhere who invited men and women to receive God's pardoning grace. Lives *were* changed, and as a byproduct *of evangelism*, people were lifted and society was made more humane. Seeing it happen, Wesley could only exclaim, 'What hath God wrought!'

Notes

Introduction   *Frank Baker*

1. Mary Pendarves to Ann Granville, 4 April 1730: 'I honour *Primitive Christianity*, and desire you will let him know as much' (Wesley, *Letters*, Oxford edition, 25:256 n.2).

2. Ibid., 25:336 and n.4; cf. p.341.

3. Wesley, *Journal*, Bicentennial edition, 18:132.

4. See *Methodist History*, Vol. 8.2, January 1970, pp.25–32, 'The Birth of John Wesley's *Journal*.

5. Wesley, *Letters*, 25:8.

6. Richard Watson, *The Life of the Rev. John Wesley*, Mason, London 1835, pp.203–4.

7. Letter to Dorothy Furly, 25 September 1757.

8. 27 January 1767.

9. Wesley's power was first questioned in the London Conference of 1763, first expounded fully in its historical setting in his annual *Minutes* of 1766, and thence transcribed into the 'Large' *Minutes* of 1770.

10. Letter to Lady Frances Gardiner, 2 November 1763.

11. Cf. his stiff reply to the recalcitrant trustees at Dewsbury, 30 July 1788.

12. Letter to Miss March, 30 May 1776.

13. Letter to 'John Smith', 25 March 1747, *Letters* 26:229–30; cf. pp.197, 210.

14. Letter to Charles, 27 June 1766. He used a form of Paul's Greek word in Acts 27.15, 17, for a ship driven before the wind.

15. *Letters*, 25:9–10.

16. Letter to Ebenezer Blackwell, 31 August 1755.

17. *Methodist History*, Vol. 12, July 1974, pp.193–4.

18. *London Quarterly Review*, Vol. 179, January 1954, pp.290–9.

19. Letter to Charles Wesley, 13 January 1774. 'Philosophy', of course, implied *natural* philosophy, or science, and he was referring to his own *A Survey of the Wisdom of God in the Creation: or, a Compendium of Natural Philosophy*, third edition, enlarged, five vols., 1777.

20. See especially Vol. II, pp.163–88.

21. Ibid., II, 189–212.

2. Wesley and the Moravians   *W. P. Stephens*

1. The Moravians were renewed in the 1720s at Herrnhut under the leadership of Count von Zinzendorf. They worked within the Lutheran

Church in Saxony, while having their own churchly life and episcopal order of ministry. They were outstanding for the emphasis they gave to overseas missionary work, and Wesley's first contacts were with Moravian missionaries. Their origins go back to the Bohemian Brethren in the fifteenth century.

2. Texts referred to in this article are as follows: *The Works of John Wesley*, edited by Thomas Jackson, 14 volumes, London 1831; *The Journal of John Wesley*, Standard Edition, edited by Nehemiah Curnock, 8 volumes, London 1909–16; *The Letters of John Wesley*, edited by John Telford, 8 volumes, London 1931.

3. Towlson sees signs of separation before the impact of Molther and regards him as the occasion rather than the cause of separation. See C. W. Towlson *Moravian and Methodist*, London 1957, pp.88, 117.

4. There were other issues – such as universal salvation (*Journal* II, 498), a collection of Moravian hymns described as 'that amazing compound of nonsense and blasphemy' (*Journal* III, 389), and their exalted view of their own church (*Letters* I, 349).

5. *A History of the Methodist Church in Great Britain*, Volume 1, edited by Rupert Davies and Gordon Rupp, Epworth Press 1965, p.xxxv.

6. John Wesley: Sacramental Theology. No Ends without the Means
Ole E. Borgen

1. For a more exhaustive study see Ole E. Borgen, *John Wesley on the Sacraments. A Theological Study*, Grand Rapids: Francis Asbury Press 1986 (reprint hereafter cited as Borgen). For the sacramental practice of the Wesleys see John C. Bowmer, *The Sacrament of the Lord's Supper in Early Methodism*, London: Dacre Press 1951.

2. Borgen, pp.46–7. Cf. also pp.36–44.

3. *The Works of John Wesley*, 14 vols, ed. Thomas Jackson, reprinted Grand Rapids, Zondervan 1958–1959 (hereafter cited as *Works*), Vol. VI, pp.417, 423; *Wesley's Standard Sermons*, 2 vols, ed. E. H. Sugden, London: Epworth Press 1961 (hereafter cited as *StS*), Vol. II, p.132, cf. Vol. I, pp.44–5, 304; Borgen, p.172.

4. *Works* VI, p.413.

5. John Wesley, *Explanatory Notes upon the Old Testament*. 3 vols., Bristol, printed by William Pine, 1765 (hereafter cited as *OT Notes*), I Chron. 21.26; Lev. 25.25; Num. 15.2; 19.2.

6. John Wesley, *Explanatory Notes upon the New Testament*, London: Epworth Press, 1954 (hereafter cited as *NT Notes*), Rom. 9.25; 1 Thess. 1.10; Heb. 2.10; 13.20.

7. Borgen, pp.44–6.

8. *Works*, VIII, p.49.

9. *StS*, I, p.259, cf. p.243.

10. *The Letters of the Rev. John Wesley, A.M.*, ed. John Telford, 8 vols, London: Epworth Press 1931 (*hereafter cited as Letters*), Vol. II, p.46, italics mine; cf. *Works* VI, p.369; VIII, p.107; Borgen, pp.82–5.

11. *StS*, I, p.242; cf. II, pp.237–8. The full text of the *Catechism* reads: '. . . an outward and visible sign of an inward and spiritual grace, given unto us, ordained by Christ himself, as a means whereby we receive the same. . . .'; Borgen, pp.49–50 n.1.

12. John Wesley, *The Sunday Service of the Methodists in North America*, London; Strahan 1784 (hereafter cited, as *Sund. Service*), pp.311–12.

13. John Wesley, *The Duty of Receiving The Lord's Supper*. Unpublished holograph, dated 1731/2, transcribed by Ole E. Borgen, 1966 (hereafter cited as *Duty of Receiving*), p.10.

14. John and Charles Wesley, *Hymns on the Lord's Supper*. With a Preface concerning The Christian Sacrament and Sacrifice. Extracted from Doctor [Daniel] Brevint, first edition, Bristol: Printed by Felix Farley, 1745, sec., III. 2, p.9. The preface is hereafter cited as Brevint (W).

15. Brevint (W), sec. III. 2–3, pp.9–10; *Works* VII, p.148.

16. *StS* II, pp.237–8.

17. *Duty of Receiving*, p.11.

18. John and Charles Wesley, *Hymns on the Lord's Supper* (see n.14 above, hereafter cited as *HLS*), hymn no. 162:1.

19. *Works* VI, pp.73–4; *Letters* IV, p.38.

20. Augustine, *First Catechetical Instruction. Ancient Christian Writers*, 34 vols., ed. J. Quasten and W. Burghardt, Westminster, Maryland: The Newman Press 1960, II, p.82.

21. Cf. *Works* X, p.192, '. . . inward grace, which added thereto, makes it a sacrament'.

22. *Sund. Service*, p.312. Wesley speaks of '. . . the senseless opinion of transubstantiation'. It is 'hurtful to piety' and goes against Scripture, sense and reason, *Works* VII, p.64; IX, p.278; X, p.151.

23. *Letters* I, p.118; *NT Notes*, John 3.13.

24. *Duty of Receiving*, p.8; *HLS*, no. 30:5; Borgen pp.58–69.

25. *StS* I, p.440; *Duty of Receiving*, p.1; *HLS*, no. 42:2–4.

26. *Works*, X, p.150; cf. p.114. Borgen, pp.69–81.

27. Brevint (W), sec. II. 1, p.4.

28. Brevint (W), sec. II. 7, p.6.

29. Brevint (W), sec. II. 5, and 9, pp.6–7.

30. Brevint (W), sec. II. 9, p.7, cf. sec. III. 2, pp.9–10.

31. Brevint (W), sec. II. 3, p.5.

32. Brevint (W), sec. II. 6, p.6.

33. Brevint (W), sec. II. 7, p.6; *HLS*, no. 94:2.

34. *HLS*, 22:1, 3; cf. nos. 25:2; 123:3.

35. *HLS*, no. 23:1–2.

36. Brevint (W), sec. II, 7, p.6.

37. John Wesley, *Sermons on Several Occasions*. Vols. I–VIII 1754–1788 (hereafter cited *Serm. on Sev. Occ*); I, p.229.

38. Article XIII, *Sund. Service*, p.310.

39. *Letters* III, pp.366–7 (italics mine).

40. *Serm. on Sev. Occ.* I, p.248.
41. *Serm. on Sev. Occ.*, I, pp.230; 249–50, cf. *Works* VIII, pp.18, 20, 62; X, p.135; XI, p.283; *St S* I, p.467.
42. *StS*, I, pp.97, 254; *Letters* III, p.322; VI, p.117.
43. *NT Notes*, I Tim. 4. 13; *Works* VIII, p.316.
44. *The Poetical Works of John and Charles Wesley*, 13 vols, London: Wesleyan-Methodist Conference Office, 1868–1872 (hereafter cited as *Poet. Works*), I, pp.233ff.; IV, pp.451 ff.
45. *Letters* I, p.86; *St S* I, pp.243, 344, 528; II, p.33.
46. *Works* VIII, pp.286, 323.
47. *The Journal of the Rev. John Wesley, A.M.*, 8 vols, ed. Nehemiah Curnoch, New York: Eaton & Mains 1909 (hereafter cited *Journal*, Curn.) I, p.330; cf. *StS*, II, pp.144, 292; *Works* VI, pp.510–11, etc.
48. *StS* I, pp.246, 248; *Works* XI, p.437; *NT Notes*, 1 Thess. 5.16–17.
49. *NT Notes*, Eph. 6.18.
50. *StS* I, pp.430–1; *NT Notes*, Matt. 6.8.
51. *NT Notes*, Eph. 6.18; II Tim. 4.5; I Peter 4.7.
52. *StS* I, p.458.
53. *NT Notes*, Matt. 4.2; *OT Notes*, Isa. 58.5, *Works* VIII, p.364.
54. *NT Notes*, Eph. 4.29; Heb. 10.22.
55. *NT Notes*, Heb. 10.25; Acts 5.11; *StS* I, p.395 (italics mine).
56. *StS*, I, p.248.
57. *Letters* III, p.79.
58. *Journal*, Curn. II, p.361.
59. *HLS*, no. 42.4–5.
60. *Works* X, p.192 (italics mine).
61. *Works* X, p.193.
62. *Works* VI, pp.66, 67, 68 (italics mine).
63. *Works* VI, p.240; X, p.190; *Poet. Works* III, pp.15, 33.
64. *Works* VIII, pp.227–8.
65. *Works* X, p.193 (italics are mine).
66. *Works* X, p.198; *Letters* III, p.36.
67. *Works* X, p.192 (italics mine).
68. *Works* VI, p.509.
69. *Works* X, p.191.
70. *Ibid.*
71. Article XVII, 'Of Baptism', *Sund. Serv.* p.312.
72. *Works* X, p.193.
73. *Ibid.*
74. *Works* X, p.195; *NT Notes*, Acts 16.15; I John 5.7; *Works* VIII, p.73.
75. *NT Notes*, Acts 16.15; cf. *Works* X, pp.196–7, 198.
76. *Works* X, pp.197–8.
77. *Works* X, pp.196–7, 199.
78. *Works* X, p.191 (italics mine).
79. *NT Notes*, Acts 22.16; *Works* VIII, pp.48, 52 (italics mine).

80. *NT Notes*, Acts 10.47; Mark 16.16; Heb. 6.1.
81. See Borgen, pp.161ff., and nn. 171, 177.
82. *StS*, I, p.194; II, p.435; *Letters* II, p.196.
83. *Works* XIII, p.476; VII, pp.77, 79, 83, 97; *StS*, p.240.
84. *HLS*, no. 92:6; cf. no. 101:2.
85. Brevint (W), sec. I, 1, p.3.
86. Brevint (W), sec. IV, 7, p.16.
87. Brevint (W), sec. III, 5, p.11.
88. *StS* I, p.253; cf. pp.242–3, 344, 528.
89. *Journal*, Curn. II, p.361.
90. *Works* VI, p.509.
91. *Journal*, Curn. III, pp.31–2.
92. *Letters* VI, p.124.
93. *StS* II, p.240; cf. Works VI, p.509.
94. *Letters* IV, p.272.
95. *NT Notes* I Cor. 10.17; *HLS*, no. 165.
96. Brevint (W), sec. V, 4, 6, pp.18–19.
97. Brevint (W), sec. II. 1, p.4.
98. *StS* I, pp.267, 295–6, 300.
99. Brevint (W), sec. V. 1, p.17.
100. *HLS* nos. 88:4; 96.3
101. *Works* VI, pp.44, 227, 230.
102. Brevint (W), sec. I. 1, pp.3–4.
103. Brevint (W), sec. VI. 2, p.21.
104. Brevint (W), sec. VI. 1, p.22. *HLS*, nos. 35.1; 67.1; Brevint (W), secs. I:1, pp.3–4: IV.8, p.16.
105. *OT Notes*, *I* Chron. 29.14.
106. *Works* VI, p.414.
107. *OT Notes*, Exod. 27.4; 29.36. Brevint (W), sec. VII.8, p.26.
108. *A Word of Advice to Saints and Sinners*, Eleventh Edition, London 1790, p.11.
109. Brevint (W), sec. VIII. 6, p.32.

7. Wesley's Legacy in Worship   *C. Norman R. Wallwork*

1. Albert C. Outler, *Evangelism in the Wesleyan Spirit*, Tidings 1971, p.55.
2. Methodist Conference, *Minutes 1786*, 1812 edition, Vol. I, p.191.
3. *The Letters of John Wesley, A.M.*, ed. John Telford, Epworth Press 1931, Vol. VII, p.239.
4. David Tripp, *The Renewal of the Covenant in the Methodist Tradition*, Epworth Press 1969, p.177.
5. John and Charles Wesley, *Short Hymns on Selected Passages of Scripture*, 1762.
6. *The Journal of John Wesley, A.M.*, ed. Jeremiah Curnock, Charles J. Kelly 1909, Vol. I, p.377.
7. Ibid., Vol. II, 1911, p.121.

8. *The Works of the Revd John Wesley, A.M.*, Wesleyan Book Room 1831, Vol. VIII, pp.258f.

9. Leslie F. Church, *More about the Early Methodist People*, Epworth Press 1949, pp.241f.

10. *Works*, Vol. VIII, pp.255–6.

11. *Letters*, Vol. 3, p.287.

12. *Works*, Vol. XIII, p.258.

13. *The Life of Mr Silas Told written by Himself* (1786), Epworth Press 1954, p.67.

14. Methodist Conference, *Minutes 1766*, 1862 edition, Vol. I, p.140.

15. James Redfearn, 'The Correspondence of Thomas Wride 1785–6', *Proceedings of the Wesley Historical Society*, 1898, Vol. 1.4, p.140.

16. W. F. Lofthouse, 'Charles Wesley', in *A History of the Methodist Church in Great Britain*. ed. Rupert Davies and E. G. Rupp, Vol. 1, Epworth Press 1968, p.125.

17. Cecil Northcott, *Hymns in Christian Worship*, Lutterworth Press 1964, p.26.

18. John Bishop, *Methodist Worship in Relation to Free Church Worship*, Scholars Press 1975, p.139.

19. Church, *More About the Early Methodist People*, pp.228–9.

20. Frank Baker, *Representative Verse of Charles Wesley*, Epworth Press 1962, p.xv.

9. John Wesley: The Organizer   *A. Raymond George*

1. See Frank Baker in Rupert Davies and Gordon Rupp (eds.), *A History of the Methodist Church in Great Britain* hereafter *HMGB*) I, Epworth Press 1965, 213–55.

2. See A. Raymond George on 'Ordination', in Rupert Davies, A. Raymond George, and Gordon Rupp (eds.) *HMGB* II, Epworth Press 1978, 143–60.

3. B. Gregory, *Side Lights on the Conflicts of Methodism 1827–1852*, London 1899, p.161.

4. John C. Bowmer, *Pastor and People*, Epworth Press 1975, pp.20–36.

5. Bernard E. Jones in *Proceedings of the Wesley Historical Society* XXXVI, 134–8; Henry D. Rack, *Proceedings of the Wesley Historical Society* XXXIX, 12–21; Henry D. Rack in Rupert Davies, A. Raymond George and Gordon Rupp (eds.), *HMGB* III, Epworth Press 1983. 156–62; John C. Bowmer, op. cit., pp.173–6.

6. Minutes of 1766.

7. *Towards a Statement on the Church*, Report of the Joint Commission between the Roman Catholic Church and World Methodist Council 1982–1986, Fourth Series, section 24.

10. John Wesley: Apostle of Social Holiness   *David Guy*

1. John Wesley, *Journal*, abridged edition, Salvation Army, Publishing Department 1905, p. 193.

2. G. M. Trevelyan, *English Social History*, Longmans[3] 1946, p.362.

3. Quoted in A. Lunn, *John Wesley*, Cassell 1929, p.139.

4. J. H. Plumb, *England in the Eighteenth Century*, Penguin Books 1969 (italics mine), p.95.

5. John Wesley, *Sermons on Several Occasions*, Epworth Press 1948, p.41.

6. Gill, *Selected Letters of John Wesley*, Epworth Press 1956, p.68.

7. John Wesley, *Sermons on Several Occasions*, Epworth Press 1948, p.546.

8. A. Briggs, *A Social History of England*, Penguin Books 1987, p.189.

9. Gill, *Letters*, p.100.

10. W. E. Sangster, *The Path to Perfection*, Epworth Press 1943 reissued 1984, p.174.

11. Lunn, *John Wesley*, p.345.

12. John Wesley, *Journal*, p.438.

13. A. J. Broomhall, *Barbarians at the Gates*, Hodder 1981, p.284.

14. David L. Edwards, *Christian England*, Vol. 3, Fount Paperbacks 1985, 65f.

15. Max Warren, *The Missionary Movement from Britain in Modern History*, SCM Press 1965, p.33.

16. L. Tyerman, *The Life and Times of John Wesley*, Vol. 3, Hodder 1890, p.44.

17. Quoted in C. Yuill, *Chosen to be a Soldier*, The Salvation Army 1980, p.18.

18. F. Booth-Tucker, *Life of Mrs Booth*, Vol. 1, The Salvation Army 1892, p.27.

19. Quoted by Max Warren, *Missionary Movement*.

20. Gill, *Selected Letters*, pp.80f.

21. Broomhall, *Barbarians*, p.355.

22. Quoted by D. Burke in *Creed and Deed. A Theology of Salvation Army Social Service*, Salvation Army: Canada 1986, p.27.

23. Edwards, *Christian England*, Vol. 3, p.66.

24. John Kent, *The Age of Disunity*, Epworth Press 1966, p.145.

25. F. Coutts, *Bread for My Neighbour*, Hodder 1978, p.67.

26. D. Burke, *Creed and Deed*, p.210.

12. Health and Healing in the Ministry of John Wesley   *Morris Maddocks*

1. *The Journal of John Wesley*, abridged by Christopher Idle, Lion Paperback 1986, entries from 21 May to 17 June 1738.

2. *Journal*, 25 May 1738.

3. *Journal*, 26 September 1749.

4. *Journal*, 4 December 1746.

5. See the *Journal* entry for 13 March 1743.

6. He had already shown interest as early as 1747, when he went with some friends 'to see what are called electrical experiments', *Journal*, 16 October 1747.

7. *Journal*, 9 November 1756.

8. *Journal*, 18/26 December 1765.

9. *Journal*, 27 June 1786.
10. *Journal*, entries for 28 June, his birthday, 1774 and 1788.
11. *Journal*, 11 August 1776.
12. *Journal*, 15 November 1786.
13. See *Journal*, 4 December 1746, quoted on p.140.
14. Proverbs 22.6.
15. A. G. Ives, *Kingswood School*, Epworth Press 1970, pp.54f.
16. Ibid., p.9.
17. *Journal*, 7 July 1739.
18. *Journal*, 5 August 1759.
19. *Journal*, 16 August 1759.

13 John Wesley and Death   *Wesley A. Chambers*

1. G. M. Trevelyan, *English Social History*, Longmans, Green and Co 1942, p.343.
2. Ibid., p.348.
3. R. F. Wearmouth, *Methodism and the Common People of the Eighteenth Century*, Epworth Press 1945, p.133.
4. *Book of Common Prayer*, liturgy for the Ministration of Public Baptism of Infants.
5. *Book of Common Prayer*, Articles of Religion, IX.
6. *Book of Common Prayer*, liturgy for the Ministration of Public Baptism of Infants.
7. John Wesley M.A., *Explanatory Notes upon the Old Testament*, Genesis 3.24.
8. John Wesley M.A., *Explanatory Notes upon the New Testament*, Rom. 7.13; I Cor. 15.55.
9. Ibid., I Cor. 15.56.
10. Ibid. Eph. 2.1.
11. Ibid. Rev. 21.8.
12. Ibid. Rev. 21.4.
13. See Rev. 22.11.
14. Ibid., I Cor 15.57.
15. Ibid. I Cor. 15.54.
16. Ibid. Rom. 5.14.
17. Ibid., Rom. 8.38.
18. Ibid., Heb. 2.15.
19. Ibid.
20. *Collection of Hymns and Psalms*, Charles-Town 1737: for Sunday XXV.
21. Ibid.: for Wednesday or Friday XV.
22. Ibid.: for Sunday XXII.
23. Ibid.: for Wednesday or Friday X.
24. *Journal of the Rev. John Wesley A.M.*, edited by Nehemiah Curnock, 18 January 1736.
25. For a full discussion of Wesley's view on hell, see D. Dun Wilson,

Proceedings of the Wesley Historical Society, Part 1, March 1963; *Journal*, Vol. 1, p.139, notes by Nehemiah Curnock.

26. *The Works of John Wesley*, Vol. 25, *Letters*, Vol. 1, 19 March 1727.

27. *Journal, ed. Curnock*, 23 November 1735: 1 January 1736: 23 January 1736: 25 January 1736.

28. Ibid., 10 July 1736: 2 January 1737.

29. Ibid., 24 January 1738.

30. Ibid.

31. Jeremy Taylor, *The Rule and Exercises of Holy Living* p.23.

32. Ibid.

33. *The Works of John Wesley*, Vol 25., *Letters*, Vol. 1, 28 February 1729/30.

34. Ibid., 28 May 1725.

35. Wesley preferred to call it the first rise of Methodism.

36. L. Tyerman, *The Oxford Methodists*, Hodder and Stoughton 1873, p.7.

37. Ibid., p.5, 6.

38. Ibid., p.77, 79; *Works*, Vol. 25 *Letters*, 5 May 1729; *Journal*, ed. Curnock, 22 February 1736.

39. Martin Schmidt, *John Wesley. A Theological Biography*, Vol. 1, Epworth Press 1973, p.225.

40. *Journal*, Curnock, Vol. 1, 14 March 1738.

41. Ibid., 27 April 1738.

42. Ibid., 26 April 1737.

43. Ibid., 9 May 1738.

44. Ibid., 10 May 1738.

45. Ibid., 24 May 1738.

46. Ibid., 6 June 1738.

47. Ibid., 31 March 1739.

48. *Explanatory Notes upon the Old Testament* by John Wesley M.A., Isa. 61.1.

49. *Modern Christianity Exemplified at Wednesbury. The Works of the Rev. John Wesley, A.M.*, 1831, Vol. XIII, p.162.

50. *Explanatory Notes upon the New Testament*, I John 4.18.

51. *Journal*, ed. Curnock, vol. 3, pp.115–16, 153, 156, 268f.

52. *The Journal of the Rev. Charles Wesley, M.A. The Early Journal 1736–1739*, edited by John Telford. Wednesday 19 July 1738.

53. *Wesleyan Magazine* for 1820, pp.464, 593ff, 623, 999ff., also *The Works of the Rev. John Wesley, A.M.*, 1831, Vol XIII, pp.471–4.

14. Wesleyan Theology   *Melvin E. Dieter*

1. *The Works of John Wesley*, third edition, reprinted Beacon Hill Press of Kansas City 1948 (hereafter referred to as *Works*, 1:103.

2. *Works*, 5:492–504.

3. *Works*, 5:501–3.

4. Albert Outler strongly affirms this in his *Theology in the Wesleyan*

Spirit, Tidings, Nashville 1975, 81–3; see especially p.82 n.27, with its reference to Martin Schmidt, *John Wesley: A Spiritual Biography*, Abingdon Press and Epworth Press 1973, II, 214.

5. See George Croft Cell, *The Rediscovery of John Wesley*, Holt, New York 1935, 341; Harald Lindstrom, *Wesley and Santification: A Study in the Doctrine of Salvation*, Epworth Press 1950, reprinted Zondervan: Francis Asbury Press 1984, 12; Kenneth E. Rowe, *The Place of John Wesley in the Christian Tradition*, Scarecrow Press, Methuchen NJ 1976.

6. *Works*, 5:502.

7. See Albert M. Lyles, *Methodism Mocked: The Satire Reaction to Methodism in the Eighteenth Century*, Epworth Press 1960, pp.117–22.

8. See Melvin E. Dieter, 'John Wesley and Creative Synthesis', *The Asbury Seminarian* 34, Summer 1984, 3–7.

9. *Works*, 5:207–8. For his reaffirmation of the sermon thirty-two years later see *Works*, 3:213.

10. Outler remarks that 'Too little attention has been paid to the implications of the fact that Wesley never discarded this sermon or even recast it', *Theology in the Wesleyan Spirit*, p.70.

11. *Works*, 1:101.

12. See Ted A. Campbell, *John Wesley's Conceptions and Uses of Antiquity*, Southern Methodist PhD dissertation 1984.

13. See especially *Works*, 5:132–34.

14. *Works*, 5:226.

15. *Works*, 8:325.

16. *Works*, 6:64–5.

17. *Works*, 6:64.

18. *Works*, 5:185–6.

15. The Relevance of John Wesley's Message for Today   *William R. Davies*

1. *John Wesley. Fifty Three Sermons*, Wesleyan Book Room, London, pp. 17, 58ff., 71, 235.

2. Ibid., p.245.

3. *The Journal of John Wesley*, Standard Edition, Epworth Press 1938 Vol 2, p.125.

4. Ibid., Vol. 1, 476. In an essay on the relevance of Wesley's message there is no space to discuss whether what happened at Aldersgate Street was salvation, assurance or both. The text as it stands suggests the latter: 'I felt I did trust in Christ, Christ alone for salvation; *and* an assurance was given me. . . .' (italics mine). However, others (e.g. Leslie Davison *Pathway to Power*, Fountain Trust, London 1971, pp.57–8) suggest the possibility of Wesley's conversion in 1725, with assurance following on 24 May 1738. Whether experienced concurrently or consecutively, these are distinct theological strands which refer on the one hand to being saved and on the other to knowing that one is saved.

5. John Wesley, *Fifty Three Sermons*, p.127.

6. *The Journal of John Wesley*, Vol. 2, p.122.

7. Cf. Luke 3.22; 4.1–3.

8. P. Tillich, *The Shaking of the Foundations*, Penguin Books 1949, p.140.

9. Ibid., p.163.

10. M. Harper, *Walk in the Spirit*, Hodder and Stoughton 1971, p.25.

11. *The Constitutional Discipline and Practice of the Methodist Church*, Methodist Publishing House, first published 1951, 61.1.

12. John Wesley, *Fifty Three Sermons*, pp.564–81.

13. *The Letters of John Wesley*, Standard Edition, Vol 5., p.333.

14. John Wesley, *A Plain Account of Christian Perfection*, Epworth Press 1952, p.81.

15. R. N. Flew, *The Idea of Perfection in Christian Theology*, Oxford University Press 1934, p.336.

16. W. E. Sangster, *The Path to Perfection*, Hodder and Stoughton 1943, pp.185ff.

17. *Plain Account* pp.41, 42, 51.

18. *Journal*, Vol 2, 323.

19. Ibid., Vol 1, p.180 note.

20. Ibid., Vol 4, p.220.

21. Ibid., Vol 7, p.333.

22. Ibid., Vol. 8, p.128.

17. Wesley as a Writer   *A. Skevington Wood*

1. George Lawton, *John Wesley's English: A Study of His Literary Style*, Allen and Unwin 1962, p.14.

2. Henry Bett, *The Spirit of Methodism*, Epworth Press 1937, pp.169–70.

3. Oliver Elton, *A Survey of English Literature 1730–1780*, Arnold 1928, Vol. II, pp.184, 212–22; Emile Legouis and Louis Cazamian, *A History of English Literature*, Dent 1930, pp.926–8.

4. *The Cambridge History of English Literature*, ed. Sir A. W. Ward and A. R. Waller, Vol. X, *The Age of Johnson*, Cambridge University Press 1913, p.368.

5. *The Oxford History of English Literature*, ed. John Buxton and Norman Davis, Vol. VIII, John Butt and Geoffrey Carnell, *The Mid-Eighteenth Century*, Oxford University Press 1979, pp.276–8, 361–2, 653–5.

6. James Sambrook, *The Eighteenth Century: The Intellectual and Cultural Context of English Literature 1740–1789*, Longman 1986, pp.41–3.

7. David Daiches, *A Critical History of English Literature*, Secker and Warburg 1960, Vol. 3, p. 662; Maximillian E. Novak, *Eighteenth-Century English Literature*, Macmillan 1983, p.110.

8. *The Journal of the Rev. John Wesley*, ed. Nehemiah Curnock, Epworth Press. 1909, Vol. IV, p.91.

9. Ibid., p.92.

10. Ibid.

11. Ibid., p.137.

12. Cf. James Downey, *The Eighteenth-Century Pulpit*, Clarendon Press

1969, pp.32–3, 58–9, 71, 136 n.1.
13. Lawton, op.cit., p.240.
14. Ibid., pp.240–65; Elton, op.cit., p.214.
15. Elton, op.cit., p.214.
16. George Sampson, *The Concise Cambridge History of English Literature*, Cambridge University Press [3]1970, p.460.
17. *The Pelican Guide to English Literature*, ed. Boris Ford, Vol. IV, Arthur R. Humphreys, *From Dryden to Johnson*, Penguin Books 1957, p.72.
18. Elton, op.cit., p.212.
19. *Journal*, Vol. I, p.83.
20. Ibid.
21. *Letters and Literary Remains of Edward Fitzgerald*, ed. W. Aldis Wright, Macmillan 1902, Vol. II, p.184; cf. Vol. III, p.87.
22. Ibid., Vol. IV, p.23.
23. Cf. *The Letters of the Rev. John Wesley*, ed. John Telford, Epworth Press 1931, Vol. I, p.xiv.
24. Ibid., Vol. VII, 377.
25. Ibid., p.392.
26. *The Works of John Wesley*, ed. Frank Baker, Clarendon Press 1976–, Vol. 25, p.28.
27. *Letters*, Vol. I, p.xiii.
28. Cf. Ibid., p.xx.
29. Downey, op.cit., p.5.
30. James H. Rigg, *The Living Wesley*, Charles H. Kelly 1891, p.135; W. Lamplough Doughty, *John Wesley, Preacher*, Epworth Press 1955, p.84.
31. John Lawson, *Notes on Wesley's Forty-Four Sermons*, Epworth Press 1946, p.1.
32. Lawton, op.cit., pp.246–9; Downey, op.cit., pp.201–2.
33. *The Standard Sermons of John Wesley*, ed. Edward H. Sugden, Epworth Press [2]1935, Vol. I, p.30.
34. Ibid.
35. *Works* (Oxford Edition), Vol. 3, pp.290–2.
36. *Proceedings of the Wesley Historical Society*, Vol. II, pp.138–9; cf. *Journal*, Vol. VII, p.73.
37. *Works* (Oxford Edition), Vol. 3, p.400.
38. Dante Alighieri, *De Vulgari Eloquentia* c. 1304; cf. Arthur P. Rossiter, *Our Living Language*, Longman, Green 1953, p.105; *Proceedings*, Vol. XXXIII, pp. 53–62; 112–17.
39. Downey, op.cit., p.225.
40. *Journal*, Vol. IV, pp.3–4.
41. *Works* (Oxford Edition), Vol. 11, p.1.
42. *Letters*, Vol. IV, p.118.
43. Ibid.
44. *Journal*, Vol. IV, p.490; Gordon Rupp, *Religion in England 1688–1791*, Clarendon Press 1986, pp.381–2.
45. *An Earnest Appeal to Men of Reason and Religion* (1743); *A Farther*

Appeal to Men of Reason and Religion (1745–1746).
    46. Elton, op.cit., p.213.
    47. John Wesley, *Explanatory Notes upon the New Testament*, Epworth Press 1929, p.6.
    48. *The Works of the Rev John Wesley*, third edition, ed. Thomas Jackson, John Mason 1829–1831, Vol. XIV, p.222.
    49. *Journal*, Vol. V., p.521; cf. *Letters*, Vol. IV, p.145.
    50. John Wesley, *Sermons on Several Occasions*, John Mason 1849, Vol. II, p.176.
    51. *Letters*, Vol. II, p.44.
    52. John H. Whiteley, *Wesley's England: A Survey of Eighteenth Century Social and Cultural Conditions*, Epworth Press 1938, p.229.
    53. Downey, op.cit., p.224.
    54. *Letters*, Vol. V, p.8.
    55. *Letters*, Vol. II, p.44; Vol. V, p.313.
    56. *Works*, Vol.25, p.130.
    57. James R. Sutherland, *On English Prose*, University of Toronto Press 1957, p.77.

18. Wesley the Communicator   *Pauline M. Webb*

    1. Letter quoted in full in L. Tyerman, *The Life and Times of John Wesley*, Vol. III, Hodder 1871, pp.130–4.
    2. Ibid., p.563.
    3. Quoted in a note in Wesley's *Journal*, standard edition, Epworth Press 1938, Vol. V, pp.188–9.
    4. Robert Southey, *Life of John Wesley*, pp.303–4.

19. Wesley the Evangelist   *Joe Hale*

    1. Nehemiah Curnock (ed.), *The Journal of the Rev. John Wesley*, New York: Eatmon R. Mains 1809, eight volumes, I, p. 442.
    2. Ibid. I, p.442.
    3. Ibid., I, p.459.
    4. John Lawson, *A Thousand Tongues*, Paternoster Press 1987, p.125.
    5. Clare George Weakley Jr (ed.), *The Nature of Revival* (from Charles Wesley's Journal), Minneapolis: Bethany House Publishers 1987, p.53.
    6. Albert C. Outler (ed.), *John Wesley*, A Library of Protestant Thought, New York: Oxford University Press, 1964, pp.14, 17.
    7. Ernest Gordon Rupp, *Religion in England 1688–1791*, Clarendon Press 1986, pp.357, 358.
    8. Curnock, op.cit. I, p.483.
    9. F. Gerald Ensley, *John Wesley, Evangelist*, Nashville: Methodist Evangelistic Materials 1958, p.41.
    10. Ibid, p.16.
    11. Outler, op.cit., preface, p.vii.
    12. Albert C. Outler (ed.), *The Works of John Wesley*, Vol. 2, Sermons II, Nashville: Abingdon Press 1985, p.187.

13. Gerald R. Cragg (ed.), *The Appeals to Men of Reason and Religion*, The Works of John Wesley, Clarendon Press 1975, p.105.

14. Ibid., p.53.

15. Outler, *John Wesley*, pp.49, 50.

16. Outler, *Works*, Vol. 2, Sermons II, p.482.

17. Cragg, op.cit., p.46.

18. Curnock, op.cit., I, p.474–7.

19. Cragg, op.cit., p.62.

20. Cragg, op.cit., p.74.

21. F. E. Holliday, *A History of Cornwall*, Duckworth ²1975, pp.264, 266.

22. Rupp, op.cit., p.339.

23. Curnock, op.cit., II, p.220–1.

24. *George Whitefield's Journals*, new edition, unabridged, Banner of Truth Trust 1960, pp.288, 289.

25. Curnock, op.cit., II, p.273.

26. Curnock, op.cit., II, p.278.

27. Curnock, op.cit., II, p.281.

28. George Hunter, *To Spread The Power*, Nashville: Abingdon Press 1987, p.57.

29. Frank Baker, *A Charge To Keep*, Epworth Press 1947, p.26.

30. F. Gerald Ensley, *John Wesley Evangelist*, Nashville: Methodist Evangelistic Materials 1958, pp.39, 40.

31. Curnock, op.cit., II, pp.211–13.

32. Curnock, op.cit., III, p.182.

33. Outler, op.cit., p.525.

34. Outler, op.cit., p.527.

35. Outler, op.cit., p.531.

36. Holliday, op.cit., p.262.

37. Holliday, op.cit., p.271.

38. Curnock, op.cit., III, p.94.

39. Holliday, op.cit., p.277.

40. Curnock, op.cit., VI, p.309, 310.

41. Curnock, op.cit., VI, p.209.

42. Cragg, op.cit., p.374.

43. Rupp, op.cit., p.448.

44. *World Methodist Council Handbook of Information 1987–1991*, ed. Joe Hale, Asheville: Biltmore Press 1987, p.101.